Assessment in Educational Reform

Assessment in Educational Reform

Both Means and Ends

Robert W. Lissitz

University of Maryland College Park

William D. Schafer

Emeritus, University of Maryland College Park

Allyn and Bacon

Boston   London   Toronto   Sydney   Tokyo   Singapore

Series Editor: *Arnis E. Burvikovs*
Editorial Assistant: *Matthew Forster*
Production Administrator: *Gordon Laws*
Composition and Prepress Buyer: *Linda Cox*
Electronic Composition: *Peggy Cabot, Cabot Computer Services*
Manufacturing Buyer: *Julie McNeill*
Cover Administrator: *Kristina Mose-Libon*
Marketing Manager: *Kathleen Morgan*

Copyright © 2002 by Allyn & Bacon
A Pearson Education Company
75 Arlington Street
Boston, MA 02116

Internet: www.ablongman.com

Between the time Website information is gathered and then published, it is not unusual for some sites to have closed. Also, the transcription of URLs can result in unintended typographical errors. The publisher would appreciate notification where these occur so that they may be corrected in subsequent editions.

Library of Congress Cataloging-in-Publication Data

Assessment in educational reform : both means and ends / [edited by] Robert W. Lissitz, William D. Schafer.
      p. cm.
      Includes bibliographical references and index.
      ISBN 0-205-33269-2 (pbk.)
          1. Educational tests and measurements—United States—Congresses.
      2. Educational change—United States—Congresses.   I. Lissitz, Robert W.
      II. Schafer, William D.

    LB3051 .A769 2002
    371.26'0973—dc21   2001022762

Printed in the United States of America

10 9 8 7 6 5 4 3 2 1   06 05 04 03 02 01

contents

p r o l o g u e

In the spring of 1999, I took a sabbatical in Greece and while visiting Athens attended a conference in honor of a faculty member retiring from a statistics department. There, as I was enjoying the conference, I thought about what an honor this was for the person who was retiring. He must have done some fine things at the University of Athens to motivate people to create a conference in his honor and to travel such distances to show their respect. That was when I realized that such an activity would be the perfect honor for Dr. William Schafer, who had just decided to retire from the University of Maryland. This book is the result of the decision to organize a *festschrift* for Bill.

The topic of the conference and the resulting book is assessment. While on leave from the University of Maryland, Bill served as the director of the State Assessment Office of the Maryland State Department of Education. In that capacity, Bill faced a number of challenges and met them all with success, but in conversations with me, we both realized that there were a large number of unresolved issues and unobtained goals. State assessment is one of the current hot buttons in America. Nearly every newspaper has an article about testing, which includes such topics as accusations of bias, allegations that too much time is allocated to testing, complaints that the right topics are not covered on the test, and questions about whether the tests are used for the right purposes, and so on. The testing endeavor attracts the attention and concerns of politicans, parents, students, and the whole professional education establishment, as well as those who report and comment on such matters. It is not hard to see why assessment is a hot button issue. It is an indicator of success (and failure) of the student and, by implication, the instructional system in which that child should be thriving. These indicators need to be fair and valid to justify so much faith in them. And it takes a lot of faith to use test results to certify competence for graduation or to allocate salary raises, just two examples of important decisions that some people suggest should be informed by test data.

When I returned to the University of Maryland from my sabbatical, I asked Bill Schafer if he would help me put together a conference, at which he would be one of those to address the audience, and then work with me to produce this book. Asking someone to help in a process that honors himself is a little awkward, but we focused on the chance to contribute to the profession to which Bill has devoted his life. Bill's continuing investment in the assessment field made the choice easy—he agreed. This book emanates from that agreement in the fall of 1999, the conference that occurred in the summer of 2000, and the addition of a series of four original papers written for this book.

The conference and the resulting book started as a festschrift but soon became an effort to influence what people actually do in the field as they work to improve the assessment enterprise. We are in a profession that is committed to facing problems and solving them, using formal approaches that are based in sound theory and carefully obtained data. This effort asked the contributors to base their chapters on sound data and the literature that exists in our field, but we asked them to do something else, too. We asked that they speculate and that they try to formulate a sense of best practice. Each of the contributors has many years of experience in the field and they have a lot to offer. This book tried to give them a vehicle for expression.

Each of the seven chapters that were part of the original conference (those by Drs. Beaton, Brookhart, Hambleton, Roeber, Schafer, Stiggins, and Wise) and the four additional chapters (those by Drs. Airasian, Diez, Stansfield, and Tindal) that were invited to be a part of the book are focused on answering an important question about assessment practice. Bill and I chose the questions and some of the contributors suggested modifications, with the intent of providing an analysis of an issue in applied assessment that would result in a set of observations and recommendations that would help a broad range of education practitioners. We hope the reader agrees that the contributors have succeeded admirably.

Robert W. Lissitz
University of Maryland

preface

The concept of this book, and its value, rests on two assumptions. One is that the potential of assessments in educational practice is very much unmet. The other is that school reform will not be effective until assessments become the focus of reform efforts. The book's purpose is to help direct that focus.

Each author was asked to postulate a new world of excellence in education and to describe what assessments will look like in that world. That is an unusual assignment for people like us. We are conditioned by our profession to be careful, making no claims that cannot be amply justified and even then expressing ourselves in language that makes it clear we understand we might be wrong. The only things we can say are true are those we ourselves see. But here, professionals steeped in that tradition were asked to speculate and describe what none of us has seen. Fortunately, all took that on as an intriguing assignment. As editors, Bob Lissitz and I marveled at their creations.

Assessment exists at numerous levels and with various scopes. Even describing all the ways in which assessments are used educationally would be a daunting task. In order to organize our thinking about topics to include here, we thought of assessments vertically, from those used instructionally by individual teachers with individual students to those used to make national and international comparisons of educational quality by policy makers. Even that is a broad range.

At the level where learning actually takes place, a teacher interacts with a student and each has assessable states and expectations during the instructional process. Susan M. Brookhart and Richard J. Stiggins explore those interactions from the perspectives of the teacher and the student, respectively. To round out building-level uses, Peter W. Airasian and Lisa M. Abrams consider the roles of assessments in schools. Mary E. Diez considers how assessment will be used in evaluating teacher candidates as well as practicing teachers.

State-level assessments are becoming more and more important. My contribution describes how state-level, large-scale assessments might be used to foster school reform. Of particular concern are problems of inclusion of all students in assessment. Gerald Tindal considers this problem from the perspective of students with disabilities, and Charles W. Stansfield and Charlene Rivera discuss approaches to the assessment of students who are non-native-English speakers.

Lauress L. Wise and R. Gene Hoffman discuss how assessment will be used to document the effects of educational reform efforts, and Edward D. Roeber considers the needs of policy makers for assessment information at all levels. Ronald K. Hambleton takes up how the data are presented to enhance interpretation, and Albert E. Beaton discusses overcoming the special problems of interstate and international comparisons.

There were many individuals and institutions contributing to the success of our work. Clearly among those are the College of Education at the University of Maryland, College Park under the leadership of Dean Edna Szymanski and the Department of Measurement, Statistics, and Evaluation under the leadership of my co-editor, Robert W. Lissitz. Also invaluable was the support of the Maryland State Department of Education, and especially

Nancy S. Grasmick, the State Superintendent of Schools, and Assistant State Superinten-dent Mark Moody. We also are indebted to our publisher, Allyn & Bacon, for its willing-ness to take this rather futuristic project on as well as for its careful and helpful work along the way.

I hope you agree that this thought-provoking collection contains more than just lip service to meaningful educational reform. And I hope you enjoy it as much as I did helping to put it together!

William D. Schafer
Emeritus, University of Maryland

Assessment in Educational Reform

What Will Teachers Know about Assessment, and How Will That Improve Instruction?

SUSAN M. BROOKHART

Duquesne University

This book is dedicated to visualizing ways in which assessments can be instrumental in effecting positive change in educational institutions. I have been asked to focus on teachers: In an ideal (or at least improving) world, what would teachers know about assessment, and how would they use that to improve instruction? Let me air my bias right from the outset. I think I was assigned one of the most important questions, because the education we all wish to improve happens in classrooms, by virtue of the work teachers and students do. Administrators make it possible for education to happen, and indeed quality classroom learning can't happen without the resources and policies they administer. But the locus of the teaching–learning experience is in the classroom, and its primary agents are teachers and students. It follows that what teachers and students know and do about assessment is critical.

The most important assessment information for classroom use comes from classroom assessments (see Stiggins, this volume). In this chapter, I have been asked to address teachers' knowledge and use of large-scale assessment information. I acknowledge that for teachers, large-scale assessment information is—and should be—secondary to classroom assessment information. Nevertheless, I can envision some important ways in which teachers' knowledge and use of large-scale assessment information would improve instruction. Some of these ways involve changing teachers' knowledge or practices, and some of them involve changing the kind of large-scale assessment information we routinely offer to teachers so that it is more useful for improving instruction.

Framework for Posing the Question: What Will Teachers Know and How Will That Improve Instruction?

Before I address this question, I need to deal with the underlying assumptions. If I just answered it, I would be participating in what Cochran-Smith and Lytle (1999) called "knowledge-*for*-practice"; that is, I would be disseminating research- or expert-based theoretical knowledge for teachers to apply to the examples and instances their classroom practice presents.

Another approach, "knowledge-*in*-practice," would eschew this whole book. Knowledge-*in*-practice elevates practical wisdom at the expense of formal theory. This approach likewise designates "experts" and "novices"—it just chooses them from a different pool (Cochran-Smith & Lytle, 1999). Teachers become the experts in a domain no one else is expected to understand. Although I understand this approach in the existential sense, it does not lead to stable, shareable knowledge. That, of course, is part of the point of this approach; it sees practical knowledge as continually constructed and reconstructed in action. Knowledge exists in and through the action of teaching, making chapters such as this one moot.

A more productive way to address this question might be to take the approach that Cochran-Smith and Lytle (1999) called "knowledge-*of*-practice." Knowledge-*of*-practice relies on teachers' communal inquiry and is very much about process, politics, and power. The first step is not up to the authors of this book; a group of teachers would decide they wanted to see how understanding and using assessment information would improve instruction in some specific way, but they would be free to use information from many sources. The point would be to see what they could learn. This learning could be shared. It would be judged not according to the canons of academic scholarship, but by its effects on improving learning for all students and improving the practice of teachers. Thus, this approach to teacher knowledge has a democratizing aspect to it.

The Knowledge-*for*-Practice Approach: What We Know

Rather than dismiss the knowledge-*for*-practice approach out of hand, I want to describe briefly what has already been written on the topic of what experts have to say about what teachers should know and be able to do. There are two purposes for this section of the chapter. First, there is actually quite a body of literature under the general theme of investigating "teacher competence" in educational measurement as defined by measurement experts. We have learned some things about teachers' knowledge and use of assessments over the past 40 years, but in this chapter, I argue that the documentation of experts' perspectives on teachers has not succeeded in improving assessment practices and instruction. I think that's because the one-way flow from expert knowledge to teacher application is not the best approach to teacher learning. Cochran-Smith and Lytle's framework helps us see that. But I would like to report selectively on the literature that effectively defines the history of the question this chapter addresses.

Second, one of the purposes of this book is to honor the career of Bill Schafer, who has long been interested in what teachers need to know about assessments in their practice. In fact, one of the first conversations I remember having with Bill was about an assessment workshop he was doing with teachers. Citing the "teacher competence in assessment" literature affords me the opportunity to cite Bill's work. Much to his credit, the Schafer articles have titles like "Assessment Literacy for Teachers" (Schafer, 1993, after Stiggins, 1991a, who also called it "Assessment Literacy") and "Essential Assessment Skills in Professional Education for Teachers" (Schafer, 1991)—much more gracious language than "teacher competence."

There are several good reviews of the literature concerning what teachers know about assessment. In 1989, the Buros–Nebraska Symposium on Measurement and Testing addressed the question, "Are our school teachers adequately trained in measurement and assessment skills?" An edited volume of papers on this topic (Wise, 1993) comprises a comprehensive review of literature about what preservice teachers are taught about measurement, what they should be taught, what they actually know, and the observed quality of their assessment practices. Two chapters are particularly relevant for our purposes: Gullickson's (1993) review of literature on teachers' attitudes and practices and the content of undergraduate measurement courses, and Marso and Pigge's (1993) review of literature on teachers' attitudes and practices and studies of direct assessments of teachers' testing knowledge. Add to these the literature review in Schafer and Lissitz (1987) about what school personnel should know, do know, and have the opportunity to learn, and an entire special issue of *Educational Measurement: Issues and Practice* (Nitko, 1991) on the topic, and we have plenty of sources for a review of this teacher-competence approach, plus the suggestion that its popularity peaked about a decade ago.

Gullickson (1993) pointed out that measurement experts have weighed in on what teachers need to know about assessment since at least the first volume of the *Journal of Educational Measurement* (Mayo, 1964). Studies of what teachers are or should be taught and what they know have generally concluded that while teachers' knowledge of large-scale testing is limited—especially in the important area of communicating assessment results, arguably something teachers should be able to do (AFT, AERA, & NEA, 1990)—their skills at gathering and using classroom assessment information are much more important. The conclusion of many authors is that measurement courses for teachers should increase emphasis on classroom assessment, and decrease emphasis on large-scale testing (Gullickson, 1993; Marso & Pigge, 1993; Stiggins, 1991b). I wholeheartedly endorse this position. Because of the topic of this chapter, however, I'd like to revisit what some of these studies have concluded about teachers' attitudes, knowledge, and needs regarding large-scale testing.

Teacher Attitudes toward Large-Scale Assessment. Schafer and Lissitz (1987) reviewed teacher surveys of the 1970s and 1980s and concluded that teachers had in general reported a positive attitude toward standardized testing. They noted that this was a well-kept secret and that popular opinion at the time assumed that teachers disliked testing (Schafer & Lissitz, 1987, p. 59). Marso and Pigge (1993) reviewed a large number of studies and concluded there were conflicting findings about teacher attitudes toward assessment. Some studies they reviewed found teachers expressed confidence in their knowledge about testing; some found an expressed lack of confidence. Many of the studies in the review were about "testing" generally. The main focus of Marso and Pigge's own work was classroom testing.

Wise, Lukin, and Roos (1991), using data collected in Nebraska in 1989, found that 77% of teachers rated themselves as "good" or "very good" at interpreting standardized test results; 82% rated themselves as "good" or "very good" at explaining standardized test scores; and 73% believed that possessing strong skills in testing and measurement was important for being perceived as professional. Impara and his colleagues (Impara, Divine, Bruce, Liverman, & Gay, 1991) found some evidence that both measurement instruction and the provision of interpretive information along with results affect teachers' actual abilities at interpreting test results.

Some studies that have taken a different approach than the one I have characterized as the teacher-competence approach have uncovered some negative teacher attitudes toward large-scale testing. Of course, what one finds depends in part on what one looks for. The teacher competency in assessment literature complements a view of large-scale testing that is understood using the language of "competency" or "minimum competency" for students. Many states have begun to talk about large-scale assessment using language about testing for "standards" or "accountability." Researchers' concerns have been about the effects of these testing programs on curriculum, instruction, and teachers.

Studies looking for these effects have uncovered more negativity in teachers' attitudes, but not about the tests themselves so much as their effects on instruction, because that is how the questions have been asked. Smith and Rottenberg (1991) found that consequences of externally mandated testing in elementary schools included a narrowing of curriculum and an increase in instructional time geared to the content and format of the tests. More relevant for this review of teacher attitudes were their findings that teachers disliked the tests, believing that they caused undue stress and fatigue for their students. Teachers' own emotional responses to tests were reported as shame and embarrassment at low scores but merely relief at high scores, based on a belief that tests measured socio-economic status as much as achievement (Smith & Rottenberg, 1991). Herman and Golan (1993), also looking at elementary schools, found similarly that testing had effects on curriculum and instruction and that these effects were more pronounced for low-SES schools. Teacher attitudes in this study were somewhat positive in that teachers reported taking responsibility for their students' learning and having some control over it. About the efficacy of testing itself, teachers were not positive, reporting disagreement with statements about testing helping with school improvement, giving useful feedback, or focusing learning goals. Rather, they reported testing caused stress for both teachers and students. Teachers in schools where test scores were improving reported more pressure from the community to raise test scores than did teachers in schools where test scores were dropping—one of the few differences found between those groups (Herman & Golan, 1993).

For our purposes, then, we can conclude that teachers have mixed attitudes toward the enterprise of testing itself, including some positive attitudes about test information that is used well. They have negative attitudes toward tests used in such a way as to have what they perceive as negative consequences for their students. They do not perceive their own knowledge about testing to be a major problem.

Instruction about Large-Scale Assessment.

Let's turn now to what others think teachers ought to be taught about large-scale assessment. I summarize this literature under the teacher-competency umbrella because this literature is about what various expert groups think teachers ought to know.

There are several approaches to the question of what teachers, either inservice or preservice, should be taught about assessment, and, taken together, they tell us quite a lot. Methods and approaches have included surveys of teachers and of measurement experts, reviews of program and course requirements, reviews of textbook contents, and observation and job analysis of teaching. As with teacher attitudes, the literature on content of instruction has been well reviewed, by some of the authors in this book and by others. Generally, surveys of teachers and the job-analysis approach have concluded by recommending more instruction, at both the preservice and inservice level, to build a repertoire of strategies for high-quality classroom assessment, and less instruction in standardized testing than is currently the case in most measurement courses for teachers. Textbook reviews or surveys of measurement experts have placed more emphasis on learning about standardized testing, although some measurement experts who have studied the classroom and its information needs do not (Airasian, 1991). Recommendations for instruction in standardized testing often include a shift away from statistical interpretation of scores and toward communication of score meaning to a lay audience (Brookhart, 1999; Schafer, 1991; Schafer & Lissitz, 1987).

Gullickson (1993) summarized the results of several survey studies he and his colleagues conducted in the early 1980s. In his summary, he compared the desired content emphases of teachers and professors by lining up the 20 content priorities rated most highly by each group. There was a match in only one of five areas, topics dealing with preparation of classroom tests. Professors reported more coverage of test statistics and analysis and of standardized test applications than teachers desired, and teachers desired more topics covered under formative and summative uses of tests and nontest evaluation practices than professors reported (Gullickson, 1993, pp. 12–13).

Are the data dated? After all, today's undergraduate teacher education students were infants in the early 1980s. In his editorial introduction to a special issue of *Educational Measurement: Issues and Practice*, Smith (1999) suggested that the lack of relevant measurement instruction has remained a problem. He wrote, "A lack of interest in the issues that concern practicing educators on the part of the measurement community puts us in danger of ceding any influence in what classroom assessments look like and how they are used to our subject-matter colleagues" (Smith, 1999, p. 4). This is part of a strongly worded argument in favor of more emphasis on classroom assessment and less on large-scale assessment in measurement courses for teachers. And even though I argued, in the same issue, for a small place in teacher education for using and communicating the results of large-scale assessments (Brookhart, 1999), I agree completely that the emphasis in such courses should be placed on classroom assessment.

The *Standards for Teacher Competence in Educational Assessment of Students* (AFT, NCME, NEA, 1990), arguably the normative reference for recommended content in assessment courses for teachers, includes seven standards. Teachers should be skilled in:

1. choosing assessment methods appropriate for instructional decisions;
2. developing assessment methods appropriate for instructional decisions;
3. administering, scoring, and interpreting the results of both externally produced and teacher-produced assessment methods;
4. using assessment results when making decisions about individual students, planning teaching, developing curriculum, and school improvement;
5. developing valid pupil grading procedures which use pupil assessments;
6. communicating assessment results to students, parents, other lay audiences, and other educators; and
7. recognizing unethical, illegal, and otherwise inappropriate assessment methods and uses of assessment information (AFT, NCME, NEA, 1990).

Standards 3, 4, 6, and 7 include skills that apply to large-scale assessment, including administering, interpreting, and communicating assessment results, using information for decision making, and recognizing unethical practices. The recommendations of Schafer (1991) and Stiggins (1991b) both parallel these content areas; although they differ in the amount of emphasis they put on teachers developing skills related to large-scale assessment, they both acknowledge teachers' need for these skills.

Knowledge of Large-Scale Assessment. Some studies have actually investigated teachers' knowledge about assessment. Two methods have been used: tests of assessment knowledge or reviews of teachers' assessments themselves. The latter studies have led to conclusions about teachers' need for instruction in classroom assessment (Marso & Pigge, 1993). More relevant for our review are the studies in which teacher knowledge was tested, because these have included questions about standardized tests as well as classroom assessments.

Gullickson (1993) pointed out that one of the strongest arguments for teachers knowing about standardized tests is simply that they are given in almost all schools. Teachers are the first point of contact for parents who call the school and would logically be the first person parents would ask about their children's test results (Brookhart, 1999). This means that teachers are in a good position to help with community education about test score meaning and use. As of December 1998, 48 states had some form of large-scale assessment in place; many had assessment programs in several subjects (Council of Chief State School Officers, 1998). So this argument remains current.

Marso and Pigge (1993) reviewed studies that concluded teachers were not very knowledgeable about interpreting large scale assessment results. Plake, Impara, and Fager (1993) reported the results of a national study of teacher competencies related to the *Standards* and found that regarding large-scale assessment, teachers were more successful at questions about administering tests and about recognizing unethical practices than they were at interpreting and communicating results. In a study in the state of Virginia, interpretation of score reports was also a problem, although providing interpretive information on printouts helped teachers (Impara et al., 1991). Among the conclusions Impara and his colleagues drew, one is particularly interesting for us: "If score reports contained only instructionally relevant information, some problems in score interpretation might disappear. For example, if NCE scores were not on the reports, teachers would not need to know what these scores mean, and the reports might be less intimidating to teachers (and parents)" (Impara et al., 1991, p. 18).

This conclusion hints at something important. Four decades of studies of the teacher-competence variety—that is, using the knowledge-*for*-practice approach where experts define what teachers should know about assessment and then study how well teacher knowledge and practice aligns with this definition—have not succeeded in raising "competence" to "standard." And while this chapter is about assessment, I'm not sure that taking the competency approach and testing teachers about educational psychology, or human development, or any of the other theoretical bases for education would fare any better. Cochran-Smith and Lytle's (1999) framework suggests we need a new approach.

The Knowledge-*of*-Practice Approach: Looking Toward the Future

Recall that the knowledge-*of*-practice approach to theoretical and practical knowledge starts with teacher inquiry. Experts are not rejected—their studies may be consulted—but teachers' questions drive their own learning agendas. Knowledge can be shared, but it is not "owned" by experts. It is communal, and its function is to improve instruction as teachers define that. At present, I'm afraid, expectations for what teachers might want to learn about how assessment can improve instruction are not high. Quoting Cochran-Smith & Lytle (1999, p. 293): "Sometimes—if they work from an inquiry stance—teachers begin to challenge and then alter or dismantle fundamental practices such as . . . [list includes] testing and assessment. . . ." Part of the reason for that may be that the assessment information readily available to teachers does not meet their instructional needs. In this paper, I will be arguing for two kinds of changes: changes in teacher knowledge and use of assessment information and changes in the kinds of information routinely presented for large-scale assessments.

One additional point about posing the question What will teachers know?: We need to understand the "teachers" in that question collectively. Positive change in educational institutions, including improvement of instruction in individual classrooms, will not happen simply by giving individual teachers more knowledge, skills, assessment information, or anything else, for that matter. Positive change in educational institutions will be based on teachers and students, administrators and parents, working together. In Cochran-Smith and Lytle's vision of knowledge-*of*-practice, teachers work together to gather information, share and test ideas, and reflect upon their joint learning. "The idea of *inquiry as stance* is intended to emphasize that teacher learning for the next century needs to be understood not primarily as individual professional accomplishment but as a long-term collective project with a democratic agenda" (Cochran-Smith & Lytle, 1999, p. 296).

So how can testing and assessment, often described as a hegemony of authorities and especially of testing companies (Gallagher, 2000), provide information or input for collaborative teacher projects that have equity and democratization—especially in terms of providing equity of educational opportunity for all learners—as their main goals? Or can they? This is the real question hiding under this paper's title question. Here, then, are some possibilities. Remember that the validation of these ideas rests with the practice of thoughtful teachers. The logical next step would be to inspire and support some teacher inquiry along these lines.

The goal would be improving instruction and educational opportunity for students by helping identify appropriate student learning goals and by helping answer teachers' questions. To the extent that assessment data can be organized to answer the questions that groups of teachers would have, as opposed to answering the questions administrators and researchers would have, the democratization of education is enhanced and teaching is strengthened. Administrators and researchers have their own legitimate needs for information, which are currently better served by information from large-scale assessments than are the needs of teachers. My point here is that teachers' needs for information by and large are not currently served by the way data from large-scale assessments are presented.

Teachers' main concerns center on their students' learning. To the extent that assessment information is used to identify appropriate learning goals for individuals and groups of children, to monitor their progress toward them, and to adjust instruction accordingly, the goals of educational opportunity are advanced and teachers' concerns are served. Teachers who wish to use assessment information to identify appropriate learning goals for students and monitor student progress would benefit from at least four things:

- Fewer thoughtless and hurtful uses of norm-referenced analyses
- Accurate progress-oriented analyses
- More criterion-referenced uses of data
- Score reports that meet teachers' information needs

Thoughtless and Hurtful Uses of Norm-Referenced Analyses. The public loves the sorting and ranking that numbers seem to call forth by their very existence. Numbers, after all, are how we count things and put them in order. This natural reaction to numbers is exacerbated by the unwitting (or maybe scheming and diabolical, but I doubt it) provision of information that begs for one analysis over another. For example, the Pennsylvania

System of School Assessment (PSSA) tests math and reading at grades 5, 8, and 11, using a test that was developed from state standards (Pennsylvania Department of Education, 2000). But the scores that are provided to the public on the PDE Web site are means, by school, with the note that 1,300 is the mean score; no disaggregated scores are presented, nor are measures of variability (PDE, 2000). About the only thing one can do with that information is to rank schools. Ranking, even ranking using "standards-based" scale scores, is inherently a norm-referenced function. The Pennsylvania Department of Education literature "strongly discourages" using test results for ranking schools but then provides the data in a form useful for little else.

In a special section of the Sunday, February 6, 2000, paper, the Pittsburgh *Tribune-Review* published "Grading our high schools—How your kids' school stacks up." The special section included a set of articles highlighting educational programs in Allegheny County. The county has 43 school districts, including the Pittsburgh city schools, and 53 public high schools. The program descriptions were interesting, but the article that stirred up the community centered around a table titled "High, low performers." This table listed the top 13 and bottom 13 schools, ranked according to the difference between their mean PSSA score (combined 11th-grade math and reading) and their predicted score after controlling for the percent of students at the school who received free or reduced-price lunch. Thus, the "high performers" were high schools that scored higher than expected and the "low performers" were schools that scored lower than expected, given their percent of free or reduced-lunch recipients (Houser, 2000).

Put aside statistical considerations such as why they used only the 53 high schools in the county when data were available for the whole state. Put aside, if you can, what conclusions about either education in Allegheny County or the PSSA, or both, can be drawn from the fact that 79% of the variance in school-level scores countywide was explained by the percent of free and reduced lunch. My story here is about the educational consequences of doing this very norm-referenced thing. The consequences were not anything that would "help schools further identify strengths and weaknesses and foster improvement in academic programs" (PDE, 2000), as the state claims is one of the purposes of the test. Actually, just the opposite happened, if I can assume that the time and money spent on damage control and spin was time and money that could have been spent on educational planning and instruction.

Two of the schools listed in the low performers chart contacted me. One asked if I would do a "workshop on raising test scores," which I declined to do. Another asked if I would write a memo interpreting the study that the school administration could present to its school board, which I did do. Whether your ethics would have been the same as mine, I think you can see that neither of these activities actually contributed to the education of children, either directly or indirectly. And yet my educational administration colleagues tell me that bad press about test scores is one of a very few things that can get a superintendent fired quickly, ranking right up there with mismanagement of funds and criminal activity. So this damage control approach was realistic.

The reporter who had written the special section had published his e-mail address in the paper, so I took the opportunity to send him a copy of my memo. I am sure the readers of this paper are aware of the obvious points I made in the memo: that ranking schools begs much more important questions; that it is inherently unhelpful because by definition any list must have a bottom as well as a top, no matter what the level of absolute performance; that it ignores progress over time; and that it ignores the performance of various subgroups within the school. The reporter's response was about the "public's right to know." There's where we had to agree to disagree. He counted the rankings as "information," and I agree the public has a right to information. But for me, data that have consequences that obviate the purpose of measuring in the first place are invalid and therefore don't count as "information" (Messick, 1989). What was the ranking of the high school in the community where this reporter lived? You guessed it: a high performer.

Now as long as we do that kind of thing to each other and to our children, no matter what principles of public information we invoke, how do we expect teachers to view large-scale assessment positively? The risks are just too great. In the landmark work in which he launched the terms *formative* and *summative* evaluation a third of a century ago, Scriven (1967, p. 41) wrote, "Anxiety about 'evaluation,' especially among teachers or students, is all too frequently an illicitly generalized response originating in legitimate objections to a situation in which an evaluation was given a role quite beyond its reliability or comprehensiveness." As long as even some people delight in the sport of ranking, even good and dedicated teachers will find it difficult to get motivated to learn the legitimate uses of large scale assessment.

Accurate Progress-Oriented Analyses.   Assessment information that would contribute most to teachers' knowing about the learning of their children would, of course, be high-quality classroom assessments tied directly to instructional targets (Stiggins, this volume). The large-scale assessment information that would contribute most to teachers' knowing about the learning of their students would not be the class-aggregated data that is now presented to teachers on their class-level printouts. These class-level printouts are meant to signal something about general level of instruction or general level of student achievement, but they can't really do the one without being controlled for the other. Thus confounded, class-level printouts don't help very much for instructional decision making. More useful for instructional planning would be individual data plotted over time, showing progress for the individual students. In this section, I consider the short-term question of what teachers might learn about progress from available norm-referenced information. In the long term, what teachers really need is to chart progress with sound criterion-referenced information, which is discussed in the following section.

Using even norm-referenced assessment information to monitor students' progress over time could inform expectations for students and the pacing of instruction better than one-shot status reports do. For example, the reading teacher of a sixth-grade student with a reading comprehension grade-equivalent score of 5.2 knows that the student may have trouble comprehending the sixth-grade reading lessons, but she doesn't know much else. If the student's fourth- and fifth-grade reading scores had been GEs of 3.7 and 4.5, she might suspect that the student is struggling but falling behind and thus slow the pace of instruction and provide extra practice for new concepts. If the student's fourth- and fifth-grade reading scores had been GEs of 4.2 and 5.1, the teacher might suspect that pace of instruction is not the problem, but rather something about the content of last year's instruction or something else about last year in particular. These two patterns would send the teacher looking for two different kinds of additional information, potentially identifying two different problems and adopting two different solutions. Without the longitudinal data, the two scenarios look the same to the sixth-grade teacher.

Whether progress is due to instruction, student aptitude, student effort, or all three, knowing something about individuals' learning curves would be more useful in constructing groups for cooperative learning, for designing individual educational plans for some students, and for making general decisions about instructional pacing than the current status reports testing programs furnish. Is there a way for testing companies that service the same districts year after year to construct a database by student identification number and prepare printouts that chart individual progress, including previous years' test data? That might even help business, because doing this would require using the same test in successive years.

Absent such progress reports, teachers and other school personnel who wish to look at student progress have a hard time doing that in a meaningful way. One of the most common approaches to charting progress over time is to look at a student's percentile rank from year to year, expecting it to stay about the same if students are making "normal" progress. This approach makes intuitive sense, and school personnel often do this because it seems the obvious thing to do with the scores provided. Because variability in achievement increases over time, students with stable percentile ranks below 50, who are showing "normal" improvement, get further behind in terms of grade equivalent as time goes on. That is, they make less than one year's worth of expected progress during one year in school. Students with stable percentile ranks above 50 get further ahead in terms of grade equivalents (Nitko, 2000). And yet this is the approach teachers most commonly take if they do analyze progress.

If teachers saw a student consistently performing at, say, the 27th percentile over time and did not know this principle, they might think the student was making expected progress. They might not take opportunities to reteach and review, or to enrich and expand, instruction. Similarly, if teachers saw a student consistently performing at, say, the 73d percentile over time, they might also think the student was making expected progress, not realizing that, in fact, this student's achievement was increasing each year by more than expected for one year in school. This particular misconception leads to more severe instructional consequences for the students below the 50th percentile than those above.

The better score metric to chart over time, of course, is the scale score. Different standardized tests have different names for this. Some call it the scale score, some the developmental scale score, some the expanded scale score. However it is called, the score to which I refer here is the score on the scale that spans all levels of a test or family of tests constructed for the very purpose of investigating progress over time. It has wonderful statistical properties and works very well. I think the reason it is not used more, and better, is the ironic fact that the very score that is best for charting progress creates the most accurate, but least interpretable, graph! Scale scores use the arbitrary scale created to be the "yardstick" to report reading comprehension, math computation, and so on. Percentile ranks, although the wrong things to chart, have the concrete referent "percent of the norm group scoring below" that most teachers understand. Looking at a scale score, however well analyzed, doesn't give a teacher any useful benchmarking information.

This leads us, of course, to grade-equivalent scores, which *are* useful for charting individual progress over time. This use is limited, however, and not well understood. One year of grade-equivalent increase is expected for each year in school, but that expectation is normative. It is based on the achievement of a typical student in that grade; it is *not* based on the graded curriculum. Grade-equivalent scores are routinely misinterpreted in this way. We have a great educational task, not only teaching teachers that grade equivalents only reflect that the student scored the same as the average student at that grade, and not that he or she knows what students are supposed to do in that grade, but also of equipping teachers with the language and skills they will need to communicate the meaning of grade-equivalent scores to students and parents. I think there's a message in this persistent misinterpretation of grade equivalents that has shown itself resistant to all manner of careful explanations and educational efforts.

I think the misinterpretation of grade-equivalent scores is a cry for criterion-referenced information (more about this in the following section). What teachers and parents really want to know about their children is whether and to what degree they are learning the material presented to them in school. Along comes a score called "grade equivalent," which seems to be exactly what is called for! A mix of wishful thinking and need for information creates a powerful motivational climate and readiness for learning . . . or mislearning, in this case. A careful, rational explanation of what grade-equivalent scores really mean, without offering any serious alternatives for the information the teachers and parents actually seek, seems a weak counteroffering. Thus, although better use of the norm-referenced measures, grade equivalents and scale scores, that exist for charting progress over time would be beneficial, better criterion-referenced information would be even more so. What teachers most need to know for their instructional decisions is what students know and can do, not how they stack up to a norm group.

Another difficulty with charting progress over time is the way test results are presented—as status reports. Students, teachers, and administrators receive printouts after a test administration. Even people who understand how grade equivalents should be used to chart progress over time cannot do it unless they take the printout and some scratch paper to the office and look up previous grade equivalents. That requires time, access, and some charting or graphing skill; if one or more of these is in short supply, then the information provided by the testing company, however longitudinally intended, cannot be used that way.

Do teachers really care to learn how to chart progress, and why? Do they care to learn to chart progress for individuals with grade equivalents and for groups of students with average scale scores translated into grade equivalents? I have some anecdotal evidence that they do. I recently spoke at a state-level conference of charter schools. Whatever one's opinions about charter schools, the important thing to note here is that charters that cannot demonstrate appropriate progress on many measures, including standardized tests, lose their charters and their funding and must close. Thus, knowing how to present standardized test information is a life-or-death issue for charter schools.

The session on using standardized test data was well attended. The participants were amazed to learn how percentile ranks work over time. They asked so many questions that we occupied the room too long and were asked to leave. They were grateful to know how the developmental measures, scale scores or grade equivalents, worked. And since many of their schools included a large portion of what the conference was calling "at-risk" students, the fact that students with low percentile ranks gradually fall behind in grade equivalents if they remain at the same percentile was a particularly interesting piece of information to them. And it was new information!

I was curious, because I was speaking to an audience that had studied education. Most of them had taken introduction to measurement courses of one kind or another.

Obviously, the information, if learned, didn't stick, and just as obviously most of them wished it had. I suggested that most of them had probably learned at least some of that information and forgotten it because they didn't see a use for it at the time. I wish you could have seen the looks on their faces. Information that people have no use for is information they forget or never really learn in the first place. One cannot answer questions that people are not asking.

Criterion-Referenced Uses of Data.   Teachers use a model of instruction that is based on identifying appropriate learning goals and helping students achieve them. The most appropriate kind of assessment information for this model of instruction is information about the degree to which students have achieved standard learning goals, whether defined by state standards, district curriculum, general public consensus, or teacher decision making. Some large-scale assessments provide this kind of information to some degree, but better criterion-referenced information is required if it is to serve as useful input to improving instruction and educational opportunity for students. If better criterion-referenced information were available, the short-term suggestions about better longitudinal use of norm-referenced information in the previous section would not be necessary.

Teachers do need to learn some things about criterion-referenced assessments. They need to understand the nature of the comparisons made between student performance and particular standards and the accuracy with which a student is classified into a performance level. Needed measurement skills for teachers might include things like interpreting scores and confidence bands and generalizing to the construct and not beyond. "Multiple measures" is a catchphrase many repeat knowingly. The number of measures alone, though, isn't the issue. It's knowing *which* measures to use to measure what constructs. Needed language and communication skills might include things like knowing how to express performance information without sounding judgmental. Most important for improving instruction, teachers need to develop a repertoire of instructional responses to various kinds of student performance.

If the goal is to improve instruction, however, developers of assessments must do their part. Testing companies and states need to provide more interpretable criterion-referenced scores. Percent correct on short subscales of basic skills tests are not the kind of criterion-referenced data that will help improve instruction. The norm-referenced information from large-scale tests, and even the criterion-referenced information from most criterion-referenced tests geared to large chunks of the curriculum, is not the right information on which to base most instructional decisions. More fine-grained and diagnostic criterion-referenced measures might be helpful, although many would argue that the best source of this kind of information is classroom assessment. Scale scores on assessments that purport to be based on standards are not helpful as criterion-referenced information either, until validation studies tie scores on the assessments to discernible levels of student performance.

Wiggins (1998) suggested an interesting alternative for grading student progress: reporting both "grades" and "scores" on student report cards. Grades would be the classroom-based measures that report student achievement based on classroom instructional objectives and expectations, in context. Scores would be criterion-referenced performance measured against some external standards. Students and their parents and teachers, Wiggins argued, need to know both how well students did what they were asked to do in the classroom and how well that translated into progress on some measure that is comparable across classes. I would add that teachers should be intimately involved in the planning of the assessments from which the scores would come, not hired and "trained" as they currently are in their role in norm-referenced test development, but truly part of the design.

I think this combination of grades and scores and the integration of external criterion-referenced assessments into the evaluation of classroom instruction is an interesting idea, worth pursuing, that has the potential to improve instruction. Whether it would is an empirical question that both teachers and researchers would need to answer, starting with the teachers. The first step would be for some educators who are intrigued by the possibility of how this might work for them to try it.

I alluded earlier to what I think is the inherent message in the persistent misinterpretation of grade-equivalent scores. Teachers and parents want to know the degree to which students are learning what they are asked to learn in school. The term *grade equivalent* sounds like the right thing, even though it isn't. I believe the "scores" on standards-referenced assessments that Wiggins calls for *would* fit this purpose. The desire for useful information is a powerful motivator; therefore, if I had to speculate about which aspect of assessment would be the first, best candidate for teacher inquiry about using assessment to improve instruction, it would be the development of standards-referenced assessments for agreed-upon curricular goals.

Since curriculum is written and delivered at the district level, perhaps that is the level where these assessments might develop, although districts might borrow and share assessment tasks or items, scoring rubrics, and exemplars. State standards-based tests do not have a good history of being based on teacher inquiry and curricular intentions; rather, they tend to be initiated by legislators and state officials. It is groups of teachers within districts that have the best chance of standing together as communities of inquirers. Teachers typically do not work with colleagues across districts in the same way as they do within districts.

Focused or Selective Reporting of Achievement.　　Elementary teachers' main concerns are, in general, more child-centered than secondary teachers, who are more subject-centered. For secondary teachers, access to the data they want without having to wade through data they don't is worth thinking about. Even elementary teachers, who may be interested in scores in all subjects, have a lot to look at on the typical printout. Computers may be the key here. If some sort of data look-up function were possible from the desktop, without signing out a student's folder from the office and then locating the appropriate information, more routine use might be made of large-scale test data.

It is also worth revisiting Impara and his colleagues' (1991) question about providing only scores that teachers really need in printouts for individual students. NCE scores (their example) would also be my first candidate for removal from the printout. They don't tell teachers about students' positions in the norm group directly, as percentile ranks do. Their function has been to be an interval-level data point in research studies; historically, they were developed for research into Title I programs for want of a better way to compare disparate standardized test scores. They were, if you will, a proxy for equating studies. But their mere existence tempts people to do things with them that are much more of a stretch than solving the practical evaluation problem for which they were invented. I recently attended a workshop for school administrators where I heard a national consultant advocate using NCE scores to compute gain scores by subtracting last spring's score from this spring's score—or, in areas where summer losses were large, spring minus the previous fall—and reporting that as a measure of "progress." My worry here is not just that the result would be statistically imprecise. The reporting of such noninformation is dangerous to the extent that people think it is real information that says something about their schools. Decisions about curriculum and instruction should be based on the best available information. Including information on a printout implies that it is useful for something.

Conclusion

I have used two different conceptions of teacher knowledge, knowledge-*for*-practice and knowledge-*of*-practice, in two ways: (1) as heuristics for understanding our own approaches to teacher knowledge about assessment and (2) as part of the argument that we need to change our approach to teacher knowledge about assessment if we really want teachers to use assessment information to improve instruction. I have not even mentioned the next logical piece of the puzzle, namely, what *students* will know about assessment and how *that* will improve instruction (Stiggins, this volume). This discussion has been about teachers and their need for information and understandings that will help them make the thousands of professional decisions each day that translate into educational opportunity for their students. I reviewed literature about what experts already know about teacher knowledge and use of assessments: knowledge-*for*-practice. I have made what I hope are some useful suggestions for thinking about the future, recognizing that progress will be based on teachers' questions: knowledge-*of*-practice.

These suggestions comport generally with the *Standards for Teacher Competence in Educational Assessment of Students* (AFT, NCME, NEA, 1990), especially Standard 3, about interpreting assessment results; Standard 4, about using assessment results; and Standard 6, about communicating assessment results. But these suggestions nudge the *Standards* a little, too, because they suggest that not only do teachers need to learn how to interpret and communicate assessment results but that some changes in the reporting of large-scale assessment results are needed, as well, to support our vision of effecting positive change in educational institutions in the new century. And most important, these suggestions turn the use of the *Standards* document on its head, because I have suggested that we should stop emphasizing what teachers need to *know* and start emphasizing what teachers *need* to know. Those who would help teachers learn about large-scale assessment, or any assessment for that matter, must realize that they need to cede ownership of the process. It doesn't matter what is interesting to us or what we think teachers need. We need to start listening to teachers' questions and understanding the problems they must solve. We need to be there with relevant information, even if that means changing the way assessment results are reported. We need to stop implying that if only teachers were more "competent," somehow assessment results would be used properly and education would necessarily improve. And we need to do all that without letting go of basic points about valid uses of assessment information, for that is where we genuinely do have something to offer to teachers. Just don't expect them to take our word for it. We need to listen.

r e f e r e n c e s

Airasian, P. W. (1991). Perspectives on measurement instruction. *Educational Measurement: Issues and Practice, 10*(1), 13–16, 26.

American Federation of Teachers, National Council on Measurement in Education, & National Education Association. (1990). *Standards for teacher competence in educational assessment of students.* Washington, D.C.: Authors.

Brookhart, S. M. (1999). Teaching about communicating assessment results and grading. *Educational Measurement: Issues and Practice, 18*(1), 5–13.

Cochran-Smith, M., & Lytle, S. L. (1999). Relationships of knowledge and practice: Teacher learning in communities. *Review of Research in Education, 24*, 249–305.

Council of Chief State School Officers. (1998). *Key state education policies on K-12 education.* Washington, DC: Author.

Gallagher, C. (2000). A seat at the table: Teachers reclaiming assessment through rethinking accountability. *Phi Delta Kappan, 81*, 502–507.

Gullickson, A. R. (1993). Matching measurement instruction to classroom-based evaluation: Perceived discrepancies, needs, and challenges. In *Teacher training in measurement and assessment skills*, ed. S. L. Wise, pp. 1–25. Lincoln, Neb.: Buros Institute of Mental Measurements, University of Nebraska-Lincoln.

Herman, J. L., & Golan, S. (1993). The effects of standardized testing on teaching and schools. *Educational Measurement: Issues and Practice, 12*(4), 20–25, 41–42.

Houser, M. (2000). Grading our high schools. *Pittsburgh Tribune-Review*, 6 February, D1–D2.

Impara, J. C., Divine, K. P., Bruce, F. A., Liverman, M. R., & Gay, A. (1991). Does interpretive test score information help teachers? *Educational Measurement: Issues and Practice, 10*(4), 16–18.

Marso, R. N., & Pigge, F. L. (1993). Teachers' testing knowledge, skills, and practices. In *Teacher training in measurement and assessment skills*, ed. S. L. Wise, pp. 129–185. Lincoln, Neb.: Buros Institute of Mental Measurements, University of Nebraska-Lincoln.

Mayo, S. T. (1964). What experts think teachers ought to know about educational measurement. *Journal of Educational Measurement, 1*, 79–86.

Messick, S. (1989). Validity. In *Educational Measurement.*

3d ed. Edited by R. L. Linn, pp. 13–103. New York: Macmillan.

Nitko, A. J. (1991). Editorial. What are we teaching teachers about assessment and why? *Educational Measurement: Issues and Practice, 10*(1), 2.

———. (2000). *Educational assessment of students.* 3d ed. Englewood Cliffs, N.J.: Prentice Hall.

Pennsylvania Department of Education. (2000). PA assessment test results. Available online: http://www.pde.psu.edu/esscores.html.

Plake, B. S., Impara, J. C., & Fager, J. J. (1993). Assessment competencies of teachers: A national survey. *Educational Measurement: Issues and Practice, 12*(4), 10–12, 39.

Schafer, W. D. (1991). Essential assessment skills in professional education of teachers. *Educational Measurement: Issues and Practice, 10*(1), 2–6, 12.

———. (1993). Assessment literacy for teachers. *Theory into Practice, 32*, 118–126.

Schafer, W. D., & Lissitz, R. W. (1987). Measurement training for school personnel: Recommendations and reality. *Journal of Teacher Education, 38*(3), 57–63.

Scriven, M. (1967). The methodology of evaluation. In *Perspectives of curriculum evaluation*, eds. R. Tyler, R. Gagne, & M. Scriven, pp. 39–83. Chicago: Rand McNally & Company.

Smith, J. K. (1999). Editorial. *Educational Measurement: Issues and Practice, 18*(1), 4.

Smith, M. L., & Rottenberg, C. (1991). Unintended consequences of external testing in elementary schools. *Educational Measurement: Issues and Practice, 10*(4), 7–11.

Stiggins, R. J. (1991a). Assessment literacy. *Phi Delta Kappan, 72*, 534–539.

———. (1991b). Relevant classroom assessment training for teachers. *Educational Measurement: Issues and Practice, 10*(1), 7–12.

Wiggins, G. (1998). *Educative assessment.* San Francisco: Jossey-Bass.

Wise, S. L., ed. (1993). *Teacher training in measurement and assessment skills.* Lincoln, Neb.: Buros Institute of Mental Measurements, University of Nebraska-Lincoln.

Wise, S. L., Lukin, L. E., & Roos, L. L. (1991). Teacher beliefs about training in testing and measurement. *Journal of Teacher Education, 42*(1), 37–42.

2

Where Is Our Assessment Future and How Can We Get There from Here?*

RICHARD J. STIGGINS

Assessment Training Institute, Portland, Oregon

*A paper presented at a conference entitled, "Assessment in Educational Reform: Both Means and Ends," sponsored by the University of Maryland, College Park, Md., June 5–6, 2000.

Public policy makers at all levels seem to believe that the way to get effective schools is to threaten students, teachers, and administrators with severe public and very personal sanctions if standardized test scores don't go up. In their need to appear to be wrestling with important social issues, they hold educators and students accountable for test scores. In doing so, these officials disregard research on when the human mind learns most easily and frequently ignore strong warnings from the measurement community about inappropriate use of test scores. They appear to be unaware of the fact that not all students face the challenge of state assessment with the same desire or confidence. In doing so, they risk damage to a sizable proportion of the student population. It is possible that the assessment instruments and procedures that we have created for public accountability are doing more harm than good for certain students—that is, they are causing these students to learn less, not more. We seem unable to accommodate the reality that not all students confront the challenge of the externally imposed examination with the same hope of success.

The point is not that standardized tests are inappropriate. They can serve very productive purposes at many different levels in the school improvement equation when used in proper ways by assessment-literate users. But so few policy makers or professional educators understand what it means to use assessment properly that the development of productive assessment environments (that accommodate differences among students) remains, as it has for decades, beyond our collective reach. If we continue in this manner, the inept use of assessment will contribute more to the demise of public education than to its enhancement.

In this paper, I offer an alternative vision of the relationship between assessment and effective schools. After exploring the problem in greater depth, I will suggest solutions that promise a more powerful role for assessment in school improvement in the future than we have experienced in the past. To begin with, in describing this optimistic vision, I will outline what I believe is a very strong assessment foundation that we have been working to put in place in recent decades. Then I will describe in detail a shift that must take place in our beliefs about assessment and its role in achieving effective schools if we are to succeed in achieving my vision of excellence. And finally, I will outline the specific work to be done to create an assessment future that promises to maximize the learning of the largest possible proportion of our students. But first, consider the problem.

The Evolution of Assessment Problems

In response to public concern in the 1960s, those in positions of political responsibility for the quality of schools implemented local, state, and even national school reform initiatives. They began to hold schools publicly accountable for their quality, and those demands have continued to intensify ever since. Virtually every school reform initiative implemented over the decades has relied heavily on assessment as a force for accountability, that is, to motivate change and to serve as the index of school success. As a result of this demand for evidence of school effectiveness, over the past few decades we have invested billions of dollars in the production, administration, and use of standardized tests. There are several reasons why we have made those investments.

First of all, we want an objective, uninvolved third party to design and conduct the assessments, so as to assure us of unbiased evidence of effectiveness. We haven't trusted local educators to provide credible data. Besides, to determine if school districts or districts across states are helping students learn, the achievement data must be comparable across classrooms and over time. Thus, the assessments must be the same—that is, standardized across contexts. Further, we believe that threatening schools (administrators, teachers, and students) with public embarrassment for low test scores will intimidate them into trying harder. The result of increased effort, we believe, will be greater learning, yielding more effective schools. Finally, we are a competitive society. Many believe that pitting one school or district against another by using a common test will result in greater effort, more learning, and more effective schools.

The strength and impact of these beliefs about the role of assessment in school improvement can be seen in the unrelenting march toward layer upon layer of standardized tests that has unfolded over the past 50 years:

- In the 1940s, we began with nationally standardized college admission tests.
- In the 1950s and 1960s, we extended this kind of testing across the nation and into every grade level with the birth of districtwide accountability testing programs.
- In the 1970s, we added statewide testing programs, beginning the decade with 3 of them, ending that decade with 37, and standing at 48 today.
- In the 1970s and 1980s, we added a national assessment program.
- In the 1990s, we have become enamored with international assessment programs.

Understand that no layer was eliminated once in place; only new layers were added. It is as if policy makers at all levels operated on the blind faith that if we just test at enough levels or at the right level, we will find the magic assessment key to better schools. Also note that as time progressed the locus of assessment moved further and further from the place where learning happens, in the classroom and in the relationship between student and teacher. *Nowhere during the past 50 years has attention been paid to the quality of classroom assessment.* Consider the total costs of these programs over the years. We have to have invested billions across levels over the decades.

The fact is that standardized tests make valuable contributions to school improvement. Critically important decision makers rely on the data from such assessments to inform decisions that impact school quality. These decision makers include policy makers, overall program planners, and those who muster resources to support classroom instruction. Our point is not to impugn the contributions of district, state, national, or international assessment. Rather, we seek to point out that these are not the only decision makers whose choices influence the nature and impact of schooling. In fact, we believe that the most crucial decisions are made by students, teachers, and parents day-to-day in the classroom and the living room. And standardized test scores will not meet their information needs. Assessments that happen just once a year are not likely to be of much help to those who must make decisions every three or four minutes. Assessments that provide broad portraits of student achievement are not likely to help those who need high-resolution microscopes. Assessments that produce results two months after the test is taken are not likely to be of value to those who must make decisions right now.

What evidence of student achievement can these assessment users tap to inform their choices? They must turn to the evidence derived from day-to-day classroom assessment.

These are the data that teachers tap to diagnose student needs, evaluate instructional interventions, and assign report card grades, for example. These are the data that students turn to in order to see if they're getting it, to determine what help they need, to judge whether the learning is worth the effort, to decide whether to try or give up in hopelessness. These are the data that parents must rely on to show them when, where, and how to invest family resources to help their children grow and succeed.

But here is the problem: Because we have been so obsessed with standardized testing and have been continuously investing so much money at so many levels, no resources remain to ensure the quality of day-to-day classroom assessments (Schafer & Lissitz, 1987; Stiggins & Conklin, 1992). As a result, even in the year 2000, we cannot ensure the accuracy of teachers' day-to-day classroom assessments. Only 14 of the 50 states require competence in assessment as a condition of certification to teach, and no state certifies that competence. Only three states require competence in assessment as a condition of being licensed as a principal, and no state certifies that competence. So teacher and administrator training programs have been notorious over the decades for not preparing practitioners to accurately assess the achievement of their students. As a result, we have a national faculty unschooled in the principles of sound assessment—an activity that will command as much as a third of professional time and energy.

Imagine the plight of the student mired in a classroom in which inept assessment is leading the teacher to misdiagnose individual and group needs, rely on ineffective instructional interventions, or even assign report card grades that systematically misrepresent student achievement. There is not a once-a-year standardized test yet invented that can overcome the dire consequences for the learner. Imagine graduating medical doctors who have not been trained to interpret the results of the laboratory tests they request—indeed, who don't even know what tests to request. This is the state of classroom assessment affairs in the United States today.

We know that teachers and administrators need to know about assessment to be effective. We know what they need to know and how to teach them. We at ATI have designed professional development materials and experiences that impart those assessment understandings in supremely flexible and economical ways. Now all practitioners need is the opportunity to become assessment literate as a school. But board members, legislators, state department of education personnel, and superintendents seem unaware of the need to allocate the resources needed to make that possible. For every dollar we spend on standardized testing programs, we should be allocating another to ensure the quality of our day-to-day classroom assessments. We must balance our assessments. If we continue to ignore the power of classroom assessment as a school improvement tool, we deprive teachers of a set of tools that have been proven to raise student achievement to unprecedented levels. But more important, if we continue to ignore classroom assessment as a school improvement priority, we continue to place students directly in harm's way.

Building on a Strong Foundation

We can overcome these problems and build a truly productive assessment future by building on a very strong three-part foundation. Each part is in place now and is ready to carry its share of the load. But what is needed is the desire to change course.

The first part of that foundation is our deep understanding of our valued expectations for academic achievement. We know what needs to be taught and assessed. The second part is the truly impressive array of assessment methods that we have at our disposal. We have the tools to do the assessment job right. And the third part is a highly refined set of quality control standards by which to judge the appropriateness of any marriage of achievement targets and assessment methods. In short, we know how to evaluate the quality of any assessment. From here, we can grow. Let's consider each of these in greater depth.

Clear Targets

One part of the foundation of a strong assessment future is mastery learning models, which were developed a half century ago. The idea was advanced that the social function of schools might be shifted from sorting students to ensuring the attainment of specific competencies. An educational system that held the amount of time to learn constant while permitting the amount learned at the end of that time free to vary was reconceived to permit time to learn to vary, holding the amount learned constant. This kind of thinking brought with it the potential for a fundamental shift in the role of assessment in the schooling process. Assessments that had traditionally been designed and built to yield a dependable rank order of students might be redesigned to provide dependable evidence of content mastery. We began to explore a new measurement model, criterion-referenced assessment.

Both of these shifts aligned the school mission and assessment more closely with the reality that teachers face day-to-day in the classroom. The teacher's job is to maximize the development of each individual student. The role of assessment is to assist in that process. By their very nature, teachers have always sought to maximize learning, not the dependability of their rank order of students. So as the concept of mastery learning has evolved through its various incarnations over the past 50 years, from behavioral objectives to minimum competencies to outcomes-based education and finally to standards-driven schools, the mission of schools has moved closer to the natural inclination of teachers. And as assessments have aligned more and more closely with specified achievement standards, they have provided teachers with the ever-more-complete portrait of student achievement that they need to guide instruction.

As a result of this evolution, specialists in all of the academic disciplines have worked diligently and effectively over the past half century to define more precisely the achievement standards that underpin their field of study. So our collective visions of what it means to master content knowledge, reason productively, read, write, speak, and solve mathematics or science problems are all far clearer than ever before. In addition, specialists in the various disciplines have assembled a variety of developmental continuums that define the ascending levels of academic competence through which students must progress to meet ultimate standards of excellence. All of these deeper understandings provide teachers with a much stronger vision of what they are to assess day-to-day in the classroom. The clearer the target, the better will be the quality of the assessment. Now the challenge we face is that of placing these visions of academic excellence and the capacity to assess them on a daily basis in the hands of every teacher. More about that later.

Impressive Assessment Options

The extremely good news is that our healthy evolution has not been limited to achievement expectations and general measurement models. It also has extended to specific assessment formats. This does not mean that we discovered a broad array of new assessment methods. During the past century only one new kind of assessment appeared on the scene, the *selected response* method developed in the 1920s. All other currently popular methods had already been in use for a long time.

The methods that we have at our disposal are impressive in their diversity and potential power. We have in hand a variety of selected response formats, including multiple choice, true/false, matching, and short-answer fill-in. We can turn to *essay assessments* in which students respond to focused assignments by constructing original written responses that teachers evaluate by applying exercise-specific evaluation criteria. We can rely on *performance assessment* methods—assessments in which students demonstrate performance skills or product development capabilities that also are evaluated using specific criteria. And finally, we can use assessments that are based on direct *personal interaction* between examiner and examinee, such as interviews, discussions, or oral examinations.

The healthy evolution to which I refer is the broad base of acceptance that has emerged for the use of the full range of available methods. Although the selected response method dominated the assessment process through the middle decades of the century and we have seen a trendy shift in interest in performance assessment in recent decades, all available methods have credibility today. In fact, the emerging popularity of subjective assessment methods has caused us to analyze them carefully and develop far clearer guidelines for their use than we have ever had before. This gives teachers access to the wide range of potentially powerful methods that they need to cover the variety of achievement targets they must assess day-to-day in the classroom. The challenge we face is that of placing these tools in teachers' hands to permit their use in everyday classroom assessment in practical terms. Again, I will address this challenge in detail later.

Standards of Assessment Quality

Not only do we understand what we wish to assess and the methods we can use but we also know how to judge if we do it well. In technical terms, that means we have defined clear and appropriate standards of validity and reliability. But more important, we know how to translate our technical standards into commonsense terms that can be applied in any assessment context. I will describe the commonsense standards now and explain their importance later.

We can frame the key attributes of sound assessments in the form of five standards.* These are the criteria by which we must judge the quality of our classroom and standardized assessments.

---

*These standards of quality are described in teacher-friendly terms in my introductory text, *Student-involved classroom assessment* (2001).

Standard 1. Quality Assessments Arise from and Accurately Reflect Clearly Speci-fied and Appropriate Achievement Expectations for Students. Knowing precisely what we are asking students to master is important because different targets require differ-ent assessment methods. In any assessment context, we must begin the assessment devel-opment process by defining a clear vision of what it means to succeed. Do we expect our students to

- Master subject matter content, meaning to *know and understand?*

   Does this mean they must know it outright?
   Or does it mean they must know where and how to find it, using references?

- Use knowledge to *reason* and solve problems?

- Demonstrate mastery of specific *performance skills*, where it's the doing that is im-portant?

- Use their knowledge, reasoning, and skills to create *products* that meet standards of quality?

Because there is no single assessment method capable of assessing all these various forms of achievement, one cannot select a proper method without a sharp focus on which of these expectations is to be assessed.

Standard 2. Sound Assessments Are Specifically Designed to Serve Instructional Purposes. We cannot design assessments without asking who will use the results and how. Table 2.1 lists the important users of assessment in schools, each of whom needs different information at different times to answer different questions. To provide quality information for teacher, student, and parent at the classroom level, we need sound class-room assessments. To provide useful information at the levels of policy or instructional support, we need high-quality standardized tests. Because of the differences in informa-tion needs, we must begin each assessment event with a clear sense of whose needs we are meeting. Otherwise, our assessments are without purpose.

Standard 3. Quality Assessments Accurately Reflect the Intended Target and Serve the Intended Purpose. Because we have several different kinds of achievement to assess, and because no single assessment method can reflect them all, we must rely on a variety of methods. The options include *selected response* (multiple choice, true/false, matching, and fill-in), *essays, performance assessments* (based on observation and judgment), and direct *per-sonal communication* with the student. Our assessment challenge is to match a method with an intended target, as depicted in Table 2.2. Our professional development challenge is to be sure all concerned with quality assessment know and understand how the various pieces of this puzzle fit together.

Standard 4. Quality Assessments Provide a Representative Sample of Student Performance That Is Sufficient in Its Scope to Permit Confident Conclusions about Student Achievement. All assessments rely on a relatively small number of exercises to permit the user to draw inferences about a student's mastery of larger domains of

TABLE 2.1   Examples of Assessment Users and Uses

Classroom Level

Assessment User	Sample Questions
Student	Am I succeeding?
	Am I improving over time?
	Do I know what it means to succeed here?
	What should I do next to succeed?
	What help do I need to succeed?
	Do I feel in control of my own success?
	Does my teacher think I'm capable of success?
	Do I think I'm capable of success?
	Is the learning worth the effort?
	How am I doing in relation to my classmates?
	Where do I want all of this to take me?
Teacher	Are my students improving?
	Is it because of me?
	What does this student need?
	Is this student capable of learning this?
	What do these students need?
	What are their strengths that we can build on?
	How should I group my students?
	Am I going too fast, too slow, too far, not far enough?
	Am I improving as a teacher?
	How can I improve?
	Did that teaching strategy work?
	What do I say at parent–teacher conferences?
	What grade do I put on the report card?
Parent	Is my child learning new things—growing?
	Is my child succeeding?
	Is my child keeping up?
	Are we doing enough at home to support the teacher?
	What does my child need to succeed?
	Does the teacher know what my child needs?
	Is this teacher doing a good job?
	Is this a good school? District?

Instructional Support Level

Assessment User	Sample Questions
Principal	How do we define success in terms of student learning?
	Is this teacher producing results in the form of student learning?
	How can I help this teacher improve?
	Is instruction in our building producing results?
	Is instruction at each grade level producing results?
	Are our students qualifying for college?
	Are our students prepared for the workplace?
	Do we need professional development as a faculty to improve?
	How shall we allocate building resources to achieve success?

(continued)

TABLE 2.1 *(continued)*

Mentor teacher	Is this new teacher producing results? What does this new teacher need to improve?
Curriculum director	How do we define success in terms of student achievement? Is our program of instruction working? What adjustments do we need to make in our curriculum?
Special Services	Who needs (qualifies for) special educational services? Is our program of services helping students? What advice does this student need to succeed?

Policy Level

Assessment User	*Sample Questions*
Superintendent	Are our programs of instruction producing results in terms of student learning? Is each building principal producing results? Which schools deserve or need more or fewer resources?
School board	Are our students learning and succeeding? Is the superintendent producing results?
State Department of Education	Are programs across the state producing results? Are individual school districts producing results?
Citizen/Legislature	Are our students achieving in ways that prepare them to become productive citizens?

Source: Student-Involved Classroom Assessment, 3/e, by R. J. Stiggins, © 2001. REPRINTED BY PERMISSION OF PEARSON EDUCATION, INC., UPPER SADDLE RIVER, NJ 07458.

achievement. A sound assessment offers a representative sample of all those possibilities that is large enough to yield dependable inferences about how the respondent would have done if given all possible exercises. Each assessment context places its own special constraints on our sampling procedures. Our quality control challenge is to know how to adjust the sampling strategies to produce results of maximum quality at minimum cost in time and effort.

Standard 5. Sound Assessments Are Designed, Developed, and Used in Such a Manner as to Eliminate Sources of Bias or Distortion That Interfere with the Accuracy of Results. Even if we devise clear achievement targets, transform them into proper assessment methods, and sample student performance appropriately, there are still factors that can cause a student's score on a test to misrepresent real achievement. Problems can arise from the test, the student, or the environment where the test is administered.

For example, tests can consist of poorly worded questions, place reading or writing demands on respondents that confound evidence of the mastery of the material being tested, have more than one correct response, be incorrectly scored, or contain racial or ethnic bias. The student can experience extreme evaluation anxiety or interpret test items differently from the author's intent, as well as cheat, guess, or lack motivation. Any of

TABLE 2.2   Aligning Achievement Targets to Assessment Methods

Target to Be Assessed	Assessment Method			
	Selected Response	*Essay*	*Performance Assessment*	*Personal Communication*
Knowledge Mastery	Multiple choice, true/false, matching, and fill-in can sample mastery of elements of knowledge	Essay exercises can tap understanding of relationships among elements of knowledge	Not a good choice for this target—three other options preferred	Can ask questions, evaluate answers, and infer mastery—but a time-consuming option
Reasoning Proficiency	Can assess understanding of basic patterns of reasoning	Written descriptions of complex problem solutions can provide a window into reasoning proficiency	Can watch students solve some problems and infer about reasoning proficiency	Can ask student to "think aloud" or can ask follow-up questions to probe reasoning
Skills	Can assess mastery of the prerequisites of skillful performance—but cannot tap the skill itself	Can assess mastery of the prerequisites of skillful performance—but cannot tap the skill itself	Can observe and evaluate skills as they are being performed	Strong match when skill is oral communication proficiency; also can assess mastery of knowledge prerequisite to skillful performance
Ability to Create Products	Can assess mastery of of knowledge prerequisite to the ability to create quality products—but cannot assess the quality of products themselves	Can assess mastery of knowledge prerequisite to the ability to create quality products—but cannot assess the quality of products themselves	A strong match can assess: (a) proficiency in carrying out steps in product development and (b) attributes of the product itself	Can probe procedural knowledge and knowledge of attributes of quality products—but not product quality

Source: Student-Involved Classroom Assessment, 3/e, by R. J. Stiggins, © 2001. REPRINTED BY PERMISSION OF PEARSON EDUCATION, INC., UPPER SADDLE RIVER, NJ 07458.

these conditions could give rise to inaccurate test results. Or the assessment environment could be uncomfortable, poorly lighted, noisy, or otherwise distracting. Part of the challenge of being assessment literate is being aware of the potential sources of bias and knowing how to devise assessments, prepare students, and plan assessment environments to deflect these problems before they ever impact results.

As we look to the future, we have much to bank on. Specialists in all academic disciplines have responded to the demand for high standards with thoughtful efforts to define what they mean by "academic excellence," and the results have been positive. We have the capacity to take more students to higher levels of competence faster than ever before. In addition, we are open to tracking their progress using a wider array of assessment methods than ever before. And we are more sharply focused on what it means to do a good job of assessment—we can monitor and adjust our assessments with precision.

With all of this on our side, one might ask, why is it that our assessment house is in such disarray. As it turns out, there are good reasons.

Redefining the Bond of Assessment to Student Motivation*

Even in the face of such immense positive potential, however, we struggle with assessment. For instance, we remain consistently out of balance in our concern for the quality of classroom and standardized assessment. We remain an assessment-illiterate school culture at all levels and in society in general. Our strong belief in "assessment for intimidation" is driving students into hopelessness. We continue today, as we have for decades, to place our students directly in harm's way, doing at least as much harm with our assessments as good.

To understand how this can happen and what to do about it, we must carefully examine our societal beliefs about what role assessment should play in the development of effective schools. We hold several strong values about this, and the assessment environment that has emerged in American schools over the past 50 years is a direct reflection of those beliefs and values.

In addition to informing decisions, as mentioned previously, we also believe that assessment should motivate learning. We believe in motivating by holding people accountable: Produce or get out. Assessment isn't just the gauge of production, the fear that it generates drives learning, we contend. Once again, we can see the strength and impact of these beliefs in the demand for public accountability in school improvement as demonstrated by the unrelenting march toward layer upon layer of standardized tests that I described earlier:

- In the 1940s, we launched national standardized college admission tests to ensure fair competition for access to higher education. Today, families and school districts spend millions on test preparation courses in the hope of raising scores.
- In the 1950s and 1960s, we extended testing across the nation and into every grade level with districtwide accountability testing programs, with some states and districts attaching grade-level promotion decisions to scores.
- In the 1970s, we added statewide testing programs, beginning the decade with 3 of them, ending that decade with 37, and seeing that number at 48 today. Now many states attach promotion, graduation, and certificate of mastery decisions to these scores.

I contend that this progression has unfolded in part because of our societal belief that these high-stakes tests can serve motivational purposes. This is part and parcel of our strongly held societal belief that the way to maximize learning is to maximize anxiety. Most of us grew up in classrooms in which our teachers purposely sought to keep us

---

*This redefinition is presented in more complete detail in Stiggins (2001).

guessing, uncertain, and vulnerable to the consequences of assessment, because they believed that this would keep us focused, striving, and learning. It is in this sense that the assessment process fuels the engine that drives instruction and student learning. That engine is student motivation. We understand that the students who learn are those who want to learn. And assessment is the great intimidator that will make that happen.

Or will it? This leads us to the age-old question, How do we help our students want to learn? I submit that the proper use of assessment has historically represented and will continue to represent a large part of the answer. The desire to succeed in school can be enhanced or destroyed more quickly and permanently through our use of assessment than through any other tools we have at our disposal. Therefore, I have concluded that the teacher's most important challenge is to manage the relationship between assessment and student motivation effectively.

Let me defend this proposition. How can we help our students want to learn? We have evolved answers to this question over the years, and each reconsideration of the question has led us to more powerful answers. Let me share that historical perspective.

Reward and Punishment as a Path to High Achievement

The theory of learning that has exerted greatest influence on school efforts to motivate is known as *behaviorism*. Proponents of this theory explain how or why we learn as a function of schedules of rewards and punishments (Skinner, 1974). We tend to repeat behavior that is positively and regularly reinforced within our environment. Behavior that is repeatedly punished is likely to be extinguished and to disappear. Therefore, by manipulating rewards and punishments we can encourage learners to repeat academically productive behavior and to eliminate behavior unlikely to result in learning. This theory of motivation has spread so deeply into our classrooms and into society at large that it has now become an unquestioned "truth."

In the classroom, assessment traditionally serves as the primary source of evidence upon which to base the doling out of rewards and punishments. High test scores and grades are thought to reinforce the behavior that resulted in substantial learning, while failing test scores and grades are supposed to punish, and thus extinguish, the behavior that resulted in insufficient learning. Sounds like a pretty straightforward way to promote the pursuit of academic excellence, does it not?

However, another social psychologist, Kohn (1993), cautions that this seductive simplicity belies the underlying truth that motivation is not all that straightforward. That is, using grades as rewards and punishments does not motivate learning in productive ways. Indeed, he contends, they have just the opposite effect. Relying on a comprehensive review of decades of research, Kohn concludes that the use of extrinsic sources of motivation, such as stars, stickers, trophies, and grades, can bring students to believe that learning activities are not worth doing in their own right, thus undermining students' natural curiosity to find out how and why things work as they do. Among others, he cites the research findings of Condry (1977), who concluded that people do the following when offered rewards:

. . . choose easier tasks, are less efficient in using the information available to solve novel problems, and tend to be answer oriented and more illogical in their problem-solving strategies. They seem to work harder and produce more activity, but the activity is of a lower quality, contains more errors, and is more stereotyped and less creative than the work of comparable nonrewarded subjects working on the same problems (quoted in Kohn, 1993, pp. 471–472).

Assuming that these researchers correctly describe what is at least a very complicated relationship between behaviorism and student motivation—and they provide a compelling body of research to defend their position—we are forced to ask the question, If test scores and grades don't necessarily result in greater learning, how then shall we encourage our students to strive to attain academic excellence?

Causal Attributions as a Path to High Achievement

Part of the answer may lie in the work of Weiner (1974), who developed a theory of motivation that expands on the idea of reward and punishment in a very interesting manner. He contends that we are driven by an internal reality or filter that helps us interpret who is in control of, or responsible for, our personal successes and failures. This is called *attribution theory.*

Basically, those students who attribute their academic successes to their own ability and hard work are said to have an internal locus of control over those successes. They see themselves as able. Thus, when faced with a learning challenge, they are likely to feel in control of the situation, to anticipate future success, and to invest whatever it takes to succeed. However, there also are those who attribute the reasons for their successes to others. Their interpretation holds that success in school probably resulted from good luck or the hard work of a good teacher. In their minds, they are not in control of the reward and punishment contingencies; someone else is. These students have an external locus of control.

As we face the challenge of encouraging students to put forth the effort required to become productive learners, we must strive to develop within them a sense of pride at having tried hard. If we can use the communication system to show them that hard work can pay off with success (you can get high grades for putting forth effort), they will be in control of the reasons for their success. This will prepare them to face new challenges with confidence and provide the motivation to succeed. In this sense, our goal is to help students feel as though they are in charge of their own academic successes; if they try, they have the resources to learn. In a very real sense, this represents the school version of the American dream. Hard work is its own reward. Pull yourself up by your bootstraps with hard work. We value this because we feel, logically, that those who try to learn succeed more than those who don't try. In reality, however, just as with behaviorism, life is more complicated than this set of values would imply.

The connection of effort to achievement is relatively easy to make for the academically successful student. But what about the students who fail to achieve and who attribute that failure to their own lack of ability? What do we do with students who try hard and fail anyway? How do we keep them from giving up in the face of insurmountable odds? How do we keep these students from feeling unable to control their own well-being in school? The bottom line is, how do we keep them from giving up on themselves and on their teachers? Further, how do we deal with students who attribute the reasons for academic failure to a system that is "out to get them," to drive them from school? Or students who lack the courage to risk trying out of fear that they might not succeed, because of uncertainty about who really is in control? Where does the motivation come from for these students to invest whatever it takes to find some level of academic success?

Maintaining Self-Worth as a Path to High Achievement

The answers to these questions may lie in the work of Covington (1992), which centers on the concept of student self-worth. He points out that school presents students with a special "ability game" that can be difficult to win. "In this game, the amount of effort students expend provides clear information about their ability status. For instance, if students succeed without much effort, especially if the task is difficult, then estimates of their ability increase; but should they try hard and fail anyway, especially if the task is easy, attributions to low ability are likely to follow" (pp. 16–17). Covington's perspective is that students' prime objective in schools is to maintain a sense of ability, a sense that they can do it, if they try. But in a cruel twist of this perspective, many students consciously choose to not study and not achieve because if they try and fail they damage that internally held and publicly perceived sense of capability, the basis of their self-worth. They feel it is better to maintain at least some degree of uncertainty, and therefore some degree of self-esteem, by not investing in the system.

Of course, not all students see themselves or school in this self-doubting way. Some are distinctly more positive in asserting an internal locus of control. Covington (citing Skinner, Welborn, & Connell, 1990) differentiates between success- and failure-oriented students. This orientation influences how they see themselves in the competitive arena of the classroom:

> When children believe that they can exert control over success in school, they perform better on cognitive tasks. And, when children succeed in school they are more likely to view school performance as a controllable outcome. . . . Children who are not doing well in school will perceive themselves as having no control over academic success and failures and these beliefs will subsequently generate performances that serve to confirm their beliefs (Skinner et al., 1990, as cited in Covington, 1992, p. 38).

So far, this sounds just like Weiner (1974). However, Covington (1992) then departs from his predecessors in offering us a trichotomy of student perceptions of self-worth: (1) success-oriented students, those who are academically competent; (2) failure avoiders, who are uncertain about the probability of success; and (3) failure acceptors, who see themselves as doomed from the outset. As I describe these, tune into the role that assessment plays in the evolution of a student's academic self-concept.

Success-oriented students feel capable of success in the classroom. Their frequent success on classroom assessments reaffirms this self-concept. But when failure does occur in school (a rare occurrence), they quickly infer that they didn't try hard enough or didn't understand the task well enough to perform well on it. In this sense, failure is not a threat. It does not lead to a sense of incompetence but rather one of ignorance: "There must be something I missed, something correctable if I just work harder and smarter." In the face of failure, they rely on their sense of their own ability to define the problem in a manner that leaves them feeling guilty but optimistic. As a result, they continue to try and do better the next time. Under all circumstances, they feel safe because they have desensitized themselves to the potentially negative effects of evaluation. They have the inner resources to take the risk of trying to learn new things.

Those without the ability to risk comfortably will stop trying and stop learning. According to Covington, they can become "failure avoiders." These are self-doubting, apathetic students who, when faced with an academic challenge, tend to think that they just aren't smart enough to succeed. This pessimism contributes to a lack of effort. When failure results, it reinforces feelings of inadequacy. This leads to greater feelings of shame and pessimism, which, in turn, yield more poor performance. To make matters worse, these students can extend this counterproductive self-concept even to those occasions when they succeed. Their internal sense of low ability can leave them worrying that they really didn't deserve the high grade. Further, they can become concerned that someone might discover that they are really only high-achieving impostors. They lack any sense of pride in accomplishment that would be reassuring about future prospects of high grades, thinking instead that they were just lucky to do well this time. In effect, they can snatch defeat from the jaws of imminent victory, resulting once again in a kind of pessimism that promises more poor performance in the future. Under no circumstances do these students feel safe, making it very difficult for them to risk trying something new or something that might require a stretch on their part. This is where the academic apathy comes from. Covington (1992) points out that these students are not "unmotivated" at all. Rather, they are highly motivated, but to do things that are counterproductive from an academic achievement point of view.

And, to complete the picture, we also can find failure-accepting students in a similar situation. They are even more trapped than failure avoiders. These students have experienced so much failure over such a long period of time that they have given up completely on themselves and school. There is no desire to "try" left in them, and thus they are assured of virtually never succeeding academically. As a result, they are constantly bombarded with compelling evidence of their own "stupidity." Soon they become numbed to the onslaught and become mental dropouts. Covington refers to this as *learned helplessness.* Even if they happen to succeed at something, these students are sure to credit blind luck, disregard any message of possible competence, and remain enmeshed in a tangle of doom. Such students feel absolutely no control over what happens to them in school and therefore are always vulnerable. Taking the risks needed to learn is not only beyond their reach, it's also beyond their frame of reference.

As it turns out, *confidence* is the key to student success in all learning situations. In the behavior management system, where tests and grades are used as rewards and punishments, some students gain confidence and learn to continue to take the risks of trying to learn more. But others lose confidence and stop trying. In other words, if we assume that our traditional motivation system is working well or can work well for all students, we are being naive. If our assessment practices continue to reflect this naivete, we will continue to lose those students who give up in hopelessness.

Why Is This Important?   To see why, this is important, think about the profound changes that are taking place in the mission of schools. Most of us grew up in schools whose mission was to sort us from the highest achiever to the lowest. The index of school effectiveness was the dependability of the rank order of seniors at the end of high school. But in the 1980s and 1990s, the business community began to say, "We hired those who were very high in your rank order and they couldn't read or write well enough to do the job. Besides, our students don't score as high as students from other nations on international assessments. Just sorting them is not enough anymore. We demand competence. We want every student to be a capable reader, writer, math problem solver." So we began to establish achievement standards—competencies that all students must master in order to be promoted or to graduate. Thus, society's mission for its schools changed. Schools that merely sort are no longer deemed effective if all graduates do not meet prescribed academic achievement standards.

Hidden inside this shift in mission is a critical paradox. In schools where the mission is to rank students from the highest to the lowest achiever, if some students work hard and learn a great deal that's good, because they are available to occupy places high in the rank order. And if some students give up in hopelessness and stop trying along the way, that turns out to be a good thing too, because they are available to occupy places low in the rank order. The result is a dependable sorting of all students.

Now change the mission to one of ensuring competence. In this case, if some students work hard and learn a great deal, again that is a good thing. They will meet prescribed state standards. But now if some students give up in hopelessness, that becomes a distinctly bad thing, because they will not even try to meet state standards. The problem is that, as we pass the turn of the century, schools will be held accountable for increasing the proportion of their students who meet state standards. That means schools must keep students from losing confidence and giving up or they must reverse the self-concepts of those who already have developed a sense of futility in their schooling.

Here is the practical significance of this issue: Let's say we lived in a state in which policy makers had just "raised the bar" by setting very high achievement standards for all students. And further, let's say they developed a new state assessment system reflecting those standards and had administered it statewide. And finally, let's say the percent of students meeting and not meeting state standards looked like this:

MET STANDARDS	30%
DID NOT MEET STANDARDS	70%

Which group probably includes a relatively large percentage of students for whom the reward- and punishment-driven behavior management system of motivation probably worked? The 30% group. And which group probably includes a relatively large percentage for whom the traditional system of motivation did not work? The 70% group.

Now think about the assignment just mentioned. We are to take students who are in the "did not meet standards" category and move them to the "met standards" level. How do you do that when the reward- and punishment-driven behavior management system of motivation around which we have built the American educational system is not working for major segments of our student population? Under these circumstances, why would we not change the manner in which we motivate? But change to what? Are there alternatives to reward and punishment that might work for them? Indeed there are.

Tapping the Wellspring of Motivation Within.   Our collective challenge comes in two parts. We must strive to (1) keep students from giving up in hopelessness and (2) rekindle hope among those students who have lost faith in themselves as learners. It's tempting to conceive of the latter as a self-concept problem, that is, as a personal/emotional issue. If we can just raise these students' self-concepts, they will become capable learners. This is counterproductive, because it confronts the problem from the wrong direction. Rather, we conceptualize the problem far more productively if we conceive of it first as a classroom assessment problem.

If these students are to come to believe in themselves, then they must first experience some believable (credible) form of academic success as reflected in a real and rigorous classroom assessment. A small success can rekindle a small spark of confidence, which, in turn, encourages more trying. If that new trying brings more success, academic self-concept will begin to shift in a positive direction. Our goal then is to perpetuate that cycle. To see clear examples of this principle at work, view once again the movie *Stand and Deliver*. Jaime Escalante, the math teacher, uses the assessment process to put students in touch with their own emerging competence. This begins to build hope of success where there was none before, which ultimately pays off in prominent ways.

The direction of the effect is critical. First comes academic success, then comes confidence. With increased confidence comes hope in the belief that learning just may be possible. Success must be framed in terms of academic attainments that the student thinks represent a significant stretch. Focused effort with an expectation of success is essential. Students must come honestly to believe that what counts here—indeed, the only thing that counts here—is the learning that results from the effort expended. They must believe that effort that does not produce learning has no value in this classroom.

The evidence that students gain access to in order to renew their faith in themselves as learners cannot come once a year from summative district, state, national, or international assessments. That evidence must come to them moment-to-moment through continuous formative assessment in the classroom. This places the classroom teacher as assessor directly at the heart of the relation between assessment and school effectiveness. Thus, the essential school improvement question from an assessment point of view is this: Are we skilled enough to use assessment to either (1) keep all learners from losing hope to begin with or (2) rebuild that hope once it has been destroyed?

For those students for whom the management of rewards and punishments will work, teachers can rely on those methods. But what do we do when that system has lost its motivational power in the eyes of some (perhaps many) students?

Planning for a Different Assessment Future: The Case for Student Involvement.   We have alternatives to our tradition of using assessment to trigger rewards and punishments. We can turn to a constellation of three tools that, taken together, can permit us to tap an unlimited wellspring of motivation that resides within each learner. These tools are

- Student-involved classroom assessment.
- Student-involved record keeping.
- Student-involved communication.

Together, they redefine how we use assessment to turn students on to the power and joy of learning. Here's why.

The teacher's *instructional task* is to take students to the edge of their capabilities so they can grow from there. But from the student's point of view, stepping off that edge can be risky. "What if I try and fail? My parents will ground me!" So the teacher's *instructional challenge* is to help each student arrive at his personal edge with enough self-confidence and trust in the teacher to risk the failure that might result if he steps off that edge. Our students must know that when we try to grow, we may at first fail, and that is all right. The trick is to help them know that our failures hold the seeds of our later successes. In other words, we must stop delivering the message to students that failure is always and necessarily a bad thing. Sometimes for some students failure is inevitable, especially when trying something new. Everyone fails as a writer when he first tries. Wise teachers use the classroom assessment process as an instructional intervention to teach the lesson that failure is acceptable at first, but it cannot continue. Improvement must follow. Success is defined as continual improvement. We can use student involvement in the assessment, record keeping, and communication processes to teach these lessons.

Student-involved classroom assessment opens the assessment process up and brings students in as partners in monitoring their own level of achievement. Under the careful management of their teachers (who begin with a clear and appropriate vision of what they want their students to achieve), students are invited to play a role in defining the criteria by which their work will be judged. They learn to apply those criteria to the evaluation of their own practice work. And they work collaboratively to apply those standards to the work of their classmates. In short, we use student-involved assessment to help them see and understand our vision of the meaning of their academic success. The result is classrooms in which there are no surprises and no excuses. This builds trust and confidence.

Student-involved record keeping brings them into the process of monitoring improvements in their performance through repeated self-assessment over time. One way to accomplish this is by having students build portfolios of evidence of their success over time and by requiring periodic student self-reflections about the changes they see. In effect, we use repeated student-centered classroom assessments to hold a mirror up, permitting students to watch themselves grow—to help them chart and thus feel in control of their own success. This can be a powerful confidence builder.

Student-involved communication brings them into the process of sharing information with others about their success. One way to do this is through the use of student-led parent conferences. This is the biggest breakthrough in communicating about student achievement in the last century. When students are prepared well over an extended period to tell the story of their own success (or lack thereof), they seem to experience a fundamental shift in their internal sense of responsibility for that success. The pride in accomplishment that students feel when they have a positive story to tell and then tell it convincingly can be immensely motivational. Mark my words, students will feel an immense sense of personal responsibility when they know that they might have to face the music of telling their parents about the specifics of their nonachievement. They will work very hard to avoid that eventuality. That prospect can drive them to productive work.

In these three ways, we can use student involvement to help them see, understand, and appreciate their own continuing and productive journey of successful achievement. This is exactly what teachers must do to help their students understand the achievement expectations, find and follow the path of success, and feel in charge of, rather than victimized by, the assessment process. In these ways, student involvement in assessment, record keeping, and communication helps them to build the self-confidence needed to keep stepping off the edge of their capabilities into new learning adventures.

Black and Wiliam (1998) provide irrefutable evidence gathered from multiple rigorous studies conducted around the world that the use of accurate formative assessments in the classroom to provide quality feedback to students in ways that involve them in managing their own success (as just described) will yield significant increases in student learning. I know of no such research summary that reveals the power of standardized tests to impact student learning. In fact, three prominent papers suggest that, by themselves, such summative assessments can do more harm than good (Heubert & Houser, 1999; Shepard, 2000; Linn, 2000).

From their very earliest school experiences, our students draw life-shaping conclusions about themselves as learners on the basis of the information we provide to them as a result of our classroom assessments. They decide if they are capable of succeeding or not. They decide whether it is worth trying or not. They decide if they should have confidence in themselves as learners and in us as their teachers—whether to risk investing in the schooling experience. In this sense, the relationship between assessment and student motivation is complex indeed. We should not be so naive as to believe that we can force our students to care merely by threatening them if they score too low on a single state assessment. The downside risk is that such a simplistic and naive system of motivation will breed hopelessness, cynicism, and failure, not learning.

Summary: A New Role for Assessment

What if we had begun the development of our assessment systems 50 years ago with a different set of beliefs about the role of assessment in school improvement? What if, for example, we had believed that the most important decisions made on the basis of assessment results are made not by policy makers and program planners, but by students, teachers, and parents? What if we had believed, therefore, that merely having high-quality once-a-year standardized tests would not provide the evidence needed to create effective schools, rather that classroom assessments needed to be of high quality, too, because of the crucial decisions made on the basis of the information they provide? What if we had believed 50 years ago that the way to maximize learning is not by maximizing anxiety, but by maximizing students' confidence in themselves as learners? If these had been our beliefs, would our assessment systems look different today? Would schools be more, or less, effective? I believe that these questions place a frame around a far more productive assessment future than the one I see emerging today. At the very least, they deserve our thoughtful attention at the highest levels of educational policy.

A Road Map to Excellence in Assessment

I submit that the time has come to carry out a three-part action plan to explore a better way to use assessment to achieve excellence in education than what we see unfolding today. First, we must carefully analyze the full array of assessment users and uses in schools and make a commitment to meeting all of their various information needs with balanced assessment systems. This will lead us to the conclusion that we must commit to ensuring the quality of both standardized and classroom assessments. Second, we must continue our efforts to clearly and completely frame our achievement expectations so that they serve as the basis for our standardized and classroom assessments. Third, we must attend to the professional development needs of teachers, providing them with key understandings of their assigned achievement objectives and proficiency in transforming those into quality assessments. And finally, educators and policy makers alike must stop believing that one can intimidate all children into wanting to become good readers or writers. We have far better motivational options at our disposal.

Assessment Users and Uses

In schools, we find three levels of assessment users: classroom, instructional support, and policy. We covered these in Table 2.1. A school district committed to meeting the needs of all assessment users must develop plans for conducting the assessments needed to provide the required information—at all levels.

If you study the information needs of the first category of users—classroom users—it will become obvious that they will obtain the information they need from the teacher's day-to-day classroom assessments. User needs at the other two levels will be served by standardized assessments. The essential planning question is, How can we be sure all users receive relevant student achievement information in a timely and understandable form? At the classroom level, each individual teacher must develop a plan for answering this question. At instructional support and policy levels, we need a district plan. Let's consider how these play out.

Planning for Classroom Assessment. To monitor student achievement effectively and efficiently, all classroom teachers must begin each unit of instruction or course of study with a clear vision of the specific achievement targets their students are to hit. Beginning with the foundational instructional targets, teachers must understand how their students will progress over time to higher levels of academic proficiency. In what order will they master more refined structures of content knowledge? How will they come to use that knowledge productively to reason and solve problems? What performance skills will they master, and in what sequence? What kinds of achievement products will they be called upon to create? In short, at the classroom level, continuous progress curriculum must be mapped.

With this in mind, then, teachers must start their instruction with a predetermined plan for assessing whether or to what extent each student has reached the required goals. In the next section, we explore the range of assessment methods available to teachers for this purpose. But for now, we should be able to ask all teachers at any time for a written plan of targets, a written plan for the sequence of assessments to track student progress, and a status report on the completion of those assessments. Further, teachers need to weave into their plans a description of how the results are to be delivered in a form understandable to students and parents (that is, how results connect to specific targets) and in time to use for the decision making process. Since students, like teachers, make decisions of the sorts identified in Table 2.1 on a continuous basis, the feedback plan should also reflect ways to keep students in touch with their own progress all along the way. Again, this classroom level of assessment planning completed by each teacher at the beginning of each program of study asks, What targets will be assessed, when, and how will the results be used?

Planning for Standardized Testing.   This same question must guide the administration and use of standardized tests at the instructional support and policy levels. What standardized tests are to be administered at what grade levels, reflecting what achievement targets at what point in time? Further, what specific assessment users are to be served by the results? This analysis should reveal which achievement targets are being assessed and which are not, as well as whose information needs are being met by these tests and whose are not. For example, if the district administers an annual districtwide standardized achievement battery for public reporting, what targets are assessed for what students, when are the assessments administered, and what specific information/decision making needs are served? If standardized tests are used to select students for special services, which targets are assessed, when are they assessed, and precisely how are the results being used? If the district participates in a statewide assessment, what are the targets tested, at what levels, and for whose purposes? Each assessment fills in part of the district's big assessment picture. By mapping that picture, both overlaps and gaps in assessment will be revealed.

Such a plan can be developed in the form of a table with these column headings:

- Name and form of the standardized test (list each test in a battery separately)
- Students tested (grade level and time of year)
- Specific achievement targets assessed (content knowledge, specific patterns of reasoning, performance skills, product development capabilities, or some combination of these)
- Specific assessment method(s) used
- How the targets assessed (and their results) relate to the district's curriculum
- Intended users of results and decisions made based on those results
- Procedures for communication of results to all relevant users and ways to verify that they were understood, interpreted, and used correctly

The big picture of standardized testing that emerges from this analysis will reveal how the results connect to users. Each test will be connected to its place in the continuous progress curriculum. It will also become clear which valued targets are covered at strategic times and which are not. It will become clear what additional assessments might be needed to meet information needs and which assessments are redundant or without purpose and can be eliminated.

Further, this analysis will reveal how each set of test results fits into the continuous progress record of each individual student's mastery of achievement expectations—how each contributes to the evolving picture of the growing learner. Here again, assessments that are redundant, fail to align properly with the curriculum, or fail to contribute useful information can be eliminated.

Thus, this planning process, conducted at the classroom and the district level, can contribute to both the efficiency and effectiveness of the district's assessment strategy and allow it to operationalize its commitment to all assessment users.

Achievement Expectations

To assess student achievement accurately, teachers and administrators must know and understand the achievement targets their students are to master. We cannot assess (or teach) achievement that we have not defined. To reach the goal of establishing clear and appropriate achievement expectations, a school district must take three critical steps.

First, the community must agree on the meaning of academic success within its schools by asking, What do we expect successful graduates of our local educational system to know and be able to do? Second, district curriculum directors and faculty members for all grade levels must meet to decide how that general vision of success can be realized within the local curriculum. The result of their deliberations must be a continuous progress curriculum that specifies how students move along a path to competence—how they succeed from kindergarten through high school. Third, a careful audit must be conducted to be sure all teachers are confident, competent masters of the achievement targets assigned as their instructional responsibility. Although districts and communities should not anticipate major problems here, neither should they simply assume that all teachers are prepared to deliver their part of the big picture.

Let's examine how these three pieces come together as a foundation for quality assessment.

A Vision of Ultimate Academic Success.   I assume that effective schools maximize the achievement of the largest possible number of students. They are achievement-driven institutions. The greater the number of students who succeed in reaching their potential, the better the school. The more sophisticated the achievement targets they hit, the better the school. This does not mean that all students will experience the same level of academic success. In the end, there will be variation in the amount students have learned. But schools cannot be considered effective merely because they sort students according to achievement, if the result is a rank order of students who have in fact learned very little. Thus, the purpose of this guide is to offer a plan for using quality assessment processes and results to maximize student achievement.

To be achievement driven, schools must work with their communities to define their local vision of academic success. The place to start is with the articulation of achievement expectations for high school graduation. These expectations must be stated in achievement terms, not Carnegie unit, course completion, or seat-time terms. We face divergent opinions about what those targets should be. To succeed, schools must find strategies for blending the views of at least four segments of the community. Without question, schools should solicit the opinions of the "family community"—the parents who entrust their children to schools and the taxpayers who support the social institution. In addition, input must be derived from the "business community"—future employers of those successful graduates. Still other advice must come from the "higher education community"—the other destination for our successful graduates. And finally, careful consideration should be given to the opinions of those in the "school community"—the teachers who are masters of the disciplines students are to learn.

In tapping segments of community opinion, schools bring a wide range of backgrounds and experiences to bear on the question of essential learnings for students. For instance, the family community may bring input from the church, the business community will bring a sense of the future development of a technological society, the higher education community will balance that with a sense of our intellectual foundations, and the school community will bring the best current thinking about academic standards from within their particular disciplines as well as any state-level academic standards that must be woven into the mix.

The process most school districts use to achieve this synthesis of community values is a combination of community meetings or forums and community surveys of public opinion. Often, several iterations of each are needed to reach a consensus on the sense of the community—to work through heated arguments about differences of opinion. I can offer no advice as to how to make this process easy. I can say only that it is critically important.

A Continuous Progress Curriculum.   Once a community and its schools agree on their vision of ultimate success, the professional education community must take over to add the next ingredient. They must work collaboratively across grade levels to back those end-of-high-school achievement targets down into the curriculum to map out the routes that students will take from kindergarten to grade 12 to achieve success. The result of this work must be a carefully planned and completely integrated continuous progress curriculum. That means teachers from primary grades, elementary grades, middle schools or junior high, and high schools within the district must meet and divide up responsibility for helping students progress grade-by-grade through higher levels of academic attainment. It means that teachers must interact with one another and plan for the contributions to be made by each K–12 team member.

To illustrate, if students are to become competent writers, educators must specify what writing foundations primary grade teachers will need to help their students master. How will elementary teachers then build on that foundation? What forms of writing competence will middle school or junior high teachers contribute? And how will high school teachers top off writing competence that launches confident writers into work or college? Not only must each question be thoughtfully answered, all teachers must know how their contribution fits into this big picture.

This same planning process must be carried out in science, math, reading, social studies, and other disciplines. We must plan for student mastery of content knowledge, specific patterns of reasoning, performance skills, and product development capabilities as they play out within and across disciplines. Planning teams must decide who will take what responsibility for which forms of student growth. If students are to master scientific knowledge, what knowledge must be acquired in early grades? And how will later teachers reinforce and build upon prior foundations? These questions must be answered to coordinate and integrate curriculum across grade levels and school buildings within a school district.

Many districts have found it useful to work in cross-grade-level teams. These planning teams can tap into state standards and grade-level benchmarks to find appropriate divisions of content. They can also consult the standards being developed by national teams working within the professional associations of teachers, like the National Council of Teachers of Mathematics, the International Reading Association, or the National Council of Teachers of English. A continuous progress curriculum is the foundation of quality assessment, because it tells us what each teacher should be assessing to track student progress. To create such a program, teachers must meet across grade levels within a local school district and work together as teams.

Teacher Competence. By developing an ultimate vision of academic success and a continuous progress curriculum, we establish our expectations of students. Thus, each teacher receives an assignment that fits into the big picture. But this is not enough. Another necessary condition for success is that teachers be masters of the targets that they expect their students to master.

Teachers can neither teach nor accurately assess learning that they themselves have not mastered. A school district cannot afford even one classroom where this condition is not satisfied. If just one teacher is incapable of helping students master essential achievement targets, that teacher becomes a weak link in a continuous chain and will cause some students to fail because they will not have mastered prerequisites. Consequently, once achievement target responsibilities have been divided across grade levels, school districts must be sure teachers are prepared to help students succeed.

One challenging part of this is helping teachers conduct the open and honest self-reflection needed to evaluate their own preparedness. Most of us didn't grow up in an environment where it was safe to admit our inadequacies, nor has the adversarial tone that often characterizes teacher/supervisor relations made it easy for a teacher to be frank about the need for improvement. Given this history, it is essential that we strive to establish supervisory and professional development environments devoted to excellence in teaching—not just minimum competence. This takes a kind of collaboration, trust, and confidence that will permit teachers to go to their supervisors in the spirit of professional growth, ask for help in gaining greater mastery of their discipline, and get that help without being penalized for it the next time a staff evaluation comes along. This kind of environment is essential in helping teachers gain the knowledge and skills they need to be confident, competent classroom assessors.

Thus, in laying the foundation for quality assessments, we must agree on what is to be measured by answering three questions: What does the community want its students to know and be able to do when they finish? How can the curriculum be planned to take them there? How can we be sure their teachers are ready to help them complete that journey? The answers form part of the foundation of a productive assessment future.

Teacher Development

As we identify assessment users, plan to meet their information needs, and carefully spell out our achievement expectations, we must attend to another priority at the same time. We must be certain teachers have access to the highest quality, yet most efficient, professional development opportunities. If teachers are deficient in the mastery of assigned achievement targets, we must help them fill this obvious gap in competence. If teachers have not yet been offered the opportunity to become assessment literate, then that opportunity must be forthcoming. To do otherwise is to doom students in those classrooms to reduced motivation and learning.

Assessment-literate educators are masters of the basic principles of sound assessment. They know and understand the five standards of assessment quality defined previously. But more important, they are able to routinely apply those standards in their schools and classrooms. High-quality professional development programs are needed to provide that foundation—especially given our long history of failing to train teachers and administrators in assessment. The objectives of a practitioner-centered professional development program in assessment, along with highly efficient training strategies, are outlined next.

Program Objectives.   Teachers and administrators are prepared to fulfill their ongoing assessment responsibilities when they

1. Understand essential differences between sound and unsound assessment practices and commit to meeting key quality standards.
2. Understand how to meet standards of quality in all classroom, school, and district assessment contexts.
3. Understand how to use student-involved assessment, record keeping and communication as teaching tools to motivate students to strive for excellence.

Standards for Effective Professional Development.   The achievement of these objectives requires the design, development, and implementation of professional development strategies that

- Provide practical new assessment ideas and strategies in an efficient manner.
- Offer classroom practice in applying those new strategies.
- Give participants responsibility for managing their own development and promote the sense of professionalism that comes from one's own pursuit of excellence.
- Provide collegial support, whereby educators learn by sharing the lessons they have learned individually.
- Deliver benefits very quickly to those who apply lessons learned in their classrooms.
- Encourage a healthy concern for quality assessment by emphasizing its implications for student well-being and teacher effectiveness.

To satisfy these requirements, we recommend a professional development program that relies heavily on a blend of *learning teams* (also referred to as *study groups* or *study teams*) and *individual study* and experimentation by teachers as the basis of interaction and growth. In these teams, a small group of five to ten teachers and administrators agree to meet regularly to share responsibility for their mutual professional development. Between meetings, team members commit to completing assignments designed to advance assessment literacy. They might, for example, study the same piece of professional literature and try the same assessment strategies and then bring the lessons they have learned from that experience to share and discuss in the group meeting. Or team members might complete different assignments, learn different lessons, and meet to share a more diverse array of insights to the benefit of all.

Organizing for Professional Development. Many school districts have elected to begin with a "leadership study team" comprised of a few key teachers and administrators from across the organization. This team's mission is threefold: (1) to develop their own high levels of assessment literacy, (2) to devise a specific strategy for forming and offering support to multiple study groups throughout the district, and (3) to conduct an ongoing evaluation of the professional development effort to determine its impact. Another way to organize is to start a learning team in each building, blending interested administrators and teachers into the same team. This can have the effect of stimulating interest among others in that same building. As a variation on this, learning teams from different schools might agree to meet periodically in a larger collective effort.

Obviously, learning teams can be configured in any of a variety of ways. Groups might be formed on the basis of grade level (within or across levels) or within or across disciplines (math, science, arts, etc.). Learning teams might come into existence as opportunities arise, when, for example, an ad hoc committee is assembled to evaluate and consider revising report card grading or when a curriculum development team decides to deal with some underlying assessment issues. All such instances represent opportunities for developing effective assessment strategies.

Motivating Participation in Learning Teams. A district might allocate released time or extended contract time to permit teachers to be involved in any or all of these efforts. The promise of time to concentrate on one important topic long enough to internalize some new and useful ideas can be a strong motivator. This, combined with time to talk with and learn from colleagues (both very rare commodities for most educators), may be incentive enough for some. In addition, an ongoing working relationship can be established with a higher education institution to offer graduate credit for competence in assessment attained through study group work.

There are also other, more internal sources of motivation. For example, people are naturally motivated to strive for excellence when they have the opportunity to see themselves improving. One way to take advantage of this is to encourage all learning team members to build a portfolio of evidence of their own improvement as classroom assessors. This record might include a journal of self-reflection about one's evolving assessment competence and examples of assessments collected over time, with written commentary on their increasing quality. Periodically, team members might also conduct the adult version of "student-led conferences," detailing to the rest of the team their evidence of progress as assessors. In this way, teachers can model in their own adult learning environments the very kinds of student-involved assessment that is advocated for classrooms.

Assessment, Student Motivation, and Effective Schools

To illustrate the connection between assessment and student motivation in a balanced assessment system, I have selected the following short story about one student's experience.

Visualize yourself at a particularly important meeting of the school board in the district where you teach. This is the once-a-year meeting at which the district presents the annual report of standardized test scores to the board and the media. Every year it's the same: Will scores be up or down? How will we compare to national norms? How will our district compare to others in the area?

What most of those present don't realize as the meeting begins is that, this year, they are in for a big surprise with respect to both the achievement information to be presented and the manner of the presentation. To make the presentation, the chair of the school board introduces the assistant superintendent in charge of assessment.

As the presentation begins, the audience includes a young woman named Emily, a junior at the high school, sitting in the back of the room with her parents. She knows she will be a big part of the surprise. She's only a little nervous. She understands how important her role is. It has been quite a year for her, unlike any she has ever experienced in school before. She also knows her parents and teacher are as proud of her as she is of herself.

The assistant superintendent begins by reminding the board and all present at the meeting that the standardized tests used by the district sample broad domains of achievement with just a few multiple-choice test items. There is much that we value, she points out, that must be assessed using other methods. She promises to provide an example later in the presentation. Emily's dad nudges her and they both smile.

Having set the stage, she turns to carefully prepared charts depicting average student performance in each important achievement category tested. Results are summarized by grade and building, concluding with a clear description of how district results had changed from the year before and from previous years. As she proceeds, board members ask questions and receive clarification. Some scores are down slightly; some are up. Participants discuss possible reasons. This is a routine annual presentation that proceeds as expected.

Next comes the break from routine. Having completed the first part of the presentation, the assistant superintendent explains how the district has gathered some new information about one important aspect of student achievement. As the board knows, she points out, the district has implemented a new writing program in the high school to address the issue of poor writing skills among graduates. As part of their preparation for this program, the English faculty attended a summer institute on the assessment of writing proficiency and the integration of such assessments into the teaching and learning process. The English department was confident that this kind of professional development and program revision would produce much higher levels of writing proficiency.

As the second half of the evening's assessment presentation, the high school English department faculty will share the results of their evaluation of the new writing program.

As the very first step in this presentation, the English chair, Ms. Weatherby, who also happens to be Emily's English teacher, distributes samples of student writing to the board members (with the student's name removed), asking them to read and evaluate this writing. They do so, expressing their dismay aloud as they go. They are indignant in their commentary on these samples of student work. One board member reports in exasperation that, if these represent the results of that new writing program, the community has been had. The board member is right. These are, in fact, pretty bad pieces of work. Emily's mom puts her arm around her daughter's shoulder and hugs her.

But Ms. Weatherby urges patience and asks the board members to be very specific about what they don't like about this work. As the board registers its complaints, the faculty records the criticisms on chart paper for all to see. The list is long, including everything from mechanical errors to disorganization to incorrect word choice and vague ideas.

Next, the teacher distributes another sample of student writing, asking the board to read and evaluate it. Ah, this, they report, is more like it! This work is much better! But be specific, the chair demands. What do you like about this work? Positive aspects are listed: good choice of words, sound sentence structure, clever ideas, and so on. Emily is ready to burst! She squeezes her mom's hand.

The reason she's so full of pride at this moment is that this has been a special year for her and her classmates. For the first time ever, they became partners with their English teachers in managing their own improvement as writers. Early in the year, Ms. Weatherby (Ms. W, they all called her) made it crystal clear to Emily that she was, in fact, not a very good writer and that just trying hard to get better was not going to be enough. She expected Emily to be better—nothing else would suffice.

Ms. W started the year by working with students to set high writing standards, including understanding quality performance in word choice, sentence structure, organization, voice, and sharing some new "analytical scoring guides" written just for students. Each explained the differences between good and poor quality writing in understandable ways. When Emily and her teacher evaluated her first two pieces of writing using these standards, she received very low ratings. Not very good. . . .

But she also began to study samples of writing supplied by her teacher that she could see were very good. Slowly, she began to see why they were good. The differences between these and her work started to become clear. Her teacher began to share examples and strategies that would help her writing improve one step at a time. As she practiced with these and time passed, Emily and her classmates kept samples of their old writing to compare to their new writing, and they began to build portfolios. And thus, she literally began to watch her own writing skills improve before her very eyes. At midyear, her parents were invited in for a conference at which Emily, not Ms. Weatherby, shared the contents of her portfolio and discussed her emerging writing skills. Emily remembers sharing thoughts about some aspects of her writing that had become very strong and some examples of things she still needed to work on. Now, the year was at an end and here she sat waiting for her turn to speak to the school board about all of this. What a year!

Now, having set the school board up by having them analyze, evaluate, and compare these two samples of student work, Ms. W springs the surprise: The two pieces of writing they had just evaluated, first of dismal quality and then of outstanding quality, were produced by the same writer, at the beginning and at the end of the school year! This, she reports, is evidence of the kind of impact the new writing program is having on student writing proficiency.

Needless to say, all are impressed. However, one board member wonders aloud, "Have all your students improved in this way?" Having anticipated the question, the rest of the English faculty joins the presentation and produces carefully prepared charts depicting dramatic changes in typical student performance over time on rating scales for each of six clearly articulated dimensions of good writing. They accompany their description of student performance on each scale with actual samples of student work illustrating various levels of proficiency.

Further, Ms. W informs the board that the student whose improvement had been so dramatically illustrated with the work they have just analyzed is present at this school board meeting, along with her parents. This student is ready to talk with the board about the nature of her learning experience. Emily, you're on!

Interest among the board members runs high. Emily talks about how she has come to understand the truly important differences between good and bad writing. She refers to differences she had not understood before, how she has learned to assess her own writing and to fix it when it doesn't "work well," and how she and her classmates have learned to talk with her teacher and each other about what it means to write well. Her teacher talks about the improved focus of writing instruction, increases in student motivation, and important positive changes in the very nature of the student–teacher relationship.

A board member asks Emily if she likes to write. She reports, "I do now!" This board member turns to Emily's parents and asks their impression of all of this. They report with pride that they had never seen so much evidence before about Emily's achievement and most of it came from Emily herself. Emily had never been called upon to lead the parent–teacher conference before. They had no idea she was so articulate. They loved it. Their daughter's pride in and accountability for achievement had skyrocketed in the past year.

As the meeting ends, it is clear to all in attendance that evening that this two-part assessment presentation—one part from standardized test scores and one from students, teachers, and the classroom—reveals that assessment is in balance in this district. The test scores cover part of the picture and classroom assessment evidence is shared to complete the achievement picture. There are good feelings all around. The accountability needs of the community are being satisfied, and the writing assessment training and the new writing program are working to improve student achievement. Obviously, this story has a happy ending.

Can't you almost visualize yourself walking out of the boardroom at the end of the evening, hearing parents wish they had had such an experience in high school? I sure can. Can't you just anticipate the wording of the memo of congratulations the superintendent will soon write to the English department? How about the story that will appear in the newspaper tomorrow, right next to the report of test scores? Everyone involved here, from Emily to her classmates to parents to teachers to assessment director to (at the end) school board members, understood how to use assessment to promote student success and effective schools. (*Source: Student-Involved Classroom Assessment*, 3/e, by R. J. Stiggins, © 2001. REPRINTED BY PERMISSION OF PEARSON EDUCATION, INC., UPPER SADDLE RIVER, NJ 07458.)

What were the active ingredients in this success? To begin with, the faculty understood who is in charge of the learning—not them, not the principal, not parents, not school board members, but the students themselves. Therefore, assessment was never a teacher-centered activity, carried out by the teacher to meet the teacher's needs. Rather, it was a student-centered activity, in which Emily and her classmates were consistently involved in the process of assessing their own achievement repeatedly over time, so they and their parents could watch the improvement. To be sure, Ms. W controlled what was written and how it was evaluated. And she made very important decisions based on assessment results. But she also shared the wisdom and power that come from being able to assess the quality of writing. She showed her students the secrets to their own success.

In this way, Ms. W used the assessment process and its results to build, not destroy, student confidence in themselves as writers. The faculty understood that those who believe that the target is within reach will keep striving. Those who see the target as being beyond reach will give up in hopelessness.

Second, they understood that students can remain confident in expecting success of themselves only if they know and understand where they are now in relation to an ultimate vision of success. Ms. W began her program of writing instruction with a highly refined vision of what good writing looks like and she shared that vision of excellence with her students right up front. Students could continuously see the distance closing between where they are now and where they want to be. That turned out to be incredibly empowering for students.

Third, Ms. W and her colleagues knew that their assessments of student achievement had to be very accurate. The writing assignments or exercises that they gave to their students had to elicit the right kinds of writing. The scoring procedures they used to evaluate student work needed to focus on the important facets of good writing. As faculty members, they needed to train themselves to apply those scoring standards dependably—to avoid making biased judgments about student work. But as important, Ms. W understood that she had also to train her students to make dependable judgments about the quality of their own work. This represents the heart of student involvement in the assessment and improvement processes.

The final key to success was the great care taken to communicate effectively about student achievement. Whether Ms. W was discussing improvements needed or achieved in Emily's work or sharing summary information about average student performance at the school board meeting, there was never a question about the meaning of the message being sent.

I hope this is our assessment future, in which we rely on high-quality assessment to build, not destroy, students' desire to learn. We get there by providing teachers with the tools needed to do that job.

r e f e r e n c e s

Black, P., & Wiliam, D. (1998). Inside the black box. *Phi Delta Kappan, 80*(2), 139–148.

Condry, J. (1977). Enemies of exploration: Self-initiated versus other initiated learning. *Journal of Personality and Social Psychology, 35,* 459–477.

Covington, M. (1992). *Making the grade: A self-worth perspective on motivation and school reform.* New York: Cambridge University Press.

Heubert, J. P., & Hauser, R. M. (1999). *High stakes: Testing for tracking, promotion and graduation.* Washington D.C.: National Academy Press.

Kohn, A. (1993). *Punished by rewards.* New York: Houghton Mifflin.

Linn, R. (2000). Assessments and accountability. *Educational Researcher, 29*(2), 4–15.

Schafer, W. D., & Lissitz, R. W. (1987). Measurement training for school personnel: Recommendations and reality. *Journal of Teacher Education, 38*(3), 57–63.

Shepard, L. (2000). The role of assessment in a learning culture. Presidential Address, Annual Meeting of the American Educational Research Association, New Orleans, La.

Skinner, B. F. (1974). *About behaviorism.* New York: Alfred Knopf.

Skinner, E. A., Wellborn, J. G., & Connell, J. P. (1990). What it takes to do well in school and whether I've got it: A process model of perceived control and children's engagement and achievement in school. *Journal of Educational Psychology, 82,* 22–32.

Stiggins, R. J. (2001). *Student-involved classroom assessment,* 3d ed. Columbus, Ohio: Merrill Education, an imprint of Prentice Hall.

Stiggins, R. J., & Conklin, N. J. (1992). *In teachers' hands: Investigating the practice of classroom assessment.* Albany, N.Y.: SUNY Press.

Weiner, B. (1974). *Achievement motivation and attribution theory.* Morristown, N.J.: General Learning Press.

3

What Role Will Assessment Play in School in the Future?

PETER W. AIRASIAN

Boston College

LISA M. ABRAMS

Boston College

Our charge is to predict the future of school assessments. This is a difficult task for at least two reasons. First, predicting the future is always an uncertain undertaking, and second, it is very difficult to generalize across the varied types and uses of assessments in American schools. A single chapter cannot hope to examine school and classroom assessments in their full richness and in all their features, nuances, and consequences. To make our task more manageable, we divide assessments into two general types, teacher-made or chosen instructional assessments and statewide standards-based assessments. We recognize and emphasize that there are wide variations within each of these two types.

Each type deals with important issues and consequences. Both are significant in the lives of pupils and teachers, yet each is quite different from the other in a number of respects. Teacher-made or chosen classroom assessments are plentiful, normally linked to classroom instruction, and focused on the performance of pupils in a given classroom. The consequences of teacher-made or chosen assessments are focused on the classroom in the form of daily work, projects, tests, and grades. Statewide assessments are administered infrequently, linked to external learning standards developed by agencies outside of the classroom, and focused on the performance of pupils, teachers, schools, and states. The consequences of statewide assessments extend well beyond individual classrooms and pupils.

We have chosen to focus mainly on the genesis, impact, pitfalls, and future of statewide assessments. We select this focus for two reasons. First, statewide assessments are becoming the more consequential assessments, with important implications for pupils and many educators. These assessments bear examination. Second, statewide assessments are increasingly influencing what is taught and assessed in classrooms and schools. The consequences associated with statewide assessments are exerting pressure on teachers to teach and emphasize the statewide standards and their accompanying assessments. Although we examine statewide assessments, we still cannot completely ignore teacher-focused classroom instruction and assessments.

The Equality of Educational Opportunity Survey

To know where we are now and where we are going with statewide assessments, it is useful to have a perspective on their genesis. We begin our perspective with the 1966 Equality of Educational Opportunity Survey (Coleman et al., 1966; Jencks et al., 1972; Madaus, Airasian, & Kellaghan, 1980; Mosteller & Moynihan, 1972). We focus on the Equality of Education Survey for a number of reasons. Its lineage has been instrumental in the rise of outcome-based assessment, bringing a significant change in the way schools, teachers, and pupils were studied and evaluated. The issues and debate it spawned are salient to the present day. The shear magnitude of the national sample of 645,000 pupils, nearly 60,000 teachers, and over 4,000 schools that were surveyed makes it worthy of attention.

The Equality of Education Opportunity Survey headed by James Coleman took place in an educational climate that sought to determine how to provide equality of education to all American pupils. It also sought to find ways to assess progress toward this goal. Concern over educational equality was evidenced by a number of educational initiatives emanating from the Johnson White House. The *Civil Rights Act* of 1964 began the nation's War on Poverty. Compensatory education programs such as Project Head Start (1965) and the *Elementary and Secondary School Education Act* (1965) sprung up in thousands of communities. It was a time when the struggle against poverty, racial injustice, and educational inequality was being addressed at a level never before seen in America.

The Coleman survey was commissioned to examine four educational issues:

1. The extent of racial and cultural group segregation in public schools
2. The extent to which educational facilities and resources differed by racial and cultural groups
3. The extent to which pupils were learning in school as measured by standardized tests
4. The relationship between pupils' achievement and the resources and facilities in their schools

Not unexpectedly, the results of the first three questions documented achievement disparities among schools and racial and cultural groups of pupils. There were inequalities across schools and pupils. However, it was the fourth question that produced the major impact of the Coleman survey. At a time when conventional wisdom held that the inputs to education were the primary influence on the outcomes of education, the Coleman survey found little evidence of this perceived connection. A study most Americans assumed would indicate that inequality of resources and facilities in schools was impacting pupils' achievement ended with this curt and unexpected conclusion: "Schools bring little influence to bear on a child's achievement that is independent of his background and general social context. . . . This very lack of an independent effect means that the inequalities imposed on children by their home, neighborhood and peer environment are carried along to become the inequalities with which they confront adult life at the end of school" (Madaus, Airasian, & Kellaghan, 1980, 30). Coleman's analyses suggested that larger differences in school achievements occurred among pupils in the *same school* rather than between pupils in different schools.

The Coleman survey weakened belief in the presumed direct connection between school inputs and school outputs and led to a national debate over the effectiveness of schooling. The debate forced educators, legislators, and parents to rethink the prevailing conception of equal educational opportunity. Prior to the survey, equal education was defined in terms of equal access to school inputs such as new books, pleasant classrooms, audiovisual material, good teachers, new facilities, and the like. Subsequent to the survey, focus on the quality of schooling began to shift from school inputs to school outcomes. In his message on educational reform in March 1970, President Nixon commented on the presumed relationship between inputs and achievement. "Years of educational research, culminating in the Equality of Educational Opportunity Survey of 1966, have, however, demonstrated that this direct, uncomplicated relationship does not exist" (Madaus, Airasian, & Kellaghan, 1980, p. 32). For many Americans, the educational promises of the 1960s were unfulfilled. The public's belief in the power of education as a vehicle of social reform was shaken.

Further, similar results from a number of large-scale surveys of Head Start and Title I in the late 1960s and early 1970s (Picariello, 1968; Glass et al., 1970) seemed to support

Coleman's conclusions. Picariello (1968, p. 1) concluded, after analyzing the reading scores of 155,000 Title I students, that there was "... only a 19 percent chance of a significant achievement gain, a 13 percent chance of a significant achievement test loss and a 68 percent chance of no change at all" and Glass et al. (1970, p. 63) indicated that there was a higher reading gain for nonparticipants than for participants.

Although the Coleman survey and Title I studies were criticized for methodological weaknesses (Madaus, Airasian, & Kellaghan, 1980; Mosteller & Moynihan, 1972; Jencks et al., 1972), their results thrust education into the public eye. The shift from inputs to outcomes spawned by these results is echoed today in a stronger, more intrusive way that few could have predicted in 1960s. Now when we ask, How are our schools doing?, it is assumed that we are asking about the outcomes of schools measured in the form of tests and assessments of varied kinds.

A Focus on Accountability

A few years after the Coleman survey, new approaches to educational assessment emerged. At the state and local district levels, a growing emphasis was placed on assessing the outcomes of schooling. Declines in national SAT scores, increased grade inflation, social promotions, and evidence of pupils being ill-prepared for higher education and the workplace fostered a push for more rigorous pupil learning and more accountable assessments.

The response to these concerns came in the form of minimum competency testing in the 1970s and 1980s. Minimum competency testing sought to assess the outcomes of pupil learning based on prescribed basic skills and processes. The focus was on the minimum level of achievement pupils had to demonstrate to graduate from high school. Although minimum competency testing programs were implemented in a variety of ways, their essential core focused on organized efforts to ensure that public high school pupils would be able to demonstrate their mastery of a set of defined minimum skills. To attain this goal, four steps were required:

1. Identification of the minimum competencies or objectives pupils had to learn in reading, writing, and mathematics to graduate from high school.
2. Development and administration of tests to determine whether high school pupils had mastered the required minimum skills. Test results, typically from standardized tests, became the accepted yardstick for pupil graduation.
3. Establishment of standards or criterion-referenced standards of performance that determined passing and failing on the competency test.
4. Determination of the consequences of failing to master stated minimums, such as pupils being retained in grade, required to attend remedial courses, or denied a regular high school diploma.

The minimum competence skills taught and tested differed from state to state or district to district, as did the particular tests and assessments administered to judge pupils' minimum competence. Minimum competency testing was viewed as a way to help pupils who had the most educational need. In a real sense, the minimum competence testing movement emphasized a back-to-basics approach. By the mid 1980s, 34 states had adopted some form of minimum competency testing (Linn, 2000; Murphy, 1990).

A Nation at Risk:
The Imperative for Educational Reform

In August 1981, the secretary of education created the National Commission on Excellence in Education with the aim of examining the quality of education in the United States. The commission was charged to

1. Assess the quality of teaching and learning in the nation's schools.
2. Compare American schools to those of other advanced nations.
3. Assess the degree to which major social and educational changes in the last quarter century had impacted on pupil achievement.
4. Define problems that must be faced in order to attain excellence in education.

Eighteen months after the initial charge, the commission completed its examination. The results were sobering and suggested that our nation was at risk of falling behind other developed nations in educational achievement. The commission wrote, "Our nation is at risk. Our once unchallenged preeminence in commerce, industry, science, and technological innovation is being overtaken by competitors throughout the world" (*A nation at risk*, p. 5). And what was the main basis for this gloomy prediction? Educational decline and the reality that ". . . the educational foundations of our society are presently being eroded by a rising tide of mediocrity that threatens our very future as a nation and a people" (p. 5).

A great deal of data were assembled to buttress the commission's report. It indicated that an estimated 23 million American adults and nearly 13% of all 17-year-olds were functionally illiterate. The average achievement of high school pupils on standardized tests was lower in the 1980s than that of pupils 26 years earlier. SAT scores had been declining for the past 15 years. Secondary school curricula had been homogenized, diluted, and diffused to the point that they no longer had a central purpose. Schools offered intermediate algebra, but only 31% of high school graduates completed it. Grades had risen as average pupil achievement had declined. Many textbooks were "written down" to lower reading levels to accommodate increasingly poor readers. Minimum competency testing fell far short of what pupils needed to learn. Too often, it was suggested, the minimum expectation had become the maximum, leading to increased lowering of standards.

The commission proposed a number of solutions to undo the gloomy future it described. State and local high school graduation requirements should be strengthened, it said. A more rigorous, taxing, and broad curriculum was needed. The commission wanted to up the ante of academic performance from accepting the minimum to expecting more rigorous and measurable standards. "Standardized tests of achievement . . . should be administered at major transition points from one level of schooling to another. . . . The purpose of these tests would be to: (a) certify the pupil's credentials; (b) identify the need for remedial intervention; and (c) identify the opportunity for advanced or accelerated work. The tests should be administered as part of a nationwide . . . system of State and local standardized tests" (*A nation at risk*, p. 28). Minimum competency testing focused on high school graduation; the commission called for more frequent testing throughout schooling.

In the years since *A Nation at Risk*, little had changed (The Center for Educational Reform, 1998). In the TIMSS international study, American pupils ranked 19th out of 21 industrialized nations in mathematics achievement and 16th out of 21 in science. According to a poll of U.S. manufacturers, 40% of 12th-graders lacked the math skills and 60% lacked the reading skills to hold down a manufacturing job. Sixty-four percent of high school seniors reported doing less than one hour of homework per night.

Standards-Based Assessments

Most recently, statewide standards-based assessments have become the latest approach to outcome accountability. Standards-based approaches are similar in some respects to minimum competency testing, but different in others. For example, performance-based assessments were rarely used in minimum competency testing; many standards-based approaches, however, include performance-based assessments that require pupils to produce or apply knowledge, not just remember it. Further, statewide standards-based approaches typically require demonstrating greater depth of knowledge in subject areas and involve more rigorous assessments than those adopted in minimum competency testing. Minimum competency testing focused on high school competence; statewide standards and assessments generally focus on pupil assessment at multiple grade levels, most typically fourth, eighth, and tenth or eleventh. In many states, demanding standards and assessments must be met by all or most pupils, regardless of their readiness, prior performance, or disabilities. This was not the norm in minimum competency testing, although in some cases waiving a minimum competence test because of lack of readiness or disability could result in nonpromotion or failure to graduate. The stakes or consequences associated with statewide standards-based outcomes substantially surpass those of prior reforms. Depending on the state, performance on the statewide standards may have important accountability consequences for pupils, teachers, administrators, and schools (Linn, 2000). Consequences associated with poor performance on statewide assessments include nonreceipt of a high school diploma, no grade-to-grade promotion, placement in remedial classes, decreased teacher pay, failure to attain teacher certification or recertification, dismissal of school principal, and closure of nonimproving schools.

The formats of statewide standards-based assessments vary from state to state in terms of the subject areas assessed, the grade levels assessed, the methods of assessment, and the consequences of assessment performance. The growth and importance of statewide assessments have increased the importance of two state responsibilities: monitoring the state educational system and certifying the performance of individual pupils, teachers, and schools.

As of 1999, statewide standards-based approaches were spread widely across the country, and manifested various purposes and applications. Some states assess pupils in each school year, while others assess pupils at the end of several years of instruction. Forty states have set standards in all core subjects, and 34 states now include some performance-based items in their standards-based assessments, usually a written exercise. The most frequent subject areas assessed are English/language arts (48 states), mathematics (47 states), writing (42 states), science (36 states), and history/social studies (38 states). Only 13 states rely solely on multiple-choice items in their statewide assessments (Olson, 1999).

The growing complexity of managing and monitoring education is increasingly shifting control of important aspects of education from the local to the state level. Criteria for and decisions about curriculum, assessment, certification, and funding are being made at the state, not the local, level. The movement toward statewide standards and assessments has led to states assuming greater control over what once were local responsibilities.

For the most part, the public has endorsed the growth of statewide standards and assessments. There are a number of reasons for this endorsement. Testing and assessment, particularly statewide, are potent social symbols in American society. Apart from their direct impact on teachers and pupils, they have a substantial perceptual impact on the public at large. The concept of a test or assessment is meaningful to most Americans because it is in the realm of their personal experience and thus capable of evoking rich mental images and remembrances. Three such symbols are associated with tests and assessments. First, tests and assessments symbolize order and control in an educational system that often is too complex and distant to grasp or conceptualize. The public seeks some external assurance of the quality of local teaching and learning and in most cases turns to external tests and assessments to provide the evidence and objectivity it seeks. Second, the language associated with tests and assessments has a strong influence on public acceptance—language influences perception. The language of tests and assessments tends to strike a responsive chord with most Americans. Terms such as *competency, literacy, standards, excellence, fairness,* and *objectivity* command attention and support. Third, in addition to symbolizing order, control, and desirable school outcomes, tests and assessments evoke a traditional set of social and educational moral values, including hard work, "nose to the grindstone," and reward for effort among others. For many citizens, there is a symbolic message associated with tests and assessments.

Note also that for those who advocate implementation of state-based educational reforms—governors, politicians, boards of education, and others—test- and assessment-based reform has many desirable features. Compared to most other methods of educational improvement and reform, testing and assessment programs are relatively inexpensive. Tests and assessments can be externally mandated by state officials for school districts and classrooms. Tests and assessments can also be quickly implemented relative to other reform approaches. Finally, the use of tests and assessments in reform programs provides interested parties such as parents and employers with quick and tangible information about the effects of the reform. For all these reasons, tests and assessments have been widely adopted and endorsed as a viable strategy to improve and measure pupil learning.

By making the results of assessments important to decisions involving interschool comparisons, funding allotments, high school graduation, grade-to-grade promotion, placement in remedial education, teacher certification, and educational equity, society makes the assessments themselves important. As a consequence, assessment necessarily has become intertwined with social, economic, and political issues, not just educational ones. The audiences and consumers of assessment information are no longer limited to a small group of professional educators. They now include parents, politicians, employers, and others. Increasingly, support for local schools is conditioned on the answer to the question, How are our schools doing? And that answer usually depends on the latest standard test or statewide assessment results. A tightening link between test results and decision making is common in many states. Both historically and today, the consequential assessments are the ones that influence what is taught in school. The broad use of assessment results often brings into focus the goals and priorities of different social groups.

Where Are We Now?

It is 35 years or so since emphasis has been placed on the outcomes of schooling. More and more over the intervening years, educators and the public have been conditioned to seek and accept the external evidence of standardized tests or statewide assessments in assessing the status of schools and schooling. Statewide standards and assessments are logical extensions of the past three and one-half decades. In most states, they have been assigned the important role of gatekeepers to the quality of education. Although the specific standards and their related assessments vary from state to state, a number of generalizations can be made that reflect the status of today's statewide standards and assessments:

- Minimum competency testing has evolved into broader and more frequent statewide assessments that require more of pupils and teachers than in the past.
- The consequences of assessments have increased from concern solely with pupil performance to the inclusion of teacher and administrator performance. Most teacher and principal assessments are linked to pupil performance on statewide assessments. If pupils do poorly, teachers may be sanctioned, and if schoolwide performance remains low over a period of time, the principal may be sanctioned or moved to another school.
- Control in many schools and states has shifted from local school districts to the state as consequential statewide learning standards and assessments have come under state control.
- The amount of higher-level thinking skills and performance assessments such as writing essays and solving problems included in statewide assessments has increased. However, significant portions of virtually all statewide assessments do include multiple-choice and short-answer items.
- The study of statewide assessment itself has increased. As their impact on and consequences for pupils, teachers, and administrators have broadened, issues related to the validity and reliability of statewide tests have been more closely studied. The challenging task of determining meaningful and appropriate performance standards or "cut scores" to differentiate varied levels of pupil, teacher, and principal performance has also come under focus.
- The tension over what the goals and priorities of education ought to emphasize has increased. The goal of quality and the goal of equity are commonly embraced by different constituents. Should the focus be on attaining individual quality, or should it be on attaining equality of education for all groups? For example, there is ongoing conflict over how educational resources should be allocated—in equal proportions to all pupils or in greater proportions to the most needy pupils?

- A "one-size-fits-all" approach to standards and assessments has become more widely adopted. Minimum competency testing and statewide assessments typically develop a single set of statewide standards and assessments for all pupils who will be assessed. What is known of pupils' prior achievement, school quality, disabilities, and other factors that influence achievement are often ignored in the assessment process. Fairness is viewed as having all pupils take similar assessments. This leads to the question of who or what is being assessed and who or what is responsible for pupils' test performance.
- Teachers have increasingly tailored the classroom curriculum and instruction to the statewide standards and assessments.

In many respects, the past 25 years of educational testing and assessment are mirrored in today's educational testing and assessment. The intervening years have broadened and improved earlier work, but the fundamental intents, applicable strategies, and debated issues have remained quite similar over time.

Issues of Concern

In most cases, standards-based assessments are the driving force behind instruction. Statewide standards can provide notable advantages to schools, teachers, and pupils. They define what is important to teach and thus narrow the broad domain of school-based instruction. They encourage standardized topics of instruction across schools and classrooms. Standards also can clarify instructional expectations for both teachers and pupils. However, although statewide standards can provide important benefits, there are a number of concerns associated with them. Three main areas of concern are

1. Instructional homogeneity resulting from preparation for statewide assessments may not be the best approach for all pupils, given the growing diversity of classroom populations.
2. There may be lack of alignment between intended and actual instruction and between intended and actual assessment.
3. Statewide assessments and the information they provide are being used for purposes that many not be valid or reliable. In addition to assessing pupil achievement, in some states information provided by statewide assessments is being used to assess teachers and schools.

Increasing Uniformity amid Growing Diversity

The first area of concern addresses the growing heterogeneity of pupil populations and the increasing trend of including pupils with special needs in statewide assessments. This trend has introduced increased complexities into instruction. It is difficult to provide appropriate instruction to diverse groups of pupils. When planning for and delivering statewide instruction, teachers often have to prepare for pupil groups manifesting such various characteristics as lack of readiness, disabilities, lack of interest, and English as a foreign language. These and other factors increase pupil diversity at the same time that statewide standards promote homogeneity of instruction and assessment. How will teachers meet the needs of diverse pupil groups while simultaneously meeting the one-size-fits-all demands of statewide assessments? This is especially a quandary when teachers themselves are being judged based on pupil performance on the statewide assessments.

In most statewide assessments, large gaps in achievement among ethnic, language, and disability groups are common. For example, the 1999 results of the Massachusetts Comprehensive Assessment System ". . . showed that Latino and black students lagged behind whites in every category on the test and for every grade" (Vigue, 2000, p. B1). Of the eighth-graders tested, almost six times as many Latino pupils and over four times as many black pupils failed the English portion of the exam as did white pupils. Massachusetts is not alone in facing large disparities in pupil performance among racial or ethnic groups. In Texas, pupils from minority groups "pass the tests at only two-thirds the rate of whites" (Viadero, 2000, p. 1). These results have important implications for pupils, particularly if the receipt of a high school diploma is contingent on passing statewide exams. Increased dropout rates of pupils from minority groups is one such result of this growing achievement gap. Researchers on the National Board on Educational Testing and Public Policy suggest that "high stakes testing programs are linked to decreased rate of high school completion" (Clarke, Haney, & Madaus, 2000, p. 2). Two years after the requirement that pupils must pass the Texas Assessment of Academic Skills (TAAS) in order to graduate from high school, black or Hispanic pupils were three times as likely to drop out of high school as their white counterparts (Clarke, Haney, & Madaus, 2000). The combination of uniform standards and diverse pupil groups raises concern about the role and meaningfulness of statewide assessment results for different groups.

Instruction in Statewide Assessments

For the most part, statewide standards were instituted as a means of educational reform designed to raise standards and expectations for schools, teachers, and pupils. However, the instructional approaches used to teach to the standards often conflict with those required to prepare pupils to succeed on statewide assessments. Consequently, the main concern focuses on the disparity between the instructional approaches teachers are expected to employ to teach to the standards and those that teachers must implement to prepare pupils for the assessments.

Statewide standards and assessments were a response to the cry for more complex, higher-level learning outcomes. The language of statewide standards and assessments asked pupils to "think critically," "make inferences," or "problem solve." In response, teachers were expected to reject traditional forms of instruction that focused on rote memorization and to adopt constructivist strategies that targeted pupils' higher-level thinking skills. This shift required teachers to implement a new set of instructional approaches in order to align instruction to the higher-level standards and outcomes. However, in many cases the main assessments used are predominantly multiple-choice items that target memorization and lower-level cognitive skills. A recent study conducted by researchers at the Wisconsin Center for Education Research examined the relationship between instruction and large-scale assessments in 10 different states. Researchers found that "the tests . . . mainly asked students to recall facts and perform other simple procedures, while classroom instruction focused more on solving novel problems or applying skills" (Boser, 2000, p. 1). In essence, teaching to the standards in order to meet the stated goals of current assessments may not guarantee that pupils will be required to demonstrate higher-level learning.

The high-stakes consequences of statewide assessments pressure teachers to administer assessments that mirror statewide assessments and implement instruction that prepares pupils for these exams. However, extensive preparation for state assessments occurs at the expense of implementing more time-consuming instructional practices that attend to higher-level skills. For example, a survey of teachers in five school districts in North Carolina indicated that "eighty percent of the teachers in the [our] study reported that they spent more than 20% of their total teaching time preparing pupils for end-of-grade tests" (Jones et al., 1999). There is a difference between teaching to the content standards and teaching to the actual test. Statewide assessments should place greater emphasis on the instruction that pupils receive in order to meet the standards rather than on expecting pupils to know specific test items. Otherwise, in order to meet curriculum standards and prepare pupils for success on high-stakes assessments, instruction must often be narrowed in both content and complexity.

Teacher and Principal Accountability

The ways in which statewide assessments are being used is cause for concern, especially as they relate to judging teacher and principal performance. There is a marked difference between using assessments to compare pupil achievement and using the same assessments to judge teachers or principals. This practice calls into question the validity of the decisions that are made based on the results of state assessments. These assessments tell us which pupils know the most about the topics addressed in the assessments. However, the pupils' assessment results do not transfer directly to judgments about the quality of teaching and administration. There are many intervening factors that do not permit judging teacher and principal quality directly from student assessments. If state assessments are constructed with the fundamental purpose of assessing the degree to which *pupils* have achieved state standards, extreme caution should be exercised in using these results for other purposes. Using pupil test scores alone to hold teachers and schools accountable is an invalid use of the assessments and can undermine the validity of the statewide assessment program.

The Future of Assessments

We have highlighted the rise of outcome-based assessment over the past 35 years, beginning with the Coleman report. We have described the rise of minimum competency testing, the concerns emphasized in *A Nation at Risk*, and the current emphasis on statewide standards and assessments. Each succeeding approach has upped the ante of pupil performance and the consequences associated with poor performance.

At present, it seems likely that both teacher and statewide assessments will be with us in some form for a long time. Thus, rather than attempt to predict a specific direction for assessments in the future, we will provide two approaches that may be more conceptually useful strategies for thinking about approaches to and changes in assessments. The first approach consists of 10 factors or indicators that can influence changes in assessments. The second approach consists of five questions that are critical to understanding the nature of standards and assessments.

The following factors do not pinpoint specific shifts in assessments, but seek to provide guideposts to emerging trends in assessments. These 10 factors describe a contextual setting in which statewide assessments typically function. Changes in some of these factors are often harbingers of change in both statewide and teacher-made assessments.

1. Schools are basically conservative and reactive institutions, so one must look to social institutions beyond the schools to identify the stresses that produce changes in schools and assessments. Most school changes are initiated by individuals or groups external to schools. Look first at outside, not inside, changes.

2. A change in the goals, functions, or control of the educational process will produce changes in the tools used to carry out the educational process. Given the interrelation among assessments, curricula, and instruction, any single change in one of them can initiate changes in the others.

3. The crucial issues of assessments are not solely technical; they are also social, economic, and value-laden. Shifts in the distribution and redistribution of rewards and sanctions often are harbingers of change.

4. The quantity of educational assessments is inversely related to the public's satisfaction with the educational system. The greater the public's dissatisfaction with education or educators, the greater the call for more assessments to measure current status and set future expectations.

5. Debate and controversy over assessments are better understood if one keeps in mind the difference between locally determined teacher assessment and statewide assessment. Focus on the most consequential assessment to find trends.

6. Most assessments provide redundant information. What is important politically is that it is supplied in an objective manner. Generally, the results reaffirm pupils' prior performance, and for pupils to improve more is needed than just assessments.

7. The greater the consequences associated with an assessment, the greater the importance of the assessment and its influence on teaching practice. Consequential assessments influence classroom focus and instruction.

8. Given the important consequences of statewide assessments, not to teach to the test may be a greater disservice to pupils than to teach to it. This can be an ethical issue. Narrowing instruction and teaching to standards are common strategies to improve pupil performance.

9. Increasingly, understanding the debate over statewide assessments cannot be accomplished without considering which interest group is espousing an argument. Growing debate over how rewards and sanctions will be distributed involves varied and opposing groups.

10. Assessments should be judged not only in terms of their technical adequacy but also in terms of the likely social and legal implications of their use. Although technical adequacy is important in assessment, the fairness of assessment consequences is even more important (adapted from Airasian, 1987).

In conclusion, we pose five questions that may help prod thinking about current applications of standards, instruction, and assessments. These five questions raise important issues about the purpose and use of the results of statewide standards and assessments. If meaningful understanding and change in assessments are to come, they will arise from the answers to some of the following questions. If these questions are honestly and openly considered, the fundamental nature and purposes of assessments might improve. Note that we are not advocating specific changes, but we are advocating consideration of the questions.

1. How much do we really know about teaching widely varied pupils at different levels of readiness in different subject areas? The key to statewide standards and assessments is not in the standards and assessments, it is in the instruction pupils receive to help them to master the statewide standards and assessments. The links among standards, instruction, and assessment represent different levels of complexity. Defining standards and constructing assessments are essentially technologies, for which we have well-established and well-known procedures. However, this is not the case with instruction. Conducting successful instruction is much more an art than a technology, especially when instruction is focused on higher-level pupil outcomes. We can easily become enamored of our technologies and forget the contexts in which they will be applied. It is not true that if we know how to state it, we know how to make it work. If statewide assessments are to produce desired learning outcomes, teachers must be able to successfully teach varied pupils with varied characteristics in varied ways. The one-size-fits-all approach that is common to developing standards and assessments will not be similarly successful in providing instruction. A logical extension of this concern is the question of how ready we are to provide appropriate instruction for those pupils who fail or do poorly on the statewide assessments. Two critical questions that will influence the nature and success of standards-based and classroom assessments are, How much do we really know about how varied pupils with varied degrees of readiness and interest can be taught? and Are there limits to our knowledge of instruction?

2. How should we deal with time in the context of statewide and teacher-based instruction and assessment? School time is limited and schools are being asked to do more for pupils in less time. How should we use this precious commodity? As our assessments demand more and more of pupils, we have reduced the amount of time devoted to traditional academic instruction. For a number of appropriate reasons, schools have been asked to assume the teaching of a variety of socialization and functional skills. A growing array of subjects such as drug and alcohol awareness, conflict resolution, values clarification, hazing and bullying awareness, gender issues, English for daily living, and health and nutrition appear in our schools and diminish the time devoted to instruction in more academic subjects related to statewide assessments. How is instructional time best used in the face of consequential statewide assessments?

   Related to this, we know that a variety of individual differences are manifested early in life and certainly by the time pupils enter school. It seems somewhat odd, then, that many statewide assessments are initially administered to pupils at the fourth-grade level. The time between a pupil's starting school and fourth grade magnifies the variation among pupils, especially for groups that manifest early school needs. It is harder to undo four years of failure or low performance than it is one year. Would some pupils be better served if greater instructional focus is put on the early grades, with small class sizes and an emphasis on both formative and statewide assessments? Would such an approach help pupil groups who are currently performing at low levels on statewide assessments?

3. Can we meaningfully and appropriately use pupil assessment data to make consequential decisions about teachers and principals? Clearly, there are links among pupils, resources, home support, and teaching. All of these factors enter into how pupils perform on statewide assessments. Assessments provide test scores, but the scores do not describe the factors that contributed to them. Comparing pupil achievement on statewide assessments is *not* the same as comparing the quality of teaching, teachers, and administrators. Can we or should we hold teachers and principals accountable only for the factors they have some control over? At the very least, when assessments are used for multiple purposes such as judging pupils, teachers, and principals based on pupils' test scores, the validity of each purpose should be determined independently. There is no magic bullet for determining consequences for teachers and principals. If we want to broaden assessment consequences to include teachers and pupils, how can we fairly and validly make decisions about their performance? Should pupil statewide assessments be supplemented by other sources of classroom-based pupil performances?

4. What do statewide assessment scores mean? What does it mean that a pupil has passed or failed a statewide assessment? What does that tell us about overall achievement, employability, and future performance? Statewide standards, instruction, and assessments represent an insular system, which is confined to a school-centered process: Standards are constructed, instruction provided, assessments administered, and scores determined. Various scoring levels are constructed to grade pupil performance. Some states score pupil performance using a simple pass–fail, while others use multiple scoring levels such as advanced, proficient, needs improvement, and failure. What do the various cut scores mean, not in terms of the established scoring levels, but in terms of what the scoring levels indicate about pupils' future performance? What do they tell us about what a pupil can do and will do in the future? Important consequences emanate from statewide assessments, but we know little about the validity of scoring levels and the consequences associated with them. What strategies can be developed to provide information about the validity of statewide assessment scoring levels?

5. Are there additional configurations that might provide an alternative measure of pupil performance and learning? At present, a single statewide assessment is administered in each subject area assessed. In many states, the assessments are administered to pupils every three or four years. Should these statewide assessments be supplemented by other, more frequent assessment information such as teacher grades, samples of pupil work, or annual subject matter assessment at the school level? These supplemental assessments could be weighted and included as a part of

the statewide assessments. Should an infrequently administered statewide assessment be the sole consequential determiner of pupil performance and learning?

The preceding questions are intended to foster reflection and probe more deeply into what we do and don't know about the features of statewide standards-based assessments. Statewide standards and assessments encompass a variety of complex and important issues, ones that should continue to be examined. Our hope is that this chapter will illustrate there are complex issues associated with standards, assessments, and instruction that require thought. In closing, we note that although our focus has been on statewide standards and assessments, the critical, central, and most important feature of successful pupil learning is the quality of the instruction pupils receive from their classroom teachers. The outcome from desirable standards and high-stakes assessments will depend largely on the quality of instruction provided.

r e f e r e n c e s

Airasian, P. W. (1987). State mandated testing and educational reform: Context and consequences. *American Journal of Education, 95*(3), 323–412.

Boser, U. (2000). Study finds state exams don't test what schools teach. *Education Week, 19*(39), 1,10.

The Center for Educational Reform. (1998). A nation still at risk. Retrieved June 1, 2000 from the World Wide Web: http://edreform.com.

Clarke, M., Haney, W., & Madaus, G. (2000). *High stakes testing and high school completion.* Boston: The National Board on Educational Testing and Public Policy.

Coleman, J. S., Campbell, E. Q., Hobson, C. J., McPartland, J., Mood, A. M., Wienfield, F. D., & York, R. L. (1966). *Equality of educational opportunity.* Washington, D.C.: Office of Education, U.S. Department of Health, Education, and Welfare.

Glass, G. V. et al. (1970). *Data analysis of the 1968–69 survey of compensatory education, Title I, Final Report on Grant No. OEG8-8-961860 4003-(@8 .* Washington, D.C.: U.S. Office of Education.

Jencks, C., Smith, M., Acland, H., Bane, J. J., Cohen, D., Gintis, H., Heyns, B., & Michelson, S. (1972). *Inequality: A reassessment of the effect of family and schooling in America.* New York: Harper & Row.

Jones, M. G., Jones, B. D., Hardin, B., Chapman, L., Yarbough, T., & Davis, M. (1999). The impact of high-stakes testing on teachers and students in North Carolina. *Phi Delta Kappan, 81*(3), 199–203.

Linn, R. L. (2000). Assessments and accountability. *Educational Researcher, 29*(2), 4–16.

Madaus, G. F., Airasian, P. W., & Kellaghan, T. (1980). *School effectiveness: A reassessment of the evidence.* New York: McGraw-Hill.

Mosteller, F., & Moynihan, D. P. (1972). *On equality of educational opportunity.* New York: Vintage Books.

Murphy, J., ed. (1990). *The educational reform movement of the 1980s: Perspectives and cases.* Berkeley, Calif.: McCuthcan Publishing Corporation.

National Center on Educational Outcomes. (1999). *1999 state special education outcomes: A report on state activities at the end of the century.* Minneapolis: National Center on Education Outcomes.

The National Commission on Excellence in Education. (1983). *A nation at risk: The imperative for educational reform.* Washington, D.C.: U.S. Department of Education.

Olson, L. (1999). In search of better assessments. Quality Counts, '99. *Education Week,* 11 Jan., 17–20.

Picariello, H. (1968). *Evaluation of Title I.* Washington, D.C.: American Institute for the Advancement of Science.

Viadero, D. (2000). Texas testing system: Success or failure? *Education Week, 19*(38), 1, 20–21.

Vigue, D. I. (2000). Race gap endures on MCAS results. *The Boston Globe,* 19 May, B1, B8.

4

How Will Teacher Education Use Assessments?

An Assessment Scenario from the Future

MARY E. DIEZ

Alverno College

Phyllis is a teacher educator at an urban campus of a medium-sized college that maintains a strong four-year undergraduate program to prepare teachers for elementary and secondary classrooms. She has set aside an hour today before one of her advisees, Maria, is scheduled to come for an appointment in preparation for the final stages of her elementary program. Maria will bring samples from her coursework and fieldwork that she's considering for inclusion in her portfolio for admission to student teaching. If her meeting with Phyllis is successful, she will get the go-ahead to take her portfolio to a principal or teacher, who will review it in the week prior to the on-campus Portfolio/Interview Assessment Event. At the end of that Saturday meeting, Maria hopes to be recommended for student teaching.

In preparation for the appointment, Phyllis reviews both the department's paper file of Maria's work in the program and the electronic portfolio entries that chronicle her self-assessment and faculty feedback on key performances over five and one-half semesters. She smiles as she remembers her first observation of Maria in the initial field placement. Two areas of concern emerged: (1) Maria's reticence with the cooperating teacher and the fourth-grade students and (2) her difficulty in making connections between theory and practice in written reflections.

Phyllis thinks about the system support that helped Maria to gain confidence and expand her sense of herself as a potential professional in the classroom. An improvisation class, recommended by Phyllis, helped Maria learn to use her posture and her voice to connect with children and adults. Feedback from her instructors in liberal arts and teacher education classes guided her development of careful analysis and relationship making. In early classes, Maria was often asked to revise her work, after feedback, and while she was initially unhappy with what she perceived to be "extra work," she gradually built strong analytic capability and solid writing and speaking skills. Her reflections in the self-assessments stored in the electronic portfolio show quite a remarkable transformation, Phyllis notes, from global statements like "I think I did really well on this" to careful analysis of specific areas of strength and weakness, along with thoughtful reviews of how she processed the tasks and overcame any obstacles.

Maria arrives, a bit out of breath, eager to get to work. She begins with showing Phyllis her videotaped lesson, completed earlier in the week at her field site, an urban public school fifth-grade class. "My lesson is part of a long-term project with fifth-grade science," Maria explains, "with a focus on investigations. I'm really proud of how the children are making progress in being able to focus a question and gather information systematically." She pulls out a chart with notes on each student's strengths and weaknesses and her plans for the next steps, taking into account the needs of a diverse group of learners.

Part of the requirement for the portfolio is to use the college's conceptual framework to critique the lesson entry and Maria also has that section completed. "I'm amazed at how much I've learned," she tells Phyllis, "I think back to when these terms seemed Greek to me and now they're so clear—like filters that I can sift a lot of experiences through."

Phyllis compliments Maria on the quality of her analysis and assures her that the jerky movement of the camera at one point won't be a major problem for the assessors, because overall a viewer can see and hear the interactions with learners. "It's your *teaching* we want to see," she says.

Maria is clear on her "sample of work in a subject area"; she is completing a minor in mathematics along with her elementary major. She's proud of the paper on fractals that she completed for a mathematics class and especially excited about how the graphs produced by the color printer in the computer lab turned out. She also shows Phyllis a chart from her "history of mathematics" class, showing historical and cultural contrasts and contributions. They agree on the paper as perhaps the better choice, although Phyllis makes a mental note to see where else cultural awareness will be addressed in the samples.

Maria says that she is not sure about her "instructional materials sample." Two semesters ago, for an introductory education class, she created a "learning center" involving computer-based problem-solving experiences for second graders in mathematics, but she also wants to showcase a social studies simulation that she created this semester for fifth graders as part of a requirement of the social studies methods class. And from last semester's integrated arts methods course, there's a third-grade art assessment using video that she developed in collaboration with her cooperating teacher. In the art assessment, she worked with students to generate criteria and has copies of both her feedback and their self-assessments.

Phyllis suggests that Maria look at the faculty feedback on those projects and focus on larger characteristics of her work with instructional materials that she wants to highlight. "For example," Phyllis says, "do any of them show a strong integration of content and pedagogy that you could identify in setting context for the sample?" Maria decides on the computer-based problem solving, "partly because I think I should show how I work with a range of grade levels and partly because the computer is such a powerful tool for supporting individual learners."

The next entry called for is a "sample of reflective writing." "I have a lot of stuff here," Maria says, "and I like the way the sequence of reflections shows how I've grown." Phyllis agrees that it's important for Maria to see how she has changed but suggests the need to keep the reading burden manageable for the external assessor. Maria settles on a reflection she completed in response to Lisa Delpit's *Other People's Children* (1995), drawing upon the ideas in the book to reexamine her own philosophy of education statement. It is also, Phyllis notes, an explicit link to issues of cultural diversity in the classroom.

"The portfolio is shaping up nicely," Phyllis comments, with an eye on the clock; "what do you want to do with the two 'open' entries?"

"Well," says Maria, "I could go back to the instructional materials projects. But I have a poetry booklet that I helped students develop last semester. The third graders really got into the idea of publishing and the computers helped them produce something really classy. But there's also the Web page I worked on this semester with the fifth graders to inform parents about the school's curriculum and extracurricular activities. What do you think?"

Phyllis and Maria talk over the benefits of each project and agree on the poetry book (to show her range of ability to work with elementary subject areas) and the Web page (to show her integration of technology in teaching). Finally, Phyllis looks at the record of experience that Maria has prepared, listing the four schools to which she has been assigned for fieldwork and several others where she has participated in special projects as a volunteer.

Phyllis notes some places where Maria needs to check spelling or other conventions, most likely affected by interference from her first language of Spanish. Maria acknowledges that these areas are still a struggle—and "spell check doesn't always help," she complains, "especially when the wrong spelling is a real word in English."

Phyllis gives Maria the name, address, and phone number of the principal who will be her assessor and shares some tips about going to the school to deliver her materials. "Try to have enough time when you go that you can take a tour of the school if she offers one," Phyllis advises.

Before Maria leaves, Phyllis also gives her a memo from the department chair, reminding her to sign up for the required state test of content knowledge for elementary teachers. Phyllis encourages Maria to go to the special Web site that provides practice material, assuring her that her work in the program shows her solid understanding of the concepts incorporated in the test. Maria sighs, but agrees with Phyllis. "I'll never like these kinds of tests," she says, "but at least I don't feel afraid of them. I've had to do so much with my knowledge here."

Essentials of Assessment for Development

When Maria brings her samples to her advisor, she is drawing upon five semesters experience with assessment for development—what the faculty at Alverno College call "assessment-as-learning . . . a multidimensional process, integral to learning, that involves observing performances of an individual learner in action and judging them on the basis of public developmental criteria, with resulting feedback to the learner" (1994). Key to assessment for development are these elements identified by the Alverno faculty (1994), which are evident in Maria's learning and Phyllis's (and other faculty's) work with teacher education candidates.

1. *Explicit outcomes.* Phyllis and her colleagues provide a clear picture of the expectations of candidate knowledge and performance in teacher education and in the disciplinary areas through the outcomes that guide course and program development and through the dozens of assessments that candidates complete in their courses and in the field. The samples that Maria discusses with Phyllis all came from projects assigned and assessed by faculty in the teacher education program.

2. *Performance.* Assessment of candidate performance allows the faculty to have a sense not only of what candidates like Maria know but what they can do with what they know. Maria's faculty create projects that will make *visible* the teacher education outcomes of the program. For example, in methods courses and field experiences, faculty develop experiences that give candidates* practice with the outcome ability of *diagnosis*—the ability to use conceptual frameworks to look at student work in order to make decisions for the next step in the teaching–learning process. Maria's current practice of creating a "running record" in order to attend to individual student needs across a class group was preceded by several studies of individual student work both in her college courses and in fieldwork.

---

*To prevent confusion, this paper will use "candidate/s" when referring to teacher education students and reserve "student/s" for K–12 learners.

3. *Public, explicit criteria.* Criteria describe the expected quality of performance and must be met (Loacker, Cromwell, & O'Brien, 1986). Faculty know that criteria need to capture the knowledge and skills related to the disciplinary content, as well as to reinforce pedagogical skills. Through using criteria, Maria and other candidates have learned to examine their planning and decision making against the expectation, for example, that they link decisions to theoretical frameworks (e.g., in developmental psychology) and show the relationships between the evidence they present and the conclusions they draw.

4. *Feedback.* Phyllis and her colleagues know that feedback is a powerful tool in supporting candidate growth. They give descriptive feedback related to the criteria for the task so that candidates will know where they stand and what areas they need to work on. In Maria's early fieldwork, for example, feedback about her interaction with fourth graders focused on her need to project warmth and care, in order to invite students to learning. Feedback from her faculty assessors was not only descriptive of her current level of performance but also suggested what she could do to address problems in that performance.

   In many courses, Maria also experienced peer feedback, which helped her and her fellow teacher education candidates internalize the meaning of the criteria by applying them to the performance of each other.

5. *Self-assessment.* As powerful as feedback from the teacher and peers may be, self-assessment may be even more powerful, once the learner has gained an understanding of the criteria (Alverno College Faculty, 1994). With developed skill in self-assessment, learners can, in effect, become their own coaches and critics. Maria and other candidates who have become good self-assessors often initiate conversations about their performance with cooperating teachers, asking for ideas about how to improve their teaching skills. (See Appendix H in Mentkowski & Associates [2000] for a picture of how self-assessment ability develops over time.)

6. *Multiplicity.* The faculty who have worked with Maria understand the importance of having multiple forms of assessment—multiple times to practice using knowledge, multiple methods and modes of assessment, and multiple contexts. Multiple times provide the support for learning; too often, candidates bring stories from high school or other colleges recounting how they had only one chance to learn something before the teacher moved on. Multiple methods and modes are important for two reasons—candidates gets chances to express themselves in a preferred mode and every candidate is stretched in trying out new modes of expression. Using multiple contexts helps candidates to see the range of ways in which what they are learning can be applied. And multiple times to practice means that candidates have the chance to build strength and consistency of performance. Multiple modes will probably always include the more "standardized" exams like the content test required by Maria's state; the principle of multiplicity argues that these exams are just one of many ways to examine what candidates know and can do.

7. *Externality.* As a concept, externality involves perspectives outside of the otherwise "closed" community of a teacher educator and a group of teacher education candidates. One way to achieve externality is to have candidates see the relevance of their work by trying it out in real K–12 classroom settings. Another is for faculty to gain perspective by looking across a number of performances of a candidate or by bringing in others not usually involved with the class to provide feedback, as when principals and teachers participate in reviewing candidates' portfolios. Third, externality can be achieved when a group of faculty members creates an assessment that will be used across candidates in their own (and others') classes. The portfolio/interview assessment for which Maria is preparing in the scenario is such an *external* assessment, developed and revised over nearly 10 years by the faculty.

8. *Developmental nature.* Assessments need to fit the level of the candidates' development of ability and knowledge. Maria's early coursework and fieldwork built critical frameworks from developmental and learning theories and guided her to focus on central tasks and individual students. For example, she learned a specific process for diagnosing reading development, completing a miscue analysis in one-on-one reading with a third-grade student. Gradually, the assignments asked her to put more aspects together, the way they occur in classrooms, both in terms of more complex tasks (e.g., planning and implementing a series of lessons) and in terms of working with groups of learners, as she is doing in the running records of student growth in her field placement.

9. *Cumulative nature.* Two principles call for assessment to be cumulative in nature. First, the standards that guide the teacher education program (whether state standards, subject area standards, or other standards) are always larger than any one assessment or set of assessments. Because no one assessment can tell the whole story about the candidate's knowledge and skill or readiness to teach, faculty need to look across multiple performances for a picture of the candidate. Second, candidates learn and grow over time. Thus, assessment must take into account the emerging picture of the candidate's growth. Cumulative assessment allows faculty to create a balance between challenge and encouragement—building on candidates' current strengths and moving them forward into areas that need development.

10. *Expansive nature.* The teacher education faculty work with candidates with the standards in mind. Developmentally, in an early field experience, a candidate may be at the beginning of understanding how to craft learning experiences, but the faculty member's sense of *where the candidate will eventually be* guides the work. Faculty members develop assessments, then, to elicit from the candidates the most advanced performance of which each is capable. Such a design not only provides faculty with good diagnostic information but also allows the candidates to go as far as they are ready to go at a given time. In a standards-based program, of course, candidates must meet all criteria for completion of the program; however, their time line for achievement may vary.

How Likely Is This Picture of the Future?

Two Agendas Support the Scenario

Given the chance to paint a picture of the future of assessment in teacher education, I drew upon what seem to me to be the implications of two agendas that have been pursued in the last 15 years. The *professionalization* agenda was sparked by *A Nation Prepared*, which called for, among other proposals, the creation of ". . . a National Board for Professional Teaching Standards, organized with regional and state membership structure, to establish high standards for what teachers need to know and be able to do, and to certify teachers who meet that standard" (Carnegie Forum on Education and the Economy, 1986, p. 55). The professionalization focus gradually merged with an agenda focused on *the improvement of teaching and learning*, so that the National Board today sees itself as not only recognizing accomplished teachers but contributing to the improvement of teaching practice through the articulation of its standards and the development of an assessment process based on those standards (Castor, 2000; National Board for Professional Teaching Standards, 1989). Thus far (spring of 2000), the National Board has developed 16 certificate areas and 4,800 teachers have achieved national board certification.

As the National Board began its work to define standards for accomplished teaching, interest grew in the development of a set of normative standards for beginning teacher practice. Early in the labor of the National Board, a consortium of states joined together to share resources being developed for beginning teacher assessment and support and to follow the work being done by Lee Shulman at Stanford on the prototype assessments for the National Board (Ambach, 1996). The Interstate New Teacher Assessment and Support Consortium (INTASC), under the auspices of the Council of Chief State School Officers, published in 1992 a set of model standards for beginning teacher licensure designed to be compatible with the National Board and focused on both the professionalization agenda (in recognizing that beginning teachers need to demonstrate standards of knowledge and practice) as well as the improvement of teaching and learning agenda (in a focus on demonstration of practice with K–12 learners). By 2000, INTASC had developed subject-specific standards in mathematics, English language arts, and science and had begun work on standards for social studies, special education, the arts, and elementary education. INTASC is also working on the development of a series of assessments for licensure, including tests of content knowledge and teaching knowledge intended to precede initial licensure and a portfolio assessment of teaching practice to be given in the first three years of teaching.

The National Council for the Accreditation of Teacher Education (NCATE), which sets standards for teacher preparation, has unveiled a new set of standards that look more like the National Board and INTASC in their focus on normative standards and performance assessment, contrasting with accreditation's more "input-focused" approach of the past. Again, the two agendas are evident in *NCATE 2000*. For example, NCATE's Standard I requires demonstration that

> candidates preparing to work in schools as teachers or other school personnel know the
> content of their fields and demonstrate professional and pedagogical knowledge, skills,

and dispositions, and apply them so that students learn. The unit's assessments indicate that candidates meet professional, state, and institutional standards (p. 1).

Although the publication *What Matters Most: Teaching and America's Future* by the National Commission on Teaching and America's Future (1996) provides an eloquent argument for strengthening the work of these three organizations through policy initiatives at the state level and the efforts of institutions of higher education at the local level, the future of assessment in teacher education as envisioned in the scenario of Phyllis and Maria's meeting is by no means assured. As noted in the next section, key to the improvement of teacher education are the need to differentiate between types of assessment appropriate for different purposes and—implicit in that distinction—the development of a higher education culture that supports assessment for development.

Contrasts in Assessment for Different Purposes

Over nearly 15 years, with an investment of millions of dollars, the National Board and INTASC, respectively, have developed legally defensible processes to determine a candidate's certification as an accomplished teacher or eligibility for a regular teaching license. The assessments of both the National Board and INTASC are, by definition, high-stakes assessments, subject to very stringent standards to ensure accuracy and fairness of judgment (Pearlman, 2000).

Figure 4.1 provides a summary of characteristics of high-stakes assessments, which will be contrasted with a parallel set of characteristics of assessment for development in Figure 4.2. The National Board process is a good example of the former. For example, all candidates for a specific board certificate complete the same portfolio entries, with the same page limits; they complete the same assessment center exercises, with the same time constraints. Given everything that the standards call for, the portfolio, of necessity,

FIGURE 4.1 Characteristics of High-Stakes Assessments

- Aspects of the standards are selected, based on both what is judged to be important and what can be measured most effectively.
- The assessment takes place under prescribed conditions.
- The prompts and modes of response are standardized, having been developed through a rigorous process of development, pilot testing, and field testing.
- Prompts and modes may need to be "secure" (e.g., in the Assessment Center Exercises of the National Board).
- The assessment is a one-time event.
- The assessment is "summative," with a cut score that determines whether the candidate is certified or licensed.
- Cut scores are determined through a process for which assessors are trained and care is taken to ensure the reliability of assessors.
- No detailed feedback is provided to the candidate.

focuses on a narrow range of performance if one contrasts it with everything that a teacher does in the course of a year's work with students or, indeed, with all aspects of the standards for the certificate. The INTASC portfolio, which asks candidates to develop portfolio entries across 10 days of instruction, has a similarly limited range in relationship to the whole of the standards.

While the board now allows unsuccessful candidates to bank scores of 2.75 or more and to redo exercises with scores below that number, the assessment is essentially a one-time event. Retakes are another one-time event. Moreover, a candidate's scores and a generalized description of levels of performance across candidates are the only feedback provided. The INTASC support process for new teachers is intended to provide ongoing formative feedback, but this support is separate from the assessment process. Moreover, it is unlikely that detailed feedback will be provided for the INTASC assessment portfolio in most states.

Although they come may come to mind most readily, high-stakes assessments are not the only option. The description of the process of assessment for development in the Phyllis and Maria scenario is related to concepts like classroom assessment (Borko, 1997; Bryant & Driscoll, 1998; Chittenden & Jones, 1998), local assessment (Roberts, 1997), course- or curriculum-embedded assessment (Swisher et al., 1999), and assessment-as-learning (Alverno College Faculty, 1994). What I call here *assessment for development* (see Figure 4.2) provides a contrast in several ways to high-stakes assessment.

NCATE requires that teacher education programs assess candidate performance over time in a variety of ways, linking the expectations for that performance to standards from the state, the learned societies, and the institution's own conceptual framework.

Depending on candidates' developmental needs and also on their choices based on interest, individual work is not limited to a standardized set of prompts or fit into a

FIGURE 4.2   Characteristics of Assessment for Development

- A wide range of aspects of the standards can be addressed, both because there is time to do so but also because multiple modes of assessment over time can be applied.
- Conditions can vary from candidate to candidate and for the same candidate over time.
- The prompts and modes of response need not be standardized; faculty continuously develop assessments to meet the needs of candidates and refine them as they learn from their use.
- An assessment can take place over time and can be revised.
- The assessment process is "cumulative," with the body of work developing an ever-richer picture of the candidate's performance.
- Faculty who work with candidates develop a community of professional judgment through which they share understanding and apply criteria; this community of professional judgment is the source of reliability of judgment.
- Feedback is a central means for improving candidate performance.
- Self-assessment is a critical process for candidate learning.

standardized set of modes; thus, any candidate's total set of assessments would not be exactly like the set completed by others. Choice of subject matter or theoretical approach allows candidates to demonstrate their knowledge and skill in unique ways, while also gathering evidence over time related to the same standards. Moreover, the faculty can use assessment diagnostically and tailor work to individual candidate needs. Time constraints are more fluid and assessments may be refined after feedback. In a developmental mode, it makes sense for candidates to revise their work in response to feedback.

The amount of time available in a teacher education program (often two or three years) allows for the assessment plan of a program to address many aspects of the standards, including some aspects of standards that are not likely to be addressed in high-stakes assessments. And some aspects of the standards spelled out by INTASC would be assessed best in an ongoing way. For example, the expectation that candidates would develop certain "dispositions" for teaching does not seem amenable to high-stakes testing. But consider dispositions like "showing enthusiasm for one's subject area" or "respecting the opinions of others." These can be assessed over time, using videotaped discussions, class presentations, and reflective writings to look for consistent engagement in learning settings and appropriate, professional interaction with adults and children.

Feedback and self-assessment are critical factors in assessment for development. Because assessments tied to learning do not need to be "secure," faculty can provide detailed feedback in relation to the criteria for an assessment. This feedback serves the diagnostic aspect of assessment, literally "feeding into" the next level of learning and growth. And making the criteria public in advance of completing the assessment allows candidates to grow in their ability to critique their own work as well.

NCATE 2000 calls for teacher preparation to incorporate assessment over time, using multiple methods and with ongoing feedback to individual candidates. Thus, assessment for development is more in keeping with the NCATE vision for what should happen in ongoing classroom practice than are the high-stakes assessments of either the National Board or INTASC. It is not that NCATE 2000 directs teacher education to neglect high-stakes tests; rather the new standards call for a balance of classroom-embedded assessment (assessment for development) and high-stakes measures, like, for example, the state-required tests of content knowledge that Maria is preparing for.

Nor does NCATE 2000 rule out the use of some high-stakes decisions in the course of a teacher education program. Many programs have points at which candidates are reviewed for readiness to move into the next stage of the program (Lowe & Banker, 1994; Diez, 1996). In the case of the Alverno program, the decision for advancement to the next stage of development is made on the basis of both specific demonstrations (e.g., of communication performance meeting a particular level of criteria) and the cumulative picture of performance (e.g., across assessments in multiple courses).

Dangers in the Assessment Landscape

A final contrast between high-stakes assessment and assessment for development relates to the awareness of teacher educators. Most have little background or expertise in assessment of any kind (NCME, 1996); those with some background are likely to assume that characteristics of high-stakes assessments are required for all forms of assessment. In my experience in providing technical assistance to institutions developing assessment plans, the lack of conceptual background is difficult to overcome. In spite of NCATE's requirement that a conceptual framework guide all aspects of a program, some faculty in schools of education have defined the teacher education program, at least implicitly, as a collection of courses taken in any order, with little relationship to each other. My own personal "test" for the full implementation of the conceptual framework in relationship to assessment for development is to examine syllabi in a program. Since NCATE redesign, many programs have done a good job of getting the conceptual framework into the front of the syllabus, with a clear impact on the goals for courses. However, if you go further into the syllabus, the middle section is probably unchanged from the past—it often consists of a calendar with topics or readings, without any clear link to the goals. And, when you look at the final pages, faculty outline a point system as the basis for a final grade. The telling question to ask is whether a candidate could amass enough points to pass the course without demonstrating achievements of the goals at the front of the syllabus. Too often, the answer is yes.

NCATE requires both a link between conceptual framework and assessment and the use of performance-based assessment over time in the teacher education program. These requirements call for a new understanding of the relationship among standards, learning experiences, and assessment. The standards or outcomes for a program need to be examined so that they guide what happens in coursework and fieldwork in order that the demonstrations of knowledge, skill, and disposition implicit in the meaning of the standards meet those standards. The essentials of assessment for development listed previously provide a useful way to think about how to make the needed conceptual shift.

The lack of faculty knowledge and expertise in assessment may lead to at least three dangers that threaten the implementation of the kinds of assessment for development called for by NCATE 2000.

High Stakes as "the" Test of Teacher Preparation.   First, under Title II, the requirement for states to use high-stakes tests to rank teacher preparation institutions based on the performance of their graduates may push some institutions into a more high-stakes stance early in the teacher preparation program. The pressure to be close to the top of the ranking may motivate institutions to select only those candidates likely to be able to pass the test. Candidates like Maria, whose cultural and/or prior educational background may not have prepared them for high-stakes testing at the entrance to teacher education, may not get the chance to become teachers.

In contrast to using only high-stakes testing, a balanced system of high-stakes tests and assessment for development has the potential to support and nurture the learning of diverse candidates for teaching. Equally important, among *all* candidates, assessment for development is necessary for bringing novices into the professional community by developing their conceptual understanding, ethical principles, and patterns of judgment in practice. These critical aspects of teaching standards are unlikely ever to be addressed in a high-stakes testing format, but the public depends upon teacher education programs to ensure that candidates develop them. Because its constraints focus on a limited range of what the standards describe, thinking of high-stakes assessment as the only valid measure creates a serious danger that the critical aspects of professional community will be ignored.

Reductionism. Second, reductionism is a related threat to the future of assessment in teacher education because it suggests that if high-stakes assessments only look at a part of practice, then only a part of the whole is necessary in practice itself. Certainly, we see this phenomenon in the current high-stakes testing emphasis in K–12 education. Teachers complain when topics that have not appeared on tests for several years begin to appear— because in the meantime they stopped teaching those topics—even though the standards still call for their inclusion in the curriculum. Even more serious are the cheating scandals, again showing up across the country (Viadero, 2000), where the goal has been reduced from student learning to getting the answers right on the score sheet, in whatever way is necessary.

I was dismayed when, in 1998, the first summer of the INTASC Academies (designed to serve multiple audiences, from potential mentors and assessors to teacher educators), some of the teacher educators in the group fell into a reductionistic perspective. Having spent several days reviewing the beginning teacher portfolio, they remarked that now that they knew what INTASC wanted in the first year of teaching, they would focus *on just that* in their teacher preparation programs.

Reductionism, put simply, is the failure to see that a standard is always larger than any one assessment of it. In order for the narrow sample of the INTASC portfolio to be used for licensure, we have to assume that there is much more evidence available in the whole of the teacher's practice that we don't see. But unless teacher educators are providing rich and deep assessments of each candidate's work—across the aspects represented in the standards—can teacher educators and policy makers be safe in making that assumption?

The Impact of Teaching on Student Learning. Both of the first two dangers just outlined create a third issue—namely, that teacher education candidates learn as much from what their faculty do as from what they say. Standard I of NCATE 2000 requires not only that candidates demonstrate their knowledge, skills, and dispositions but also that they "apply them so that students learn" (p. 1). If teacher education programs reduce the curriculum to what's on the high-stakes test, they are modeling a practice that their candidates will take into their teaching, exacerbating the current problems with high-stakes testing at the K–12 level. Moreover, if their practice suggests that all assessment must be high stakes, rigidly standardized, and disconnected from teaching, that's what candidates will internalize. Maria and others who have experienced assessment for development, in contrast, take away a keen sense of the power of assessment for development, assessment as diagnostic and individualized, and assessment as contributing to student learning.

The Challenge of Institutional Cultures

Clearly, our future scenario faces an uphill battle because of challenges inherent in the organization and practice of institutions of higher education. As Blackwell and Diez (1998, 1999) point out in relation to redesign of master's programs to align with National Board standards and processes, several types of barriers are likely to make the realization of the assessment scenario difficult. From among those that they describe, two that are salient in this context are faculty isolation and the force of old patterns.

Isolation.   The twin agendas of professionalism and the improvement of teaching and learning envisioned by the National Board, INTASC, and NCATE require a different approach to the preparation of teachers than is often practiced in what has been called the individualistic culture of much of higher education (Putnam, 1995). Some have described schools of education, particularly, as collections of individual entrepreneurs.

NCATE standards since 1986 have required that faculty in schools of education develop a professional community, with each other, with liberal arts faculty, with teachers in K–12 schools, and with teacher education candidates. The new NCATE 2000 builds on that expectation, now requiring that faculty work in concert to implement meaningful assessment experiences through which data are gathered over time and candidates receive feedback to improve their learning. Clearly, those who have built strong professional communities are in a better position to move forward with this new initiative.

To gauge the seriousness of the challenge of developing communities of judgment, consider the meaning of the grade in higher education. While some decry the rise of "grade inflation," and others call for a 3.0 for all who would be licensed (American Federation of Teachers, 2000), does anyone pretend that a standard meaning of an A, B, or C is validly and reliably applied within an institution or across institutions? A standards-based approach to teacher education would be a first step in making visible the hidden criteria for judgment in individual faculty members' minds. Such a step must be taken to approach the development of a "community of professional judgment."

The Force of Old Patterns.   Other impediments to the changes called for in NCATE 2000 are present in the rigidified patterns of institutions of higher education. For example, in spite of considerable attention to issues of faculty roles and rewards by the American Association for Higher Education, among others, over the last 10 years, many institutions place higher value on research over teaching and the development of curriculum and assessment for teaching. Recent studies report an escalating need to conduct research in order to obtain tenure or be promoted or to remain on contract in institutions without tenure (Blackwell, 1999). And, in spite of Boyer's *Scholarship Reconsidered* (1990), acceptable research remains narrowly defined in many institutions. Nonetheless, even in settings with narrow definitions, research focusing on assessment design and implementation, for example, could serve to support both the practice of teacher education and the demands of the academy.

Whither the Future?

The stage is set. The work of the National Board for Professional Teaching Standards, INTASC, and NCATE, which is influencing state policy makers across the nation, has set forth an agenda that combines the professionalization of teaching with the need to improve teaching and learning. Will teacher educators accept the challenge? Will policy makers and teacher education practitioners avoid the pitfalls of single-measure, high-stakes tests that lead to reductionism and, ultimately, the failure of these agendas? For Maria and other teacher education candidates whose potential can be unleashed by the power of assessment for development, a lot hangs in the balance.

references

Alverno College Faculty (1994). *Student assessment-as-learning at Alverno College.* Milwaukee, Wisc.: Alverno Institute.

Ambach, G. (1996). Standards for teachers: Potential for improving practice. *Phi Delta Kappan, 78*(3), 207–210.

American Federation of Teachers (2000). *Building a profession: Strengthening teacher preparation and induction.* Washington, D.C.: Author.

Blackwell, P. J. (1999). A preliminary report on the promotion and tenure standards of schools, colleges, and departments of education: A national survey. Paper presented at the American Association of Colleges for Teacher Education, Washington, D.C.

Blackwell, P. J., & Diez, M. E. (1998). *Toward a new vision of master's education for teachers.* Washington, D.C.: National Council for the Accreditation of Teacher Education.

———. (1999). *Achieving the new vision of master's education for teachers.* Washington, D.C.: National Council for the Accreditation of Teacher Education.

Borko, H. (1997). New forms of classroom assessment: Implications for staff development. *Theory into Practice, 36*(4), 231–238.

Boyer, E. L. (1990). *Scholarship reconsidered.* Princeton, N.J.: The Carnegie Foundation for the Advancement of Teaching.

Byant, D., & Driscoll, M. (1998). *Exploring classroom assessment in mathematics: A guide for professional development.* Reston, Va.: National Council of Teachers of Mathematics.

Carnegie Forum on Education and the Economy (1986). *A nation prepared: Teachers for the 21st century—The report of the Task Force on Teaching as a Profession.* New York: Author.

Castor, Betty (2000). Kappa Delta Pi lecture. American Association of Colleges for Teacher Education Annual Meeting, Chicago.

Chittenden, E., & Jones, J. (1998). Science assessment in early childhood programs. Paper presented at the Forum on Early Childhood, Science, Mathematics, and Technology Education, Washington, D.C.

Delpit, L. (1995). *Other people's children.* New York: The New Press.

Diez, M. E. (1996), Admission and advancement in teacher education programs at Alverno College. Unpublished department chart, Alverno College, Milwaukee, Wisc.

Interstate New Teacher Assessment and Support Consortium (1992). *Model standards for beginning teacher licensure and development: A resource for state dialogue.*

Washington, D.C.: Council of Chief State School Officers.

Loacker, G., Cromwell, L., & O'Brien, K. (1986). Assessment in higher education: To serve the learners. In *Assessment in American Higher Education,* ed. C. Andelman. Washington, D.C.: Office of Educational Research and Improvement, U.S. Department of Education.

Lowe, V. J., & Banker, B. J. (1994). Preparing teachers at Asbury College: Restructuring for the 21st century. In *Changing the practice of teacher education: Standards and assessment as a lever for change,* ed. M. E. Diez. Washington, D.C.: American Association of Colleges for Teacher Education.

Mentkowski, M., & Associates (2000). *Learning that lasts: Integrating learning, development, and performance in college and beyond.* San Francisco: Jossey-Bass.

National Board for Professional Teaching Standards (1989). *What teachers should know and be able to do.* Detroit: Author.

National Commission on Teaching & America's Future (1996). *What matters most: Teaching for America's future.* New York: Author.

National Council for the Accreditation of Teacher Education (2000). *NCATE 2000 unit standards.* Washington, D.C.: Author.

National Council on Measurement in Education (1996). *NCME ad hoc committee on preservice teacher training in assessment: Final report.* Washington, D.C.: Author.

Pearlman, M. (2000). Using standards as the foundation for assessment of beginning teachers: Issues and implications. Paper presented at the American Educational Research Association Annual Meeting, New Orleans.

Putnam, R. (1995) Bowling alone: America's declining social capital. *Journal of Democracy, 6*(1), 65–78.

Roberts, L. (1997). Evaluating teacher professional development: Local assessment moderation and the challenge of multi-site evaluation. Paper presented at the Annual Meeting of the National Evaluation Institute, Indianapolis, Ind.

Swisher, J. D., Green, S. B., & Tollefson, N. (1999). Using curriculum-embedded assessment for making educational decisions: An empirical study with implications for including students with disabilities in accountability. Paper presented at the Annual Meeting of the American Educational Research Association, Montreal.

Viadero, D. (2000). High-stakes tests lead debate at researchers' gathering. *Education Week,* 3 May.

5

How Can Assessment Contribute to an Educational Utopia?

WILLIAM D. SCHAFER

Emeritus, University of Maryland

The authors of the chapters in this collection have tried to capitalize on opportunities for assessment to impact education practice. In my recent years as an educator and researcher at the University of Maryland (UMCP) and a state assessment director at the Maryland State Department of Education (MSDE), I have come to believe that assessment holds perhaps the greatest potential for positive change in schools. I am certainly not alone in that belief. But different people have different ideas about what the potential is. For example, I commonly hear that assessments can allow diagnostic–prescriptive instruction. Certainly, diagnostic–prescriptive instruction cannot be done without assessments, but do those assessments exist in usable form? I have not seen them. So what will those assessments look like and where will they come from? Answers I hear to questions like that are not usually very detailed. Mostly they call upon teachers, after training of course, to write them or perhaps to find them in curriculum materials. But I think it is naive to expect even well-prepared teachers to write the needed assessments given the on-the-job support they receive. And yet I believe that assessment in general, and large-scale assessment in particular, holds the promise we need for fundamental and effective school reform. That it does not currently deliver on that promise is the result of three disconnects that I feel we should address.

In this chapter, I will discuss those disconnects and three associated suggestions that I feel can allow large-scale assessments to have strong, positive impacts on how day-to-day instruction is done in classrooms. All these suggestions would orient our work toward facilitating the professional activities of teachers by using assessments to clarify the outcomes, or goals, of instruction and progress toward them.

These three disconnects and associated suggestions are these. (1) Because we do not now establish tight connections between the curriculum we want to deliver and widely held understandings about cognition, we should consolidate and coordinate the cognitive demands expressed in our curricular goals across disciplines. (2) Because descriptions of the results of assessments are not currently expressed in terms of what students are actually doing, we need to connect student test results to specific student achievements. (3) Because large-scale test results have little to do with either teacher activities or even teacher assessments, we need to enhance the connections between summative assessments and instruction. I will propose specific ways to move forward in each of these directions toward an assessment utopia that can profoundly change the way in which teaching is done on a daily basis.

Instruction and Curriculum

One point needs to be made at the outset. Fundamental to all I discuss here is a distinction that should be drawn between curriculum and instruction. Although the two are often thought of as interchangeable, they are very different and even depend on qualitatively different criteria for their justifications.

Curriculum refers here to the goals of education. As students go through schooling, it is intended that their capabilities change. We understand curriculum to the extent that we know what changes we want to bring about in our students. Identifying the elements of a curriculum is, fundamentally, determining what outcomes are valued. Because a curriculum is an expression of values, it should be decided through a process by which stakeholders' opinions are molded into a consensus, which means that the process is inherently a political one.

Curriculum, as I see it, should be universal within its political, consensus-building entity and not tailored to students or groups of students within such an entity (unless the tailoring is done as part of the political process). Curriculum should be a given in the classroom, not created by teachers as they perform their day-to-day roles. In other words, because it embodies the goals the community has for the school and the classroom, it should be imposed on the school and the classroom by the entity that legitimizes it politically. Because curriculum is the way we express our values about what students should learn, it depends for its justification on the process by which those values are determined. I will have nothing to say here about what curriculum should be, but I will have much to say about the features we should look for in how it is expressed.

Instruction, on the other hand, is the means by which student capacities are developed. It is probably dependent at least on student inputs, teacher characteristics, environmental capacities, and the nature of curricular goals. But what differentiates it most from curriculum for me is that it is not judged through a process of valuing. Rather, instruction is itself a disciplinary area, sometimes called *pedagogy*. Like its close ally, the discipline of learning, it may be theorized about and researched. Its goal is to develop understandings that can be used to improve students' attainments of curricula. It is a science. As such, it depends not on valuing but on empirically derived theory for its justification and is best implemented by professionals who have been trained in the applications of the theory.

An important implication of this distinction between curriculum and instruction is that we can think of formative assessments, those used to help students move toward greater achievement, as a part of instruction, and summative assessments, those used to certify achievement of instructional goals, as operationalizations of curriculum. While I am convinced that formative assessments have great value in instruction and would play a very important role in anyone's assessment utopia, I want to focus this discussion on summative assessments based on curricula. I do that because I think improved summative assessments are our most critical area of current need in educational reform. I believe that because I think curriculum must precede both instruction and assessment and I do not think the curricula we now have can satisfy the needs of either instructors or assessors, because it is not understood in the assessment-ready terms needed by both. In other words, we need better summative assessments before we can develop better formative assessments. Hence, my focus in school reform at present is on large-scale assessments.

Suggestion One: Develop Theory about the Determiners of Task Difficulty

The standard rhetoric of assessment holds that large-scale tests are intended to show what students "know and can do" in various curricular areas. No matter what the form of assessment, this measurement is made through presentations of tasks to students and observations of their performance.

The first suggestion I mentioned was to link curriculum with cognition. To do that, we must engage in a broader effort, that of understanding why assessment tasks (e.g., items) are easy or hard. I feel this problem is the next great challenge for measurement research. I will therefore discuss making curriculum–cognition linkages within the broader problem.

When done well, a task is designed as a combination of one or more curricular units with features to allow their expression. Each of these elements can serve to make the task easy or difficult. Although some research has been undertaken to study determiners of task difficulty, this seems to me to be only the beginning of the intensive, basic, theory-driven research effort we need in order to enhance the contributions of assessment to school reform, about which I will have more to say later.

There are probably three categories of determiners of task difficulty that we should focus on: (1) required access to knowledge (what students know), (2) required cognitive demands (what they can do with the knowledge), and (3) noncurricular elements, such as context, that are irrelevant to the important educational goals. Each of these will be discussed, but with more emphasis on cognitive demands.

Determiner One: Access to Knowledge

As a representation of curriculum, a task should require certain knowledge elements. What students know is probably the element most directly and therefore most easily changed through instruction. From a research point of view, this means we will likely need to take students' instructional histories into account when we study knowledge determiners of difficulty.

Some feel otherwise, but my belief is that knowledge domains are not in and of themselves more or less difficult than each other to learn, although it is certainly true that people differ in their general and specific aptitudes. Instead, what makes some knowledge areas seem more accessible to some groups of people than others is that they have a more apparent structure to these learners. For example, persons who propose mnemonic devices to help memory seem typically to be attempting to supply structure to unstructured knowledge elements. So I am guessing that we will probably find knowledge structure to be an important element that affects task difficulty and that we will probably also want to differentiate between knowing something and accessing that knowledge.

It is important to include the needed knowledge in specifying curriculum, and there are two tendencies that should be avoided when specifying it. First, the knowledge must be unambiguously defined. Teachers need to know the minimum knowledge their students must possess, and assessors need to know the limits of the knowledge that is "fair game" for their tests. Second, specifying knowledge is not enough; it is also important to specify what students are to do with the knowledge (i.e., cognition). I'll add later a third element to my conception of a rich expression of curriculum.

Determiner Two: Cognitive Demands

Please take a minute and write down an example of something the schools should teach a student to know and be able to do by the end of the fifth grade in the social studies area of economics. I chose this combination of content and grade level because it fits with an example I will use later. Don't read on until you have finished writing your example.

There are five criteria I think we should be using to decide if statements like the one you wrote are educationally sound. Now that you have your example, please evaluate it against these questions. (1) Is the content fully specified? Does it define all of the content knowledge the student needs without implying a wider scope to some people and not to others? (2) Is the needed cognition fully specified? Does it define what the student is to do with the knowledge? (3) Is it too narrow? It should allow many different representations of tasks to assess it. (4) Is it too general? All teachers should be able to agree on whether any particular task does or does not qualify as a representation of your statement. (5) Does it imply a criterion for when it has been accomplished? To do that, it should contain an expression of how well a student is expected to be able to do it, which need not necessarily be at the level of perfection. These are stringent criteria, but I will argue that they are all-important to the clear expression of the curricula that we use to describe our educational goals. I know of no curriculum at present that satisfies them. In general, the first criterion is the one that is easiest to satisfy. Perhaps your example illustrates that?

Bennett (1999) has suggested that future tests will be designed based on cognitive principles. Because our achievement tests should represent curricula and curricula should include cognition, this is a highly desirable goal. But I feel we are not currently able to understand sufficiently well what students can do to achieve that goal with the knowledge they have. There are at least two barriers that need to be overcome. The first barrier is lack of understandings about cognition on the part of teachers and the second has to do with the fragmented nature of our educational goals.

Barrier One: Cognitive Understandings.   There is no consensus on how to educate teachers about the structure of cognition. Actually, little of that kind of learning ever takes place in teacher education programs. This is probably due to three factors: the complexity of cognition, the lack of a felt need for paying attention to cognition in teacher education, and lack of understandings about how to teach for students' cognitive development. Each of these factors will be considered.

Factor One: The complexity of cognition.   That several descriptions of thinking skills and processes within the cognitive domain exist suggests that cognition is not easy to understand. Nitko (1996), for example, gives not one, but five descriptions in his introductory educational assessment text and references a source for even more. A typical teacher education program may discuss the Bloom et al. (1956) cognitive taxonomy but likely will make little use of it in other coursework. Because we do not have a shared understanding of what cognition is or how to apply cognitive theories to a broad array of educational examples, we ignore it for the most part in teacher education. As a result, few practicing teachers know about and even fewer use any representation of cognition at all. Some way needs to be found to develop a conceptualization of cognition that can be universally understood and applied by educators.

Factor Two: Lack of a felt need for attention to cognition in teacher education.   It has often been said that teachers do not fail in their principals' or other supervisors' eyes by lacking understanding of assessment. That has been posed as one reason why assessment is not represented in about half of the nation's teacher education programs. Perhaps the same could be said about cognition. When instruction in cognition is absent in teacher education, there are no negative consequences because understanding cognition is not a factor in job placement, and once teachers are hired, those who evaluate their job performance simply won't miss it, let alone demand its demonstration in the classroom.

Factor Three: Lack of understandings about how to teach for cognitive development. How do teaching techniques differ when trying to educate students to classify as opposed to explain as opposed to apply as opposed to evaluate? Until we know more about how to teach students to engage in different types of higher-order cognition such as these, it will be difficult to focus the education of teachers on thinking goals at all. Teaching candidates will naturally ask about how to develop those outcomes in students, but there do not seem at present to be satisfying answers. For example, a National Research Council (1999) review of connections between psychology and instruction made several points about how to instruct for transfer of higher-order skills, but the examples were all highly contextualized. The review did not describe generalized principles that teachers could use to help them apply these understandings selectively to their own instruction.

Barrier Two: Fragmented Goals. While cognitive theory has had little impact on the education of teachers, the subject matter disciplines have had an impact on how students are to demonstrate what they can do with the content. These influences are neither coordinated nor tested in terms of theory, although they are strongly promoted in their individual fields. A colleague at the Maryland State Department of Education, Gary Heath, calls this phenomenon the "tyranny of content." Content experts have separately described how cognition should be represented in their fields. Quite naturally, these descriptions are very different from each other. But how is thinking different if it is done with science content as opposed to social studies content or any other? To document this issue, what is needed is an analysis of the various content frameworks that do exist with an eye toward evaluating their comparability in terms of the cognitive functioning they imply.

Taking problem solving as an example, I looked at the National Assessment Governing Board (NAGB) Web site (www.nagb.org) and found the only framework for which problem solving is an explicit category is in mathematics. The NAGB defined problem solving as using knowledge in new situations (how is that different from the "application" level of the cognitive taxonomy?) and elaborated it as recognizing and formulating problems; determining whether data are sufficient or consistent; using strategies, data, models, and mathematics; using spatial, inductive, deductive, statistical, or proportional reasoning in new settings; and judging whether solutions are reasonable and correct. The science framework approached problem solving as a part of scientific investigation, which also included processes of science. However, the discussion of what constitutes scientific investigation does not focus on cognitive skills, but instead focuses on variation and control in scientific investigations. That is content, not cognition. The NAGB civics and social studies frameworks are silent on problem solving.

Yet problem solving involves skills that can, probably should, and do have meaning in any discipline. According to Marzano, Pickering, and McTighe (1993), for example, problem solving includes identification of constraints or obstacles to a desired outcome, identifying alternative ways to overcome the constraints or obstacles, selecting and testing an alternative, and evaluating the selection and suitability of alternatives. It would not be difficult to find important examples of this eminently teachable and assessable collection of skills in any content area.

Another example comes from reading. According to the National Assessment of Educational Progress (NAEP) framework, good readers are able to use what they already know to help them understand what they read; to form an understanding of what they read; and to extend, elaborate, and critically judge its meaning. This is also called *integrating* the material with the reader's prior knowledge. To me, this means looking for consistencies and inconsistencies. Material might be confirmatory, disconfirmatory, an extension, or irrelevant to elements of one's current knowledge and understandings. Except through teaching by integration of content areas, the NAEP analysis has been limited to reading and has not been replicated, at least not clearly, for the other disciplines. Yet these cognitive components seem to have direct and important application in any area where principles (perhaps called *theories*) are developed and compared with new knowledge. The extensions to the hard sciences, life sciences, and social sciences are quite obvious. Even in mathematics, much of what is taught is intended to be a tool, and thus subject also to external validation. Therefore, integration of prior knowledge with evidence, and evaluation of the quality of the evidence, is appropriate in virtually any content area but is not described in such a way that a teacher is helped even to understand that it has fundamental relevance across disciplines. More broadly, it may perhaps be better to revise our concept of this cognitive skill integrating as knowledge structures, because prior knowledge and new evidence each need to be evaluated in the process of integration (i.e., prior knowledge may be wrong and/or new evidence may not be strong). But no matter how this ability is characterized cognitively, the integration of knowledge with evidence is clearly a measurable process.

In my assessment utopia, cognition will have the same meaning across the disciplines. We might get there by identifying a common conceptualization of cognition (perhaps through an effort coordinated by NAGB). Of course, the content areas would need to collaborate on the common definition, but it should be developed with the informed participation of our best cognitive theorists. The result should at once represent the ways in which what students know can be used and be parsimonious enough for universal use across disciplines by teachers. Each discipline could focus not on alteration, but instead on elaboration of how cognitive activities are represented within its unique content area. Each might also be asked about which cognition constructs are irrelevant, but I suspect the answer will be "none." The result would be a menu of elements of cognition that curriculum designers would choose from in expressing their instructional goals. We would thereby have a language to use in communicating with other educators about cognition. For the language to be commonly understood, it needs to be taught in teacher education and professional development programs routinely. Understandings about cognition and how to instruct to achieve it should be used in the daily functioning of—and therefore become an expectation of—every teacher.

NAGB is in a unique position to provide a valuable service in facilitating this collaboration. The role of NAGB is particularly important, states follow its lead in developing their own content standards, partly because the NAGB frameworks lend legitimacy to their own efforts. NAGB could assemble a credible panel of cognitive theorists and credible representatives from each of the core disciplines in an effort to synthesize our understandings about cognition into a useful and teacher-friendly description that applies equally to all content areas. The result would benefit both curriculum developers and those who study teaching, the two external groups whose work has most impact on what happens in classrooms. One valuable first step in this process might be to evaluate the existing frameworks to see if the cognitions they contain are generalizable across the other disciplines, as suggested by my examples.

Determiner Three: Noncurricular Elements

Several characteristics of a task that are irrelevant to either the content or the cognition of an item may also influence task difficulty. These may include such features as the context of the problem, the inclusion of irrelevant information, the format of the question, and so on. I don't want to spend much time on this except to note that these characteristics need to be considered, at least enough to control them if not to study them in research into task difficulty. Because they are goal-irrelevant, we need to make sure we are not measuring students' ability to deal with them in our assessments of achievement. About the only way I know to do that is to try to understand how they influence the difficulty of the tasks in our assessments.

In order to achieve my assessment utopia we need to understand the content, cognitive, and contextual determiners of task difficulty. In that future world not only will we be able to create items that test the content and cognitions we want but also we will be able to write them for particular levels of student achievement in order to target our assessments to our student groups carefully. Quite a bit of work is needed to get there, but the goal is well worth it.

Suggestion Two: Communicate
Results in the Language of Standards

Communications about student achievement fail when they do not express what students are doing. Yet the context we normally use to attach meaning to scores is other scores. This leads to simple judgments of higher (e.g., better) or lower (e.g., poorer) but does not help us understand what students, individually or in groups, have accomplished. Although there is undeniable value in such norms, the messages they send are incomplete.

We should try to improve the ways we clarify and communicate student performance in order to enhance the understandings needed for better instruction. To do that, we need to be able to describe activities of students in a way that shows their levels of achievement. The method must be technically sound and, ideally, allow both norm-referenced and criterion-referenced judgments. But above all it must express performance in a way that creates an accurate mental image of student behavior in the minds of teachers. The intent is to help teachers, and others, envision degree (i.e., amount) of achievement by describing it in terms of the activities achieving students engage in.

While with MSDE, I worked with some of my colleagues on a device that seems to have potential to satisfy these criteria. Our work originally grew out of the interest of many teachers in the state in seeing the test papers of their students. There were at least two reasons for that interest. First, they wanted to learn what demands were being placed on their students in the accountability system. Not satisfied that their knowledge of the state's content domain was either adequate or complete, they wanted to use the test to discover the state's actualized content and performance standards. Second, they wanted to evaluate the degree of performance their own students had achieved in assessment in terms of the state standards. But student papers are not the best evidence for either purpose. Any test form is only a sampling of the content domain. The domain is richer than any test can represent. With respect to the second objective, student work, even if scored, does not carry degree-of-proficiency interpretations against state standards. Thus, such work is not informative, although many teachers likely do not realize that.

We tried to satisfy several criteria in working on a substitute scoring system. We wanted to capitalize on the item–response–theory (IRT) scaling of the assessment, and we wanted to represent both the content and process elements of the sampling plan for the domains that were being tested. We also wanted to indicate how the process demands of tasks contribute to task difficulty, and we wanted to divide each domain into instructionally meaningful content subsets. Our concept borrowed from NAEP's use of a device for mapping items to their achievement scales. Being most familiar with how this would apply to the Maryland School Performance Assessment Program (MSPAP), I will describe the device in that context. However, it should generalize straightforwardly to any assessment scaled using IRT, or, more broadly, to any assessment that places students and items on the same scale.

Four characteristics of the MSPAP are important to review here. First, it is entirely a performance assessment. All items are open-ended and many are scored with rubrics containing more than two response categories. Second, the content areas tested (reading, writing, language usage, social studies, science, and mathematics) are broken down into outcomes, which is the lowest level at which results are reported, after scaling and longitudinal recalibration at the content level using two-parameter, partial-credit models. Third, although individual scores of students are reported to schools, interpretations are recommended only for groups of students, such as for schools. Fourth, the scale of MSPAP, which originally (in 1992) was set at a mean of 500 and a standard deviation of 50, is typically broken down into five proficiency levels for each content area, and accountability decisions are based on proportions of students in the various levels. Anyone interested in further elaborations about MSPAP, including sample tasks, reports, and technical manuals, can go to the Web site www.mdk12.org to learn more.

It is easiest for me to describe this device using an example. Table 5.1 is the framework of a display that might describe the scores of a class (or other group) of students on the economics outcome within the social studies content area of MSPAP. The middle column of the table represents the possible scores (even numbers only) that make up the scale. (Eventually I would like to see such a report presented at a Web site, in which case all the scores, not just the even ones, could easily appear, the vertical limitation of the print format being eliminated.) On MSPAP, these scores are recalibrated year-to-year so

TABLE 5.1   Grade Five Economics Outcome Scores, Heuristics, and Histogram

Students	Scores	Heuristics
	676	Thoroughly explains how lack of multiple resources impacts the goods & services produced in a community
	674	
	672	
	670	
	668	
	666	
	664	
	662	
	660	
	658	
	656	
	654	
	652	
	650	
	648	Thoroughly describes the impact of economic growth on a community's standard of living
	646	
	644	
	642	
	640	Thoroughly explains the effects of supply & demand on the production of goods & services
	638	
	636	
	634	
X	632	Identifies and thoroughly describes multiple ways that goods & services are produced
	630	
	628	
	626	Thoroughly explains connections between supply & demand of goods in different community settings
	624	
	622	
	620	Thoroughly explains how other groups and places help meet a community's economic needs
	618	Thoroughly explains how environmental resources are used to produce goods & services that are in demand
	616	Explains exchanging goods and services between regions using a map
	614	
X	612	Thoroughly explains how lack of at least one resource impacts the goods & services produced in a community
	610	Identifies multiple decisions made by individuals because economic growth affects their standards of living
	608	"Identifies resources and consistently classifies them as capital, natural, or human"
	606	Uses prior knowledge to explain how student's state's present economy is related to historical and economic factors
	604	Synthesizes historical & economic information to describe supply & demand conditions in student's home state
	602	
X	600	Thoroughly explains how better transportation improves individuals' standards of living
X	598	Thoroughly explains types of goods exchanged between regions
	596	Thoroughly describes the types of goods & services provided in a given community setting
X	594	Supplies economic reasons for events in the historical economic growth of the student's home state

(continued)

TABLE 5.1   *(continued)*

Students	Scores	Heuristics
	592	Identifies and partially describes one or more ways that goods & services are produced
	590	Describes how different types of communities use their available resources to meet their economic needs
	588	Explains how production of a good or service is related to the resources needed to produce it
	586	Partially explains how environmental resources are used to produce goods & services that are in demand
	584	
X	582	Partially describes the impact of economic growth on a community's standard of living
	580	Thoroughly explains capital, natural, and human resources used by a service business in a community
	578	Identifies different economic resources of different types of communities
	576	
	574	
X	572	
	570	
	568	Thoroughly explains historical exchange of goods between student's home state and the world
	566	Identifies the economic resources of one type of community
	564	Consistently discriminates between capital, natural, and human resources
	562	Identifies resources and can usually classify them as capital, natural, or human
	560	Identifies one or more ways that goods & services are produced
	558	Partially explains the effects of supply & demand on the production of goods & services
X	556	Partially explains how lack of at least one resource impacts the goods & services produced in a community
	554	Partially explains how other groups and places help meet a community's economic needs
	552	Makes a connection between production of a good or service and the resources needed to produce it
	550	Identifies one decision made by individuals because economic growth affects their standards of living
	548	Partially describes the types of goods & services provided in a given community setting
X	546	Partially explains capital, natural, and human resources used by a service business in a community
	544	Attempts to use historical & economic information to describe supply & demand conditions in student's home state
	542	Partially explains how improved transportation improves individuals' standards of living
X	540	
XX	538	
	536	Describes how one type of community uses its available resources to meet its economic needs
	534	
X	532	Partially explains connections between supply & demand of goods in different community settings
	530	Explains how provided historical and economic information is related to student's state's present economy
XX	528	Partially explains historical exchange of goods between student's home state and the world
XXX	526	
	524	
XX	522	Usually discriminates between capital, natural, and human resources
X	520	
X	518	
	516	
	514	

TABLE 5.1   *(continued)*

Students	Scores	Heuristics
	512	
	510	
	508	
X	506	
	504	
	502	
X	500	Partially explains types of goods exchanged between regions
	498	
XX	496	
X	494	
	492	
	490	
X	488	
	486	
X	484	
	482	
X	480	
	478	
	476	
	474	
	472	
	470	

Source: I want to make sure to acknowledge the helpful work of Elizabeth Johnson at MSDE, who compiled the item locations and prepared the initial activity descriptions, which I call *heuristics*, in Table 5.1.

they maintain the same meaning. Not shown in the table are the proficiency levels that are defined on the scale. They range from 1 (high) to 5 (low); the score ranges are 622 and above for level 1, 580 to 621 for level 2 (excellent), 525 to 579 for level 3 (satisfactory), 495 to 524 for level 4, and 494 and below for level 5. Proportions of students at and above levels 2 and 3 are reported in the state accountability program. The Xs in the column on the left indicate the scores of a hypothetical class of 30 students on this MSPAP outcome. The statements at the right of the scale gave the criterion-referenced meaning of the scores, which I call *heuristics.* It is important to describe how these definitions were developed and how they were placed on the scale.

The heuristics were created from levels on scoring guides for tasks that students completed on MSPAP across several forms. Anchor statements were amplified in the scoring guides with examples of student work. The statements in the table are generalizations of the scoring guide anchors that are intended to describe as specifically as possible what students were asked to do and how well they did it without providing enough information to communicate the specific nature of the tasks. The placements of the heuristics correspond to the recalibrated score location parameter estimates for all nonzero scores. These generally are the locations from the generalized Samejima (1969) graded response model where the response probabilities are 0.5. More recently, Huynh (1998) has suggested that reporting score locations where response probabilities are 0.67 results in the most mean-ingful interpretations.

In general, the heuristics should satisfy four goals. The first three goals refer to each heuristic and the fourth refers to their use in an achievement reporting scale. First, each should be general enough to allow multiple representations of that combination of task and achievement level. It is this feature that led me to use the name *heuristic*. Second, each should be specific enough that everyone would agree whether a given example of a task-achievement level combination would or would not be an example of the heuristic. Third, each should include all the features that we know are relevant to determine difficulty from the content and cognitive sources. Fourth, the heuristics for score reporting should collec-tively be dense enough to infer meaning for all of the important score ranges along the achievement scale. Minimally, these are the ranges where most of the students are and are expected, with success, to be.

That the heuristics in Table 5.1 do not satisfy these goals should be no surprise. Al-though they certainly allow multiple representations, the range of representations is virtu-ally always too broad. That violates the second criterion. A commonly understood language of cognition could help us write heuristics that better satisfy this criterion. Fur-ther, all educators will not define *thoroughly* and *partially* in the descriptions of achieve-ment levels equivalently. This is not a problem in operational scoring of MSPAP, because scoring guides are used to elaborate the modifiers through exemplars and response cues, but for a more general audience there is an uncomfortable lack of specificity. The same is true of the content descriptions, in which terms like *resource, community*, and *historical in-formation* can be exemplified by tasks with a broad range of accessibility (i.e., familiarity and structure) to a student. We limited ourselves to three years of MSPAP assessments, so the denseness of descriptors is spotty in places, particularly at the extremes. The lower ranges of the scale are not well represented; they are defined more by what students can-not do than by what they can do. These heuristics also do not necessarily represent the important aspects of task difficulty because we do not yet know much about what they are.

The nature of the model that is used to describe difficulty has implications for the physical representation used to scale both items and persons. In this example, a single la-tent dimension is assumed. Consistency between the achievement trait and its scaling model should, of course, be evaluated empirically. A review of alternative latent models along with some extensions can be found in Cohen and Kolstad (2000). It must be remem-bered, though, that whatever representation is used must communicate clearly to teachers if it is to affect what happens in schools.

Even with its shortcomings, this prototype example does give a feel for a scale that should be useful—depending on the standard errors of the scores, of course—as a way for educators, students, parents, and the general public to understand the meaning of scores from large-scale assessments. Results from virtually any achievement test scored using a model that places students and items on the same scale can be presented in this format. For example, expressing NAEP results in such a table would be far more meaningful than the current proficiency-level descriptions and sample tasks. Commercial achievement tests also would be far more meaningful both in terms of what they test and what the tested students can do if presented using such a device.

Some measurement professionals will likely recommend using sample items in place of heuristics in reports like these. They will argue that the items themselves are operational definitions of the combinations of characteristics that lead to their placements on the achievement scale. It is tempting to agree, because the items are actual evidence of what they require. It would then be possible to scale released items and report results using actual prompts. Nevertheless, I hope this recommendation can be resisted. The power of heuristics comes in their ability to be generalized, and items do not have that property. The reporting approach I am recommending has most value when teachers can use the heuristics as a means to develop their own examples. To suggest that teachers should themselves abstract from specific items the elements that should be generalized would be going beyond what they should be asked to do. It is far more reasonable for curriculum and measurement professionals, working together, to develop the heuristics and to justify them empirically. That is not an instructional activity and should therefore not be a responsibility of a classroom teacher.

An important advantage of this system is that the heuristics do not need to be redeveloped across forms or time as long as the scores are recalibrated to retain the same meaning. After all, the scale represents a test domain, not a test form. Instead, heuristics that cover sparser regions of the scale can be sought out as the assessment program develops. However, it would be prudent to check the established heuristics to see that they are stable across forms and time to guard against scale drift. In this example, the heuristic placements are averages when tasks were repeated across different years. That occurred for 17 task–category combinations. In most cases, the locations being averaged were very close, but in three they were disparate by as many as 38 points. Two of those three were for different score categories from the same item. Of course, the better the heuristics are placed, the more useful the device.

Reporting assessment results using this sort of table would clarify for students what they able to do and what they must learn to improve their performance. Teachers could see where their students are and what they need to be able to do to demonstrate greater achievement. For each, the difference between highly ambitious goals and goals that are perhaps more realistic can be clarified.

Suggestion Three: Articulate Classroom Assessments with Large-Scale Assessments

The third connection that needs to be made is between summative assessments and the activities of teachers. Large-scale accountability assessments are being used for two purposes, to motivate instructional change and to guide the nature of the change. The former they can do quite well. But it is a common lament among practitioners that the assessments do not inform classroom activities. For instructional guidance, teachers need means that are more readily available and more frequent than even the most ambitious large-scale assessment program can be. Another approach is needed.

There should be a clear interface between large-scale assessment and instruction in classrooms. In my assessment utopia, that would be achieved through smooth transitions between formative classroom assessment, summative classroom assessment, and large-scale assessments. Two prerequisites are needed for that. The first is that the curriculum standards and student performance standards are defined by heuristics. The second is that each type of assessment is used for a clearly understood purpose.

Prerequisite One: Standards Defined by Heuristics

Since each heuristic is a statement that indicates what students are doing (cognition), what they are doing it with (content), and how well it is being done (performance), they should be an ideal mechanism to explain to a teacher exactly what is to be learned and how well it must be mastered to be determined "satisfactory" or "excellent" or "basic" or "advanced" or whatever language tags are given to performance levels. Heuristics can help a teacher envision what achievement will look like when students attain it. Thus, they provide a way to define instructional goals specifically and meaningfully. A curriculum defined by heuristics would communicate its full scope in an instructionally meaningful way to a teacher. Expressing curriculum in terms of heuristics would also force those who develop it to be precise about what is meant.

I think of heuristics as positioned in a three-dimensional model. The base, or floor, of the model is defined by content and cognition subdivisions and except for how the cognitive elements are expressed, would not differ much from a typical table of specifications. The vertical dimension is performance standards, expressed as regions on a continuum. Some of our research (Schafer et al., in press) indicates instructional benefits from generic rubrics, and this seems to support expressing performance standards in broad ways across content–cognition combinations. Indeed, it may prove possible to generalize generic rubrics across disciplines, perhaps based, ideally, on the cognition elements. Doing the latter would help teachers to reach and use the common understanding of cognition that I am suggesting.

It is probably most reasonable in this utopia to define curricula in stages, top-down. At certain points, such as grades 3, 5, and 8 and for a core set of high school courses, the heuristics to be achieved would be described by an accountability agency, such as a state. Further development would be at more local levels, such as districts, where curricula would be defined in all the grades and courses, taking care that the state heuristics would be achieved at the specified grades. Besides ensuring that the accountability heuristics are covered, the local agency might or might not augment them with either new heuristics or more demanding ones, as defined through its own political process.

Prerequisite Two: Uses of Assessments

Three types of assessments would be emphasized in my assessment utopia. First, teachers would use formative assessments to help themselves and their students understand their achievement goals and how much their students have progressed toward them. Second, teachers would use summative assessments to document student learning on sets of heuristics defined by content–cognition combinations. Third, there would be periodic checks, or verifications, on teachers' student-achievement judgments through accountability assessments, which would be sponsored by at least three levels: district, state, and national. Although recommending that curriculum be developed by a top-down approach, I think of assessments and accountability as bottom-up. Each successive level validates those portions of the more local heuristics its curriculum covers.

Assessment Type One: Formative Classroom Assessments. Because it is specific, a heuristic can be used to generate valid operational definitions. That is, it can be represented using multiple tasks and can be translated into both formative and summative assessments. Armed with behavioral descriptions of performance goals, teachers can develop formative assessments or perhaps use formative assessments developed by others (such as states, districts, or textbook publishers) that are tied to the heuristics in the curriculum. The performance-level feature of the heuristics would imply that students could understand along with teachers how well they are able to perform in the various content–cognition combinations they are learning.

Assessment Type Two: Summative Classroom Assessments. Teachers would maintain in portfolios evidence of achievement over commonly defined sets of heuristics. These would be different from the formative assessments in that they should be constructed more carefully to satisfy psychometric criteria. Each accountability agency—the district, the state, and the nation—should commit to developing multiple summative assessments for each content–cognition set of heuristics so that teachers have external resources to draw on. Further, the availability of these summative assessments should help teachers construct their own elaborations and verify their own understandings of the meanings of the heuristics. Reporting to parents might be based on these summative assessments. Reporting could be ongoing and perhaps even be done using copies of student work if the classroom-level summative assessments would not be compromised by disclosure. Reports of student achievements on the curriculum elements would be collected at the building level and summarized in school, district, and state reports. This would also provide a means of very early identification of students who are in need of enhanced or specialized instructional support and of assessing demand for different types of academic support services.

Assessment Type Three: Summative Accountability Assessments. External accountability assessments would provide verification in a standardized setting that the curriculum has been achieved. Because teachers and schools have (or at least should have) incentives for the achievement of high performance expectations by their students, there will always be concern about the validity of summative assessments by teachers. The only way I see to overcome that is to introduce third-party accountability, such as through district, state, and perhaps national assessment systems. But if these assessments are tied to the heuristics defined in the district- or state-level curriculum, and students have achieved at the performance levels documented in their portfolios, then there should be no surprises in either the content or the results of the large-scale assessment. If there are discrepancies, then principals have evidence to use with teachers to help them improve their classroom summative assessments, or perhaps to question in a constructive way the validity of portions of the larger-scale assessment.

Final Thoughts

At the outset I distinguished between curriculum and instruction. This paper has been about curriculum, only. Actually, it has described not what curriculum should be, but how it should be expressed and used. Through the use of heuristics, curriculum may be described in terms that are at once both teacher-friendly and assessment-friendly. Although some may feel this sounds a lot like scripted instruction, it is not. There is nothing here that pertains to how teachers teach. This utopia also differs from Hirsch's (2000) core knowledge conceptualization because it is more than just specification of content. Besides content, cognition, and performance are also described in heuristics.

In this utopia, assessments are embedded in a system of communication about cognitive as well as content standards and students' achievements in relation to them. In other words, the goal is to help teachers envision and document achievement through making feasible a way of expressing in generalizable terms all three dimensions of achievement: what is done, what it is done with, and how well it is done.

Another attempt to describe how tests may provide the information needed for instructional decisions (Popham, 2000), proposes four rules for those who develop accountability assessments. These will be compared with the three proposals here. Popham's first rule is that curriculum should be prioritized and that high-stakes tests should cover only those elements of the highest priority. In the present utopia, this would occur at each level that curriculum is specified. The only operationally meaningful degree of prioritization is whether a curricular element is assessed, and this decision would be made when a curriculum domain is described. In order to write tests that are tied to heuristics, curriculum and assessment professionals will need to agree on the content, the cognitions, and the degree of performance that is acceptable. Modifications (elaborations or extensions) to curricula would be made at the same times and by the same agencies as they are made to assessments. The second rule proposed by Popham is that assessment tasks should require students to use their knowledge and skills and/or to apply the criteria that will be used to judge the quality of the response. His third rule is that the knowledge and skills that a test represents should be constructed for teachers so that they understand the cognitive demands that are needed for successful performance by students.

Two points should be made here. First, when assessment tasks are tied to heuristics, the knowledge and cognitive skills of students are engaged to the extent that the tasks are valid. Second, the use of heuristics to express curriculum implies that judgments about quality of achievement can become a fundamental part of teaching as well as testing. It would be natural and desirable for rubrics that express descriptions of levels of achievement, in terms of cognitive skills, to become routine components in all aspects of classroom life.

Popham's fourth rule is that any high-stakes assessment should be reviewed to an extent commensurate with the consequences of its use. This point is well-taken no matter where tests come from or what they represent. Popham suggests five criteria. Two apply to the assessment's domain description, which should be clear and concise enough for a teacher to be willing to read it and should express the cognitive demands that students are to master. The use of heuristics to express curricula should suit both these criteria. The other three criteria are that each task on an assessment should lead to higher scores for students who have mastered its content than for those who have not, that the task be free of bias, and that the content the task assesses should be teachable. The first two apply no matter how the content domain is expressed. The last is implied by the criterion for heuristics that they should be capable of many representations but that each representation should be susceptible to consensus among reasonable teachers that it does indeed represent the heuristic.

Clearly, there is a great deal of work to be done before this vision of assessment utopia can be realized. Item difficulty needs to be better understood. Cognition needs to be defined and then agreed upon across the disciplines. Content needs to be determined and then combined with the cognition elements through a value-clarifying process nationally, in states, and in districts. Performance levels and heuristics to express them in terms of content–cognition combinations need to be developed and verified at the same time. Finally, a sufficient critical mass of assessments needs to be developed for an initial implementation of the system. A side issue is to determine whether performance levels can be expressed for cognitive elements in terms of generic rubrics that apply across disciplines. My expectation is that we will find generic rubrics not only to apply across disciplines but also to apply equally well at all levels of education. As people progress in learning, I suspect they continue to apply the same cognitive skills, but they apply them to deeper, and increasingly complex, knowledge structures.

Although the constructed-response format allows more direct access to student cognition, the selected-response format also is appropriate for these assessments. The key is to be able to represent the heuristic without irrelevant interference from task characteristics. As we develop understandings about item difficulty, that will be easier and easier to accomplish.

There are a number of reasons why this may not seem much like a utopia you want to live in. Perhaps the first thought of some is that this would imply a mandated curriculum, at least at the state level. I agree, it does. But I also suggest that wherever there exists a statewide accountability program with real consequences, there exists a statewide curriculum. That is a fact. The only difference between some programs and others is that some do not tell anyone what the state curriculum is. When it is hidden, then educators in the state are only guessing about what is fair game for the state's accountability tests. Some will guess right and some will guess wrong, and student scores will behave accordingly. That does not sound very utopian to me!

The classroom I see after these efforts are successful would be noticeably different from what it is today. The teacher would act more like a coach for the students as opposed to a determiner of their day-to-day successes and failures. Successes and failures would instead be determined using rigorous summative assessments of goals, defined by consensus curricula and made available through districts and large-scale accountability agencies. And teacher judgments of progress would be verified at accountability checkpoints in a student's schooling. Teachers would be freed of the need to make judgments about the adequacy of individual student performance and would instead make judgments about how to educate the students toward the needed levels of achievement—judgments more appropriate to ask and educate teachers to make.

I believe this is a vision of a feasible assessment utopia. I hope you agree that the proposals made here can move us in that direction.

r e f e r e n c e s

Bennett, R. E. (1999). Using new technology to improve assessment. *Educational Measurement: Issues and Practice, 18*(3), 5–12.

Bloom, B. S., Englehart, M. D., Furst, E. J., Hill, W. H., & Krathwohl, D. R. (1956). *Taxonomy of educational objectives: The classification of educational goals. Handbook I: Cognitive domain.* White Plains, N.Y.: Longman.

Cohen, J., & Kolstad, A. (2000). *Theory-consistent item response models (T-CIR models).* Paper presented at the annual meeting of the National Council on Measurement in Education, New Orleans.

Hirsch, E. D., Jr. (2000). The tests we need. *Education Week, 19*(21), 64, 40–41.

Huynh, H. (1998). On score locations of binary and partial credit items and their applications to item mapping and criterion-referenced interpretation. *Journal of Educational and Behavioral Statistics, 23*(1), 35–56.

Marzano, R. J., Pickering, D., & McTighe, J. (1993). *Assessing student outcomes: Performance assessment using the Dimensions of Learning Model.* Alexandria, Va.: Association for Supervision and Curriculum Development.

National Research Council (1999). *How people learn: Brain, mind, experience, and school.* Washington, D.C.: National Academy Press.

Nitko, A. J. (1996). *Educational assessment of students,* 2d ed. Englewood Cliffs, N.J.: Prentice-Hall.

Popham, W. J. (2000). Assessments that illuminate instructional decisions. Paper presented at the 30th Annual Conference on Large Scale Assessment, Snowbird, Utah.

Samejima, F. (1969). Estimation of latent ability using a response pattern of graded scores. *Psychometrika Monograph,* No. 17.

Schafer, W. D., Swanson, G., Bené, N., & Newberry, G. (in press). Effects of teacher knowledge of rubrics on student achievement in four content areas. *Applied Measurement in Education.*

6

How Will Assessments Accommodate Students with Disabilities?*

GERALD TINDAL

University of Oregon

*The research summarized in this chapter reflects work founded by the Office of Special Education Programs (OSEP)—Project VALIDATE (Validating Accommodations that Legitimize Individuals' with Disabilities Access to Testing in Education, CFDA #84.023F) and the Oregon Department of Education (ODE)—Development of Modified Measures. The opinions and text reported in this chapter, however, do not reflect those of either of these government agencies.

The field of research on test accommodations has expanded considerably in the past decade. Thurlow, Ysseldyke, and Silverstein (1993) provided the first summary of research describing the results from six studies completed on students with disabilities (SWD). Six years later, Tindal and Fuchs (1999) reviewed 106 studies on the effects of accommodations for SWD. In part, this increase has been due not only to more studies being conducted but also to the manner in which the field has defined the term and accorded it a priority. For example, Olson and Goldstein (1996) and Mazzeo et al. (2000) report on the participation of students with special needs in the National Assessment of Educational Progress (NAEP), reflecting a growing need for more research with more students if NAEP is truly to serve as the nation's report card. Finally, Abedi, Kim-Boscardin, and Larson (2000) recently published a book that includes summaries of research not cited in previous reviews and studies. In their report, yet another population is identified for whom test accommodations need to be considered: English Language Learners (ELL) and students for whom English is a second language.

The increase in research also may be fueled by passage of the Individuals with Disabilities Education Act (1997). Following are two quotes from this legislation, highlighting the provisions on inclusion of students with disabilities

Part B—Assistance for Education of All Children with Disabilities, Section 612 State Eligibility Subsection (a) (16) & (17)

(17) PARTICIPATION IN ASSESSMENTS
(A) IN GENERAL—Children with disabilities are included in general State and district-wide assessment programs, with appropriate accommodations, where necessary. As appropriate, the State or local educational agency (i) develops guidelines for the participation of children with disabilities in alternate assessments for those children who cannot participate in State and district-wide assessment programs; and (ii) develops and, beginning not later than July 1, 2000, conducts those alternate assessments.

Section 614. Evaluations, Eligibility Determinations, Individualized Education Programs and Educational Placements, Subsection (d)(1)(A)(v)
[IEP includes . . .] (v) (I) a statement of any individual modifications in the administration of State or district-wide assessments of student achievement that are needed in order for the child to participate in such assessment; and (II) if the IEP Team determines that the child will not participate in a particular State or district-wide assessment of student achievement (or part of such an assessment), a statement of (aa) why that assessment is not appropriate for the child; and (bb) how the child will be assessed.

This proliferation of activity has helped us clarify the variables being studied, the populations being tested, and the decisions being made. The purpose of this chapter is not only to review this research but also to draw implications for practice on accommodations and to identify the issues in conducting research on and developing policies and practices for implementation of accommodations with specialized populations. These issues are critical in addressing the question, How will assessments accommodate students with disabilities? Following an introduction that clarifies the term *accommodation*, three sections are presented. The first section addresses the obvious first line of reasoning to consider, the empirical basis for accommodations. Although research provides a good start, it also is clear that more questions than answers exist and practice needs to be considered. Therefore, the second section focuses on the manner in which decisions are made, either in terms of policy or in terms of actual implementation. In this section, the focus expands to consider a broader range of issues surrounding state standards and assessment practices, particularly as they serve as an impetus or context for accommodations. Finally, in section three, accommodations are considered within a comprehensive assessment system using an integration of assessment technologies to align performance assessments to standards.

Introduction: What Is an Accommodation?

The term *accommodations* generally has referred to changes in the way tests are administered or taken that do not alter the construct being measured (Tindal, 1998a). This definition, in one form or another, has led to further caveats. For example, as an educative concept, the following attributes may be considered as (a) reflecting controlled changes in testing, (b) useful with specialized populations, and (c) leading to similar meaning of performance or inferences to be made from the performance. Changes can be made in testing procedure or formats to provide students with disabilities and those who are English Language Learners (ELL) or of Limited English Proficiency (LEP) an equal opportunity to participate in a test situation and demonstrate their knowledge and abilities. This view immediately leads to an analysis of construct validity as a critical attribute of the concept (c, above). Usually, the term *accommodation* is contrasted with *modification*, in which the changes being made are radical and result in a different construct being measured and/or different decisions being made. With a modification, the changes generally are made to provide a student an opportunity to participate meaningfully and productively in a learning experience. However, performance on a modified assessment cannot be compared to performance on a standard assessment.

Accommodations also can be viewed from a broader perspective in which five conditions need to exist for an "appropriate" definition of accommodations (Phillips, 1994):

1. The measures must be technically adequate (have established reliability and validity).
2. Students should be able to adapt to the standard testing situation if at all possible.
3. The skill being tested should be the same regardless of any changes made in the way the test is given or taken.
4. The meaning of scores should be the same regardless of any changes being made in the manner in which the test is given or taken.
5. The accommodation should not have the potential for benefit for students without disabilities.

Finally, a practical definition from the National Center on Educational Outcomes (NCEO) includes a list of accommodation types that are sorted by a taxonomy. For example, Table 6.1 shows four categories of accommodations: (1) *timing/scheduling*,

TABLE 6.1 Assessment Accommodations from the National Center on Educational Outcomes (NCEO)

Timing/Scheduling	*Setting*
• Flexible schedule • Allow frequent breaks during testing • Extend the time allotted to complete the test • Administer the test in several sessions, specify duration • Time of day • Administer test over several days; specify duration • Provide special acoustics	• Administer the test individually in a separate location • Administer the test to a small group in a separate location • Provide special lighting • Provide adaptive or special furniture • Administer test in locations with minimal distractions • In a small group, study carrel, individually

Presentation	*Response*
• Braille edition or large-type edition • Prompts available on tape • Increase spacing between items or reduce items/page or line • Increase size of answer bubbles • Reading passages with one complete sentence/line • Multichoice, with answers following questions down bubbles to right • Omit questions that cannot be revised, prorate credit • Teacher helps student understand prompt • Student can ask for clarification • Computer reads paper to student • Highlight key words or phrases in directions **Test Directions** • Dictation to a proctor/scribe • Signing directions to students • Read directions to student • Reread directions for each page of questions • Simplify language in directions • Highlight verbs in instructions by underlining • Clarify directions • Provide cues (e.g., arrows and stop signs) on answer form • Provide additional examples	**Test Format** • Increase spacing • Wider lines and/or wider margins • Graph paper • Paper in alternative format (word processed, Braille, etc.) • Allow student to mark responses in booklet instead of answer sheet **Responses–Assistive Devices/Supports** • Word processor • Student tapes response for later verbatim transcription • Typewriter • Communication device • Alternative response such as oral, sign, typed, pointing • Brailler • Large diameter, special grip pencil • Copy assistance between drafts • Slantboard or wedge • Tape recorder • Calculator, arithmetic tables, abacus • Spelling dictionary or spell check

Presentations—Assistive Devices/Supports	*Presentations (continued)*
• Visual magnification devices • Templates to reduce visible print • Auditory amplification device, hearing aid or noise buffers • Audiotaped administration of sections • Secure papers to work area with tape/magnets • Questions read aloud to student • Masks or markers to maintain place	• Dark, heavy, or raised lines or pencil grips • Assistive devices (please specify) • Amanuensis (scribe) • Questions signed to pupil

(2) *setting*, (3) *presentation*, and (4) *response* (Thurlow, Ysseldyke, & Silverstein, 1993). *Timing and scheduling changes* address how many sessions are used to complete an assessment or the length of the sessions. *Setting changes* focus on where the assessment is given. *Presentation changes* may be in the assessment directions and/or the use of assistive devices: (a) Braille, magnifying equipment, or large print; (b) signing directions; (c) interpreting directions; and finally, (d) orally reading the directions. *Response changes* use different assessment formats or assistive devices; for example, changed spacing in the assessment materials, use of graph paper, wider lines, or wider margins; permitting an oral response; use of an alternative format (word or line processed, Braille, etc.); or permitting responses marked in a booklet instead of in bubbles on an answer sheet. Of course, these changes cannot be interpreted in a vacuum but require an analysis of the assessment being administered and the decision being made before any of these changes can be considered an accommodation.

Review of Research on Accommodations

The earliest critical mass of research appeared with NCEO and has since continued with a methodological research review by Tindal and Fuchs (1999), a meta-analysis by Chiu and Pearson (1999), and an American Educational Research Association (AERA) Special Interest Group (SIG) Yearbook 2000 (Abedi, Kim-Boscardin, & Larson, 2000).

1. Thurlow, Ysseldyke, and Silverstein (1993), the first publication, presented a summary of available empirical work on the effects of accommodations in testing students with disabilities. They reported on six research efforts, the broadest of which was conducted by American College Testing (ACT) Program and by Educational Testing Service (ETS). The latter, more significant research examined the Scholastic Aptitude Test (SAT) and Graduate Record Examination (GRE) for college admissions. This line of research led to the identification of two issues: score comparability and task comparability.
2. A second publication (Thurlow, Hurley, Spicuzza, & Erickson, 1996) provided an updated bibliography of the literature on testing accommodations and located empirical studies that examined issues of technical adequacy.
3. A companion to the 1996 bibliography of research (Thurlow, Hurley, Spicuzza, & Swaraf, 1996) provided a synthesis of major large-scale assessment issues: type test accommodations for students with disabilities (timing, format, and curriculum), legal considerations, perceptions, and conceptual concerns.

In addition to these NCEO research syntheses, a bibliography compiled by Chiu and Pearson (1999) identified all completed dissertations on test accommodations. They found 30 studies that had been completed since the original 1976 authorization of PL 94-142, the predecessor to IDEA and IDEA '97, using the following key words: *accommodations, assessments, Braille, disabilities, extra time, formats, learning disabilities, presentation,*

presentation formats, second language, test modifications, testing, timed, and *untimed.* The effects of accommodations were generally quite weak with a

> small positive effect on "target population" students . . . using general education students as a comparison group. The overall weighted mean accommodation effect size for all target population students was .16, with a standard error of 0.02 (Q = 470.97, df = 46, p < 0.01). For general education students, the overall weighted mean effect was .06, with a standard error of 0.02 (Q = 392.83, df = 30, p < 0.01). . . . Despite the positive accommodation effects, the significant Q test for homogeneity of variance revealed that the variations among the accommodation effects were large, implying that using the mean effect alone would be misleading because it would fail to portray the diversity of accommodation effects (p. 15).

Instead of a quantitative review, Tindal and Fuchs (1999) completed a methodological review of 106 published studies on accommodations. Studies were included if they had bearing on large-scale tests/measures of achievement (and not classroom criterion measures focused on instruction) whether or not it was group or individually administered. The research was sampled broadly to include both descriptive and experimental studies and students from both general and special education. Attention was given to three major issues: background and foundational research, analysis of literature by subjects and test, and analysis of research quality and summary. This research also was summarized in appendix tables with information about the authors (study number) and date of publication, description of the accommodation, subjects included in the study, test given as the dependent variable, and the findings reported from the research. The remainder of this section draws primarily from the last three reviews and is organized with three general conclusions.

In the Tindal and Fuchs (1999) review, the research studies varied considerably in terms of the subject populations being studied, the dependent measures being affected, and the (experimental) designs used to counter threats to validity. The most frequently studied accommodation was time and scheduling, with 25 separate investigations. Use of computer-based presentation also was investigated as an accommodation quite frequently, with 15 studies, and another 10 studies on the effects of using word processors. In contrast, only 1 study appeared on the effects of auditory accommodations. Few of the studies, however, had been replicated. Rather, many differences were apparent in the accommodation type and practice, the populations studied, the tests used (both accommodated and used to measure the effects of the accommodation), the quality of the research, the construct validity of the outcomes, and the consequences accrued by implementation of research in practice. The final recommendation from this report was a request that

> the process for creating policy becomes more anchored to an experimental rather than descriptive or comparative approach. In setting a research agenda, however, many more changes were being recommended in practice than the data supported. As a consequence, they recommended that researchers and practitioners collaborate more effectively and conduct broader research on various test changes. This research however

needs to be framed appropriately and executed carefully, on more diverse student populations, different tests, and with different decisions (Tindal & Fuchs, 1999, p. 97).

After nearly a decade, then, the research has begun to clarify critical issues in the way that accommodations are studied. In summarizing a program of research conducted through the University of Oregon, for example, Tindal, Helwig, and Hollenbeck (1999) described accommodations in mathematics as reflecting a growing sophistication in the way that accommodations are viewed. Initially, the focus was on finding a differential effect (à la Phillips, 1994) using a group design. Basically, an experimental group (of both general and special education students) received an accommodation and a control group (again comprising two groups of students) received a standard administration. Outcomes supporting an accommodation would reflect a significant difference between special and general education on the standard administration and no such difference on the accommodated version. In essence, the accommodation wiped out differences in access between the two groups.

Tindal et al. (1998) report an example of this kind of research. In this study, when students with IEPs in math had the math test read to them, they were not significantly different in their math multiple-choice test (MCT) performance than low-ranked general education students. In contrast, when students with IEPs in math read the math MCT themselves (as in a standard administration), their scores were significantly lower than low-ranked general education students. This differential effect justifies the use of this accommodation (see Westin, 1999, for similar findings) because a (reading) disability no longer impedes performance.

The research was refined in a subsequent study reported by Helwig et al. (1999). They found no overall differential effect; with a careful follow-up analysis, however, they found an effect for students who were low in math and reading when responding to certain types of problems. In particular, an effect was found for problems that had many words and more verbs. From this study, it appears that accommodations need to interactively reference specific populations and particular problem types.

Another example of this refinement of research on accommodations was reported in a recent study from Hollenbeck et al. (in press). They reported an effect with math problems in which student self-paced reading benefited students with IEPs in math more than teacher-paced reading. In this study, two groups of students received a read-aloud accommodation using a crossed design (with students in both special and general education serving as their own comparison and rotating through both a computer self-paced and a video, teacher-paced treatment). With this study, it became apparent that many accommodations have represented confounded treatments and often include multiple components (for example, reading aloud and pacing), the effects of which are ascertained separately.

In summary, the research on accommodations is becoming better defined by articulating critical variables. Clearly, populations need to be specifically described as well. Rather than referencing the disability, however, it may be important to reference the skill proficiencies. Furthermore, the tests that are being accommodated also need to be more explicitly described, given that total performance is really a composite obtained only from summing across many different items. Accommodations may work with some but not other items. And as more research accumulates, differential item functioning may need to be included as part of the analysis (see Koretz, 1997). Finally, research needs to investigate all of the components of an accommodation. In using the database from the Abedi, Kim-Boscardin, and Larson publication (2000) and Web page (http://aerasig.cse.ucla.edu), it is possible to isolate these variables more efficiently and interactively.

Policies and Alignment of Standards, Measurement Systems, and Outcomes

Unfortunately, many states simply list the allowed and nonallowed accommodations as an exhaustive domain with little reasoning behind their inclusion or exclusion. The listings neither cite the research nor describe the relationship between the accommodation and the test. Much of this work has been organized and summarized by NCEO in its descriptions of large-scale assessments since the early 1990s. Using policy document reviews and survey–interview research, the results have indicated the following (Thurlow, Scott, & Ysseldyke, 1995):

- States differ remarkably in the kinds of tests being used as part of their large-scale assessment programs. Different kinds of testing and measurement formats are used within large-scale assessment programs, ranging from published, norm-referenced tests using multiple-choice formats to performance assessments using portfolios and work samples that are scored with rubrics and scoring guides.
- Similar terms often have very different meaning or different terms have similar meaning. Great confusion exists in the meaning of changes made in the ways that tests are given or taken. For example, some states consider the following terms to have the same meaning while other states distinguish among them: *accommodations*, *modifications*, *alternate assessments*, and *alternative assessments*.
- Participation of students with disabilities varies considerably across districts and states, rarely coming close to 100%. Furthermore, the formulas used to gauge participation rates differ. The percent can be based on the number of students in general education, the number of students in special education at the time the December 1 child count is taken, the number of special education students in the schools at the time tests are given, or the number of students taking any or all of the state tests.
- Very few state policies provide explicit procedures and strategies for including students and providing appropriate accommodations, modified tests, or alternate assessments, when deemed necessary. Generally, the Individualized Educational Program (IEP) team is assigned responsibility for ascertaining whether or not an accommodation is needed, with little guidance provided about the criteria for making such a decision.

To illustrate how assessments will accommodate students with disabilities, therefore, two state examples are described in this section. Both examples rely on assessment systems that are well designed and include diverse standards in the basic skills, an array of different measurement systems, and a range of accommodations for specialized populations. Yet, they also represent typical problems in most states, most notably the lack of linkage between the standards, the measurement systems, and the accommodations or alternate assessments for students not fitting into the standard assessment.

Washington Large-Scale Assessment System (assessment.ospi.wednet.edu/)

According to the Washington Office of the Superintendent of Public Instruction (SPI) Web site, the Educational Academic Learning Requirements (EALRs) consist of outcomes in eight content areas. In the language arts areas, for example, the following standards are specified.

Reading.   The student understands and uses different skills and strategies to read. The student understands the meaning of what is read. The student reads different materials for a variety of purposes. The student sets goals and evaluates progress to improve reading.

Writing.   The student writes clearly and effectively. The student writes in a variety of forms for different audiences and purposes. The student understands and uses the steps of the writing process. The student analyzes and evaluates the effectiveness of written work.

Communication.   The student uses listening and observation skills to gain understanding. The student communicates ideas clearly and effectively. The student uses communication strategies and skills to work effectively with others. The student analyzes and evaluates the effectiveness of formal and informal communication.

As an example of how these standards (and others) are translated into assessment systems, the first standard in reading is more concisely specified as

1. using word recognition and word meaning skills to read and comprehend text such as phonics, context clues, picture clues, and word origins; roots, prefixes, and suffixes of words,
2. building vocabulary through reading,
3. reading fluently, adjusting reading for purpose and material,
4. understanding elements of literature—fiction such as story elements, use of humor, exaggeration, and figures of speech, and
5. using features of non-fiction text and computer software such as titles, headings, pictures, maps, and charts to find and understand specific information.

These skill areas are then broken into levels of performance for ascertaining mastery or passing. For example, the first standard includes (among other benchmarks)

- Benchmark 1—Use meaning, context, and pictures to comprehend story.
- Benchmarks 2 & 3—Integrate appropriate reading strategies to adapt reading to different types of text.

Measurement Format.   The Web site describes the assessment system as having "four major components: state-level assessments, classroom-based assessments, professional staff development, and school and system context indicators." State assessments include multiple-choice tests and performance assessments (both brief and extended tasks) with example passages and questions provided exemplifying the standard that needs to be passed. Eventually, a Certificate of Mastery is awarded students who pass the most advanced level. Beginning in 2006, seniors are required to have this certificate to graduate.

Accommodations.   In the state of Washington, the purpose of accommodations is to provide equity, not an advantage, and are either specified for all students or specifically for special populations if the IEP or 504 plan specify their use. It is recommended that all accommodations be used in the classroom prior to their introduction in the test.

For all students, the following accommodations are allowed in scheduling and timing, as noted in their policy documents.

- Administration of the assessment may be spread over the three-week testing window.
- Students may be provided more testing time, frequent breaks, and adjusted materials to fit their attention span.
- Students are allowed to continue working on each subtest as long as they are productively engaged. Time for individual students may vary considerably on a performance assessment.
- The assessment may be administered at a time of day most beneficial to the student(s).

For *students with an IEP or Section 504 plan* that documents a disability affecting reading or written communication, the following accommodations are allowed.

- Answer orally, point, or sign an answer. A scribe can record a student's response verbatim (e.g., from written dictation or audiotape) without interpretation, translation, or corrections.
- Use appropriate physical supports or assists (e.g., easel, magnifier, arm or stabilizer guide, text–talk converter, communication device to indicate responses, noise buffers, FM or other sound amplification device to assist in hearing directions, slantboard, or wedge).
- Use a reader to read math assessment items verbatim in English.
- Use a computer or word processor for recording responses (with no spell check allowed) when a computer is indicated for written communication.
- Isolate portions of the assessment page to focus student's attention (mask).
- Use math manipulative (except calculators) as indicated. Use calculators only as specifically permitted in test directions.

Summary.   The assessment system in the state of Washington contains broad standards with a complex mix of both selection and production tasks and a list of accommodations that appear quite appropriate. At the same time, the lists of accommodations do not make clear how the accommodations have bearing on the tasks and are not inclusive of other accommodations that could be used. Little rationale is given for the use of accommodations, and their relationship to either the standard or the measurement format is left implicit.

Colorado Reading and Writing (www.pde.psu.edu/pssa/esstand.html)

The language arts standards in Colorado are quite similar to those in Washington state in the identification of basic skills:

1. Students read and understand a variety of materials.
2. Students write and speak for a variety of purposes and audiences.
3. Students write and speak using conventional grammar, usage, sentence structure, punctuation, capitalization, and spelling.
4. Students apply thinking skills to their reading, writing, speaking, listening, and viewing.
5. Students read to locate, select, and make use of relevant information from a variety of media, reference, and technological sources.
6. Students read and recognize literature as a record of human experience.

These standards are then further articulated into more specific behaviors. For example, the first one (reading and understanding a variety of materials) is expanded to describe using comprehension skills (e.g., previewing, predicting, inferring, comparing, etc.), connecting what students already know with what they are reading, adjusting reading strategies for different purposes, using word recognition skills, and increasing vocabulary through reading. For each standard a rationale is provided for the knowledge and skill set.

Each standard is then further operationalized with grade-level expectations. For example, for the first standard (reading and understanding a variety of materials) when students leave fifth grade, they are expected to summarize long passages, draw inferences from context, compare and contrast information, monitor themselves in their use of various strategies, identify sequential order (in expository text), use a variety of recognition skills to understand unfamiliar text, use a dictionary, paraphrase key ideas, and confirm meaning. This list is longer than that posited for fourth graders and does not include any notion of skills reserved for later grades (i.e., recognition and use of text structure in sixth grade). The list is both very reasonable and yet uses verbs that are very open in their interpretation for measurement or demonstration.

Measurement Formats.   The Web site includes a sample passage with a multiple-choice question that serves as an exemplar of a selected-response question assessing the first benchmark in Standard 1. This benchmark focuses on "the use of comprehension skills such as previewing, predicting, inferring, comparing and contrasting, re-reading and self-monitoring, summarizing, identifying the author's purpose, determining the main idea, and applying knowledge of foreshadowing, metaphor, simile, symbolism, and other figures of speech." In addition, an open-ended question is included, providing an example of a short constructed-response question that assesses the first benchmark in Standard 4. This benchmark assesses whether the student can "make predictions, analyze, draw conclusions, and discriminate between fact and opinion in writing, reading, speaking, listening, and viewing. Both short and extended constructed-response questions are scored with a specific scoring rubric (or scoring method) developed for each question."

Accommodations.   The definition of an accommodation for the state test takes note of issues about allowable access and unfair advantage. Five criteria are listed in explicating the need and use of accommodations, including prior use, content specificity, possible consequences, need for multiple accommodations, and need based on both primary language and disability. Accommodations are then listed that must be documented (nine in all) and that do not need to be documented (eight in all). These allowable accommodations are listed in table format. One of them involves extended time that is more than 10 minutes in a session. "Any student who may need more than one hour to complete a test session should be identified ahead of time and, preferably, should be administered the assessment in separate settings. This accommodation should be documented *only* if the student actually takes more than 10 extra minutes to complete the session. Additionally, students can take the test in more, but shorter sessions. When the total testing time exceeds 60 minutes, documentation is required."

Summary.   Again, as in Washington state, the standards are incontrovertible, the measurement system is a complex mix of selection and production responses, and the list of accommodations appears thoughtful but is unrelated to the standards or the measurement formats. In addition, no principles are stated for explicating the rationale behind those accommodations that are included or those excluded. Although the accommodations are very reasonable and some even obvious (e.g. use of Braille, signing, and rereading the directions), others are not so clear in their relationship to the standard or the measurement system used to ascertain proficiency on the standard. Furthermore, the outcomes from the application of benchmarks, which leads to the decision of passing or not passing, are not directly embedded in the assessment system.

Summary of Standards, Measurement Systems, and Decision Making on Accommodations

The standards of these two states in particular, and most states in general, are likely reasonable. In fact, when schooling is viewed as a compact with the public, it is unlikely that anyone would dispute the standards. A problem appears to arise, however, from the operationalization of the standards in the form of specific performances on tests and measures and the controlled use of specific accommodations (or their disallowance). Typically, the standards are quite neutral with respect to these methodological issues of measurement, as the verbs used could be considered to reflect both content and performance standards. In the end, states have used both traditional multiple-choice tests as well as performance tasks to determine whether students are performing at satisfactory levels of proficiency. Nevertheless, accommodations are listed that appear to provide comparability in the performances of students yet often do not distinguish clearly between different measurement formats. Furthermore, a problem arises in the disjunction among the standards, the measurement formats, and accommodations that are allowed or disallowed.

Such variation in testing policies and programs, reflecting different standards and assessment systems, is complicated by a further problem: the variation in teacher knowledge and skill. In a recent survey of teachers, Hollenbeck, Tindal, and Almond (1998) reported that the majority of teachers (regardless of whether they worked in general or special education) lacked knowledge about specific accommodations. If their survey of allowable accommodations were viewed as a test, only about 50% of the items were answered correctly. Furthermore, teachers' decisions were not differentiated according to level of student disability. Such a finding may not be surprising given the level of skill and knowledge about testing and measurement in the profession generally. Nevertheless, teachers are assigned the responsibility of ascertaining whether an accommodation is needed, either directly or through participation in an IEP team.

Because appropriate testing decisions on high-stakes tests must be made for students with disabilities and because teachers are expected to function as "measurement competent educators" who can "evaluate student performance in a fair and meaningful way" (Siskind, 1993a, p. 233), all teachers must be knowledgeable about assessment and assessment-related concepts. However, significant deficits in teachers' knowledge concerning high-stakes testing are evident. Most of teachers' knowledge about testing and measurement comes from "trial-and-error learning in the classroom" (Wise, Lukin, & Roos, 1991, p. 39). Furthermore, knowledge deficits are not specific to general education teachers. Shepard's (1983) research documents that neither school psychologists nor teachers of the learning disabled were likely to be competent in their knowledge and application of assessment. Corroborating Shepard's conclusions, Siskind (1993b) reports that special educators are not well informed about assessment and assessment procedures either.

Returning to the central question, then, how will assessment accommodate students with disabilities? The answer lies in the articulation of the relationships among the standards, measurement formats, and decision making for accommodations. In part this articulation will require practical procedures as well as effective professional development and dissemination. Any general policy eventually translates into a practical decision-making process, requiring considerable professional development. Standards need to be operationalized so that teachers can see the connections between the generally vague standards and the specific indicators and outcomes. Furthermore, they need to know how policy is implemented in practice so that the constructs being measured can be described and accommodation decisions clearly explicated, including both a list of allowable accommodations as well as the principles behind such allowances. The impetus for this practical suggestion comes from the kind of data reported next.

In March of 1998, a survey on large-scale testing was distributed to every teacher in the state of Oregon (Tindal & Glasgow, 1999). The project, sponsored by the state educational union, focused on four issues: professional development needs (what do you need to be successful?), curriculum and instruction (what has happened in the classroom?), communication (how is test information used?), and interpretations and decision making (what do the test results mean?). The survey had statements to which the teacher could react on a scale from 1 (strongly disagree) to 5 (strongly agree). The areas receiving the greatest attention from teachers dealt with developing alternative learning options for students not meeting state standards. In addition, uniform agreement was demonstrated in the *strong interest* in more professional development in aligning the curriculum to the skills and knowledge on the test, teaching essential skills for student success on open-ended performance tasks, creating allowable test changes for special needs students, and developing appropriate work samples. Teachers generally thought they *were interested in some* professional development in judging traits on open-ended performance tasks, scoring work samples, and interpreting students' state test performance to parents. For example, on two items relevant to accommodations, teachers responded to the statement "I would like to participate in training related to (a) development of alternative learning options [see Table 6.2] and (b) creating allowable test changes" [see Table 6.3]. For both issues, few teachers were in the moderate to strong agreement categories.

Unfortunately, the profession is being placed in the untenable position of needing to make decisions to support students in the absence of clear guidelines or consistent procedures. When students fail a high-stakes test, therefore, a number of questions arise. How should the student be tested to ascertain attainment of the standard? How limiting is the measurement format for the student? What accommodations can and should be used in overcoming these measurement limitations? What is the "cause" of failure? How could the student be assessed in a more fair and equitable manner? Who should make such decisions? What information should be used and valued when making these decisions?

The remainder of the chapter addresses these questions with a proposal in which the technology of assessment is complemented by classroom measurement and observation systems. In this proposal, teachers develop and interpret student performance on tasks that can be developed and interpreted by them, without requiring the psychometric features of most large-scale assessment programs. Yet, these classroom systems are related to and embedded in the large-scale assessment programs. In this manner, then, the standards are made accessible through a multiple range of formats, ensuring that students have an adequate opportunity to learn and teachers have an appropriate database with which to make informed decisions.

TABLE 6.2 Frequency Count of Teachers Expressing Interest in Training on Developing Alternative Learning Options for Students Who Do Not Meet State Standards

		Count	*Percent*
Strongly Disagree =	1	697	10
	2	765	11
	3	1380	19
	4	1899	26
Strongly Agree =	5	2469	34
Does Not Apply		266	
Do Not Know		71	

TABLE 6.3   Frequency Count of Teachers Expressing Interest in Training on Creating Allowable Test Changes for Special Needs Students

		Count	Percent
Strongly Disagree =	1	1013	14
	2	1140	16
	3	1704	24
	4	1464	21
Strongly Agree =	5	1760	25
Does Not Apply		342	
Do Not Know		97	

From Issues to Options: Development of a Comprehensive* System

In this final section, I address the development of a comprehensive assessment system that interleaves curriculum-based measurement (CBM) into state testing programs. Although it is tempting to think that the problem is exacerbated by adding yet another measurement format into statewide assessment systems, given multiple measures both within and across any one large-scale assessment program, I believe this solution is appropriate for two reasons. First, CBM provides teachers with an assessment technology that is "doable" in an efficient manner and to which they have access. Second, the power of CBM is in the value added to an extant measurement system and its predictive value in helping both identify and forecast problems as well as track progress. Therefore, the answer to the question, How should we accommodate students with disabilities?, needs to address the following issues:

- Development of a technically adequate measurement system that samples important behavior in the classroom and allows teachers to ascertain specific skills, some of which may well be access skills for performance on large-scale assessments, and ensuring that the measurement system is predictive of performance on large-scale tests.
- Making decisions about using accommodations or modified and alternate assessments with curriculum-based measures and monitoring programs for types of error (false positives, in which teachers incorrectly recommend the use of an accommodation, and false negatives, in which teachers fail to recommend an appropriate accommodation).
- Systematically evaluating the use of accommodations, perhaps eventually fading out specific classroom supports as student performance indicates.

*Dr. Patricia Almond should be credited with the use of the term *comprehensive* as part of an effort to unify a state's assessment program, allowing teachers to make choices about the specific technologies used to document student performance on state standards.

Technically Adequate Measurement

The first requirement for any decision to accommodate students is that it be based on technically adequate data. Of course, reliability, defined as consistency, is needed. Yet, as Linn (1994) has noted in summarizing the research on performance assessments, "Most results suggest that the error of measurement due to tasks is a bigger stumbling block than errors due to raters" (p. 10). This statement is based on the following research: Shavelson, Baxter, and Gao (1993); Shavelson, Baxter, and Pine (1992); Dunbar, Koretz, and Hoover (1991); Mehrens (1992); Miller and Legg (1993). Gentile (1992) found that nearly half of the students sampled performed differently on NAEP writing assessments than on school performance tasks, with two-thirds doing better on NAEP. Finally, two other studies report on the influence of tasks and raters in performance assessments and on improving reliability more substantially by adding more tasks (and testing time) rather than by adding more raters: Baxter et al. (1992) (in this study, performance assessments were moderately correlated with multiple-choice tests and with each other) and Saner et al. (1994). Brennan and Johnson (1995) reported, "the realism of performance assessments comes at the cost of limitations in generalizability of the results" (p. 12). In the end, work samples and collections of evidence that are incorporated into portfolios may be excellent examples of performance assessments that are instructionally useful and valid for making decisions about what and how to teach. Their use in making high-stakes decisions, however, is problematic in that they lack sufficient reliability (comparability across tasks).

In contrast to ill-structured performance assessments, CBM provides a systematic way to document student performance using brief production tasks. A general and comprehensive definition of CBM would be as follows: brief tasks (from one to five minutes) in which students actively read, write, spell, and compute, using standardized administration and scoring procedures that employ sensitive metrics capable of showing change over time and evaluating instructional effects. Examples of CBM include oral reading fluency (see Tindal & Marston, 1996), computation and application probes in mathematics (see Fuchs et al., in press, for mathematics measures used with accommodation decision making by teachers), and written-expression story starters (Tindal & Parker, 1991). The research literature supporting CBM typically addresses criterion validity using other accepted measures and monitoring student performance to develop effective instructional programs (Tindal, 1998b).

In using CBM as part of a comprehensive assessment program that accommodates students with disabilities, two lines of research and practice can be identified. First, CBM in the basic skill areas is used in a predictive manner for understanding how students can, with accommodations, best participate in large-scale testing programs. Second, CBM can serve as an alternate assessment for those students who would benefit little by participating in the standard testing program, even with accommodations. The remainder of this chapter provides examples of both uses of CBM, as a comprehensive solution that allows large-scale assessments to accommodate students with disabilities.

In a recent field-based project, CBM was implemented twice (mathematics) and thrice (reading) during the year in reading and mathematics with all students in grades 2 and 3 (Tindal & Crawford, 1999). In the spring, the Oregon State Assessment (OSA), a multiple-choice test, was administered to all third graders as part of the statewide testing program. At the end of the school year, we compiled all the test data into a single file and completed several analyses. First, we conducted simple correlations between the CBM reading and math and the OSA reading and math scores for approximately 100 students. Then, we ran regression analyses to predict achievement on the OSA using the CBM scores as predictors. The relationship among the CBM oral reading fluency measures was extremely high and between any of them and the state (OSA) multiple-choice test scores reasonably high, providing evidence that the same construct (reading) was being assessed. In math, the results were similar though less strong when the two math lab performances were compared to each other and to the state test (see Table 6.4).

When we ran the regression analyses, we found the CBM oral reading fluency measure to be a strong predictor of performance in reading as well as in math, with a significant percentage of the variance accounted for. All three oral reading fluency measures (fall, winter, and spring) accounted for most of the variance on the state multiple-choice test (46% in the fall, 48% in the winter, and 47% in the spring). Given that only a single one-minute sample of reading was being used to predict performance on a long and time-consuming test (as much as six months into the future), this amount of accountable variance is remarkable. In mathematics, the same regression analysis also resulted in significant predictive capacity for the CBM, though the findings were less strong. In the fall lab, only 16% of the variance could be accounted for, although the spring results were more encouraging, with 43% of the variance accounted for with the use of the math lab. The most surprising finding in math, however, was the significant amount of variance accounted for by reading proficiency (oral reading fluency): Fully 38% of the math multiple-choice test performance could be accounted for by the students' reading proficiency. Clearly, this finding reflects the need to consider reading as an accommodation in math multiple-choice testing, if the purpose is to understand the student's mathematics proficiencies (see the earlier discussion of the effects of using this accommodation).

In summary, it appears that CBM reading and math measures are technically adequate in terms of alternate-form reliability and criterion validity. These results actually fit into a much larger research program that has been conducted for the past 20 years (beginning with the early work of Deno; see the special issue of *Exceptional Children*, 1985,

TABLE 6.4   Correlations between Curriculum-Based Measures and the Oregon Statewide Assessment (OSA)

Reading	*OSA*	*Fall—Fluency*	*Winter—Fluency*
OSA			
Fall—Fluency	.677		
Winter—Fluency	.711	.905	
Spring—Fluency	.697	.928	.917
Math	*OSA*	*Fall Lab*	
OSA			
Fall Lab	.404		
Winter Lab	.555	.637	

vol. 53). In most of this work, other forms of reliability have been investigated (alternate form, test, retest, inter and intra judge) as well as both types of criterion validity: concurrent and predictive. See Marston (1989) and Tindal and Marston (1990) for a description of the investigations focused on technical adequacy.

Making and Evaluating Decisions to Accommodate Students

All statewide tests require some kind of basic access skills of reading, writing, and computing. Multiple-choice tests in math require calculating, computing, and reading skills. Open-ended math tests and math work samples (used in portfolios) require problem solving, calculation, and writing skills. Writing tests and portfolio work samples both require writing as well as reading. Reading tests require reading primarily but any work samples also are likely to require writing as well. For each of the tests in each of these subject areas, a decision needs to be made whether a student should take the test in a standard-accommodated manner or whether a modification should be made and an alternate assessment administered.

For example, a student may need either more time or a scribe when taking an open-ended math test. This decision can be made on the basis of a five-minute sample of writing. Such an accommodation would be justified if the student were performing at the 10th percentile rank in the number of words written per minute when compared to a normative sample of comparable students. Such normative standards are relatively easy to establish with CBM and have been extensively described in the literature (see Tindal & Marston, 1990). In this case, a change in administration may be appropriate for a math performance task in which the student is expected to write an answer to an open-ended problem. The problem that the student is facing is sheer production fluency, and either (a) the amount of time needs to be extended or (b) a scribe needs to write the answer. However, a reading and math multiple-choice test may not require extended time or a scribe, though some other accommodation for these tests may be necessary for other reasons. In this example here, accommodation decisions need to be specific to a measure and not simply generic, as noted in the Colorado assessment system. Probably the best way to document student need is to use a formal screening measure to determine the student's performance on critical access skills. In the example here, with the student needing modifications for tasks requiring writing production, such a determination may have been made on the basis of low proficiencies in letter and word formation or in minimum fluency on a brief writing probe.

Another example of formally collecting CBM data to help render an accommodation decision is in the reading of math tests. Many students cannot read the math problems on the multiple-choice test, in which case performance is likely to be impeded. A screening measure would help determine just how fluent the student is in reading. A range of reading tasks could be assembled and administered, such as reading from grade-level passages, reading from off-grade passages, and reading controlled words (e.g., consonant–vowel–consonant words) or functional words (critical community words like *stop, walk, men, women, up,* and *down*). Depending on the degree of skill, a decision would then be made about recommending an accommodation. This documentation would be placed in the student's file to determine a recommendation and also would be used to help structure practice in the classroom (e.g., reading story problems to the student).

Both of these examples provide strategies for using CBM to help make decisions about an accommodation. In the spirit of IDEA '97, however, such a decision needs to be made by a team of professionals (including the parents, as well as general and special education teachers). It is likely that each of these individuals form conclusions from past experience with the student. To help ensure that their experience is explicitly known, therefore, it is best to supplement CBM data with other information when making decisions. Three such sources of data include analysis of process skills used in classroom (permanent) product performance, direct observations of classroom conditions, and anecdotal descriptions from secondary sources.

Analysis of Test Process Skills Required for Performing. For multiple-choice tests, students need to have skill in reading a problem with alternate selections listed below, selecting the one that best answers the question, and then marking a bubble on an accompanying sheet that corresponds to the same letter as the (appropriate) selection listed below the problem. For any open-ended or performance tasks, students need to write connected text. For young students and those with moderate disabilities, these tasks reflect quite a chain of behaviors. Teachers, therefore, need to establish the degree to which the tasks completed in classrooms reflect requisite skills necessary for participating in statewide testing. To do so, they may ask various questions designed to highlight similarities and differences in the skills required to perform in the classroom versus those needed to perform on a large-scale assessment.

- Does the student systematically orient pages, turn them, and manipulate books and bubble sheets? If students cannot manage the paperwork portion of the test, information cannot be collected on their skill or knowledge.
- How different are the tasks used in large-scale assessments from those typically used in the classroom, and how should these requisite skills be taught to students? Testing with a multiple-choice format is often not common in early elementary grades and therefore may need to be taught directly. The writing and editing process may need to be taught if students are unfamiliar with the writing process.
- What requisite skills are needed for completing work samples in the classroom, and how relevant are these skills for participating in a large-scale assessment? In many classroom assignments, students have access to a rich assortment of resources, lessening the need to perform from memory or without help. In the statewide testing situation, such resources are not available and students need to know how to function with minimum supports.
- Does the student read and understand text? When students are dysfluent readers, it is not possible for them to complete many items that require them to read. Can the student read fluently at or near grade level? All multiple-choice tests require reading, which may be fine for the reading test but actually may be irrelevant when other areas are being tested (i.e., math, content knowledge). Any accommodations based on extending time likely would be ineffective in helping the student complete the test. Reading is the problem, not time.

- What is the student's primary language? How long has the student been in English-speaking programs? All testing needs to be given either in the student's native language or through a side-by-side or bilingual translation. In what language are the classroom materials written?
- Can the student form letters and numbers and write connected text? All work samples and open-ended tasks require more than single-word or short responses. For this portion of the test, such a skill deficit could interfere with the analysis of what a student knows and can do. How much of the classroom environment relies on or helps students become proficient in such an access skill?
- Can the student use appropriate tools (pencils and erasers, pens, measuring devices, calculators, protractors, etc.)? When allowed, it is important for students to use as many tools as possible.

With work samples collected and annotated, and the conditions and process for completion noted, documentation would be assembled for making a recommendation to accommodate a test or develop a modified administration/measurement. Because such process analysis comes from the classroom, it provides a ready connection to the testing environment.

Observation of Classroom Conditions Required for Performing. To complete any statewide test, students need to work independently, with attention, for a sizable amount of time. The question is whether the conditions of the classroom are consistent with the conditions of the testing. Students need to be provided sufficient opportunity to participate in testlike conditions or their performance may not be generalizable from the classroom to the testing environment. Listed next are some exemplary questions that can be asked to determine whether changes should be made in the way the test is given or taken.

- In general, students need to participate in tasks (in both the classroom and on the test) that require them to sit quietly, listen to directions, work independently, read text, and select or write responses. Are the conditions for completing classroom tasks different from the testing conditions? Can the student work independently for 45 to 60 minutes? Most of the statewide tests take about this amount of time in one sitting to complete and being unaccustomed to performing for this amount of time is a clear problem. Many classrooms use project-based learning or cooperative groups, allowing students to come and go as they please, talk to their partners, and otherwise control the pace of work completion. In either case, most statewide testing is far different and requires students to be acclimated to independent work on tasks in one setting.
- How much prompting and support do students need to complete classroom tasks, and how similar are such prompts and supports to the accommodations and modifications that appear on the state list of those deemed acceptable? Many students complete classroom work dependent on teachers' pacing and support. In a statewide test, such support may modify the administration. For example, cues to students are considered a modified administration, even though most teachers probably tell students during instruction, "Watch the signs on the math

problems," and "Don't forget to carry on the double-digit math problems." This kind of prompting is undesirable in the actual testing situation unless the student's needs are such that it is deemed necessary and it therefore reflects a modified measurement.

- Can the student work within a whole-class setting? While most testing is group administered, considerable variation is allowed in the physical setting, as long as there is no differential advantage provided (e.g., posters on the wall reflecting inappropriate cues for the answers).
- Does the student follow directions with multiple steps arranged in a sequence? Many of the state tests have directions given only at the beginning of the test and then require the student to remember the steps while they complete several subsequent problems. This feature relates as much to memory and concentration as it does to content learning.
- What is the student's schedule? How much time is spent in instruction in various academic skills as well as in general or special education settings? When students take the statewide test, it may be important to be in a room in which they have traditionally been taught and tested with familiar examiners.

The answers to these questions help establish access to an environment in which the student can concentrate and remain on task. Any number of further questions could be asked, so at this point, the most important issue is simply the congruence between the teaching and testing settings. When large differences exist between them, poor performance may be explained partially by a lack of familiarity with the process, potentially invalidating the outcomes.

When using observations to help document student need, note should be taken of the conditions during which the observations are made and the stability or durability (duration or frequency) of the observations, both across settings and individuals. For example, teachers may want to qualify information by reference to observations being made during certain activity structures (e.g., teacher lectures, demonstrates, asks questions, etc. while the student is expected to listen, perform, or answer, respectively) over a few days of data collection (Parker, Hasbrouck, & Tindal, 1989). However, when the observations are made across settings or by different individuals, and they result in the same conclusions, support for student need is stronger.

Anecdotal Observations from Secondary Sources.   Probably the least trustworthy, but nevertheless important, source of information is that reported from secondary sources. This information must be considered but should be used with caution. The primary reasons for qualifying secondary information is that (a) often it is collected in ways that are unknown or ill defined, and (b) it includes implicit judgments that reflect a subjective orientation.

For example, a teacher may report in a transfer student's record that the student had a very difficult time being attentive in class and appeared unable to maintain attention for more than a few minutes without making any disruptive comments. This note, however, may reflect any number of different classroom settings and contingencies and may reflect the teacher's classroom management practices, as well as the teacher's expectations or tolerances, as much as it does the student's capacity.

Fading Out Accommodations Where Possible. The dilemma with accommodations is that they can both be needed as a permanent prosthetic or used temporally for a brief period of time. Many accommodations, particularly those used with sensory and physical impairments, are considered necessary for life. In contrast, for students with high-incidence disabilities, accommodations may be needed as part of an instructional support that can be faded out. Reading math tests, for example, has been shown to be an effective accommodation for elementary-age students (see Tindal et al., 1998; Westin, 1999). As part of an instructional program, such assisted reading also has been shown to be an effective intervention in teaching students to read (see Shany & Biemiller, 1995). Such a practice may eventually, however, need to be faded out so students may participate in more "authentic" tasks, as described in the Curriculum and Evaluation Standards for School Mathematics (National Council of Teachers of Mathematics, 1989).

Summary

In summary, the question How will assessments accommodate students with disabilities? can be answered with reference to the three areas reviewed in this chapter: research, policy, and practice. All three need to be incorporated into a comprehensive assessment program. Furthermore, all three are needed to substantially address the question. Assessments can accommodate students with disabilities by specific reference to the research. It simply is not possible to say that "research shows. . . ." Rather, specific studies need to be cited, with consideration given to the type of test investigated, the population of students receiving the accommodation, and the quality of the design. Even with such specificity, the answer needs to be qualified by noting that few studies have been replicated. Assessments also can accommodate students with disabilities by specific reference to the policy standards that employ specific measurement formats and decision-making practices. All three components need to be related, however. Furthermore, the profession needs to be knowledgeable and capable of making decisions within this policy context beyond simple reference to descriptive admonitions (listing allowed and disallowed accommodations) by providing comparative and quasiexperimental justifications. Finally, assessments can accommodate students with disabilities through the adoption of a comprehensive assessment system that provides a range of measurement tools that are correlated and that provides teachers information for decision making. To accommodate students with disabilities, these correlated indicators need to be predictive of performance on the large-scale assessment and provide early warning signs that students may be having difficulty. In this capacity, "opportunity to learn" standards can be invoked to provide linkages with both content and performance standards. These correlated indicators also can serve as technically adequate measurement systems in their own right, providing a more sensitive measure of performance and progress. With time and teaching, students can be brought from an alternate assessment to one that reflects an accommodation.

The research summarized in this chapter reflects work funded by the Office of Special Education Programs (OSEP)—Project VALIDATE (Validating Accommodations That Legitimize Individuals' with Disabilities Access to Testing in Education, CFDA #84.023F) and the Oregon Department of Education (ODE)—Development of Modified

Measures. The opinions and text reported in this chapter, however, do not reflect either of these governmental agencies.

r e f e r e n c e s

Abedi, J., Kim-Boscardin, C., & Larson, H. (2000). *Summaries of research on inclusion of students with disabilities and Limited English proficient students in large scale assessments: SIG Yearbook*. Los Angeles: UCLA–CSE/CRESST.

Baxter, G. P., Shavelson, R. J., Goldman, S. R., & Pine, J. (1992). Evaluation of procedure-based scoring for hands-on science assessments. *Journal of Educational Measurement, 29*(1), 1–18.

Brennan, R. L., & Johnson, E. G. (1995). Generalizability of performance assessments. *Educational Measurement: Issues and Practice, 14*(4), 9–12.

Chiu, C. W. T., & Pearson, P. D. (13–16 June, 1999). Synthesizing the effects of test accommodations for special education and limited English proficient students. Paper presented at the Large Scale Assessment Conference, Snowbird, Utah.

Dunbar, S. B., Koretz, D., & Hoover, H. D. (1991). Quality control in the development and use of performance assessments. *Applied Measurement in Education, 4*, 289–304.

Fuchs, L. S., Fuchs, D., Eaton, S., Hamlett, C., & Karns, K. (in press). Supplementing teacher judgments of test accommodations with objective data sources. *School Psychology Review*.

Gentile, C. A. (1992). *The writing students do in school: The 1990 NAEP portfolio study of fourth and eighth graders school-based writing*. Washington, D.C.: National Assessment of Educational Progress.

Helwig, R., Rozek-Tedesco, M., Heath, B., Tindal, G., & Almond, P. (1999). Reading as an access to mathematics problem solving on multiple choice tests for sixth grade students. *The Journal of Educational Research, 93*(2), 113–125.

Hollenbeck, K., Rozek-Tedesco, M., Tindal, G., & Glasgow, A. (in press). An exploratory study of student paced versus teacher paced accommodations for large scale math tests. *Journal of Special Education Technology*.

Hollenbeck, K., Tindal, G., & Almond, P. (1998). Teachers' knowledge of accommodations as a validity issue in high-stakes testing. *The Journal of Special Education, 32*(3), 175–183.

Individuals with Disabilities Education Act Amendments of 1997, P. L. 105–17, 105th Congress, 1st session.

Koretz, D. (1997). *The assessment of students with disabilities in Kentucky* (CSE Technical Report No. 431). Los Angeles, Calif.: Center for Research on Standards and Student Testing.

Linn, R. (1994). Performance assessment: Policy promises and technical measurement standards. *Educational Researcher, 23*(9), 4–14.

Marston, D. (1989). A curriculum-based measurement approach to assessing academic performance: What it is and why do it. In *Curriculum-based measurement: Assessing special children*, ed. M. Shinn, pp. 18–78. New York: Guilford Press.

Mazzeo, J., Carlson, J. E., Voelkl, K. E., & Lutkus, A. D. (2000). *Increasing the participation of special needs students in NAEP: A report on 1996 NAEP research activities*. Washington, D.C.: National Center for Education Statistics.

Mehrens, W. A. (1992). Using performance assessment for accountability purposes. *Educational Measurement: Issues and Practices, 11*(1), 3–9, 20.

Miller, M. D., & Legg, S. M. (1993). Alternative assessment in a high stakes environment. *Educational Measurement: Issues and Practice, 12*(2), 9–15.

National Council of Teachers of Mathematics. (1989). *Curriculum and Evaluation Standards for School Mathematics*. Reston, Va.: Author.

Olson, J. F., & Goldstein, A. A. (1996). Increasing the inclusion of students with disabilities and limited English proficient students in NAEP. *Focus on NAEP, 2*(1). Washington, D.C.: National Center for Education Statistics.

Parker, R., Hasbrouck, J., & Tindal, G. (1989). *Activity structures observation system*. (Resource Consultant Training Module No. 1). Eugene, Oreg.: University of Oregon.

Phillips, S. E. (1994). High-stakes testing accommodations: Validity versus disabled rights. *Applied Measurement in Education, 7*(2), 93–120.

Saner, H., Klein, S., Bell, R., & Comfort, K. B. (1994). The utility of multiple raters and tasks in science performance assessments. *Educational Assessment, 2*(3), 257–272.

Shany, M. T., & Biemiller, A. (1995). Assisted reading practice: Effects on performance for poor readers in grades 3 and 4. *Reading Research Quarterly, 39*(3), 382–295.

Shavelson, R. J., Baxter, G. P., & Gao, X. (1993). Sampling variability of performance assessments. *Journal of Educational Measurement, 30*, 215–232.

Shavelson, R. J., Baxter, G. P., & Pine, J. (1992). Performance assessment: Political rhetoric and measurement reality. *Educational Researcher, 21*(4), 22–27.

Shepard, L. (1983). The role of measurement in education policy: Lessons from the identification of learning disabilities. *Educational Measurement: Issues and Practice, 2*(3), 4–8.

Siskind, T. G. (1993a). Modifications in statewide criterion-referenced testing programs to accommodate pupils with disabilities. *Diagnostique, 18*(3), 233–249.

Siskind, T. G. (1993b). Teachers' knowledge about test modifications for students with disabilities. *Diagnostique, 18*(2), 145–157.

Thurlow, M., Hurley, C., Spicuzza, R., & Erickson, R. (1996). *Resources: Students with disabilities in national and statewide assessment* (Minnesota Report 7). Minneapolis, Minn.: National Center on Educational Outcomes.

Thurlow, M., Hurley, C., Spicuzza, R., Sawaf, H. (1996). *A review of the literature on testing accommodations for students with disabilties* (Minnesota Report 9). Minneapolis, Minn.: National Center on Educational Outcomes.

Thurlow, M., Scott, D., & Ysseldyke, J. (1995). *A compilation of states' guidelines for accommodations in assessments for students with disabilities* (Synthesis Report 18). Minneapolis, Minn.: National Center on Educational Outcomes.

Thurlow, M., Ysseldyke, J., & Silverstein, B. (1993). *Testing accommodations for students with disabilities: A review of the literature* (Synthesis Review 4). Minneapolis, Minn.: National Center on Educational Outcomes.

Tindal, G. (1998a). *Models for understanding task comparability in accommodated testing.* Washington, D.C.: Council of Chief State School Officers, Assessing Special Education Students—State Collaborative on Assessment State Standards.

Tindal, G. (1998b). Assessment in learning disabilities with a focus on curriculum-based measurement (pp. 35–66). In *Learning about learning disabilities*, eds. J. Torgeson, B. Wong. San Diego, Calif.: Academic Press.

Tindal, G., & Crawford, M. (1999). Curriculum-based measures as predictors in large-scale assessments. Unpublished data.

Tindal, G., & Fuchs, L. S. (1999). *A summary of research on test changes: An empirical basis for defining accommodations.* Lexington, Ky.: Mid-South Regional Resource Center.

Tindal, G., & Glasgow, A. (1999). Oregon Education Association: Teacher survey of statewide testing in Oregon. Unpublished report, University of Oregon.

Tindal, G., Heath, B., Hollenbeck, K., Almond, P., & Harniss, M. (1998). Accommodating students with disabilities on large-scale tests: An empirical study of student response and test administration demands. *Exceptional Children, 64*(4), 439–450.

Tindal, G., Helwig, R., & Hollenbeck, K. (1999). An update on test accommodations: Perspectives from practice to policy. *Journal of Special Education Leadership, 12*(2), 11–20.

Tindal, G., & Marston, D. (1990). *Classroom-based assessment: Evaluating instructional outcomes.* Columbus, Ohio: Charles Merrill.

———. (1996). Technical adequacy of alternative reading measures as performance assessments. *Exceptionality, 6*(4), 201–230.

Tindal, G., & Parker, R. (1991). Identifying measures for evaluating written expression. *Learning Disabilities: Research and Practice, 6*, 211–218.

Westin, T. (1999). *The validity of oral presentation in testing.* Montreal, Canada: The American Educational Research Association.

Wise, S. L., Lukin, L. E., & Roos, L. L. (1991). Teacher beliefs about training in testing and measurement. *Journal of Teacher Education, 42*(1), 37–42.

7 How Will English Language Learners Be Accommodated in State Assessments?

CHARLES W. STANSFIELD

Second Language Testing, Inc.

CHARLENE RIVERA

George Washington University

The Improving America's Schools Act of 1994 (IASA) requires states and districts to adopt standards-based education systems based on the expectation that *all* students, including English language learners (ELLs),[1] will reach high academic standards. IASA also requires states to implement assessment systems by the 2000–2001 school year that will allow all students the opportunity to demonstrate their skills and knowledge. Assessment is an essential element of standards-based systems because it provides measurement of the degree to which individuals, schools, and districts have reached the standards.

As IASA implementation deadlines arrive, many states are developing new assessment policies that take a variety of approaches to the participation of English language learners. One of these approaches is to allow the use of accommodations. Accommodations are changes in the test or testing situation that address students' special needs and that provide students access to the test to enable them to demonstrate academic knowledge. Accommodations are intended to level the playing field for students who receive them, but not to provide an unfair advantage. Because of their limited English proficiency, it is ELLs' special linguistic needs that should to be addressed through testing accommodations.

Federal legislation mandates that all students participate in statewide assessments, but it neither requires nor prohibits the use of accommodations for students whose first language is not English; these decisions are left to the states. This chapter presents a description and discussion of state policies regarding the accommodation of English language learners in statewide assessment programs during the 1998–99 school year. The data is taken from a recently completed study, funded by the Office of Bilingual Education and Minority Languages Affairs, *An Analysis of State Policies for the Inclusion and Accommodation of English Language Learners in State Assessment Programs during 1998–99* (Rivera et al., 2000).[2] This chapter focuses on two related research questions that were addressed in the study:

1. What are states' accommodations policies for ELLs?
2. What are states' score reporting policies for ELL students who receive an accommodated version of a state assessment?

Methodology

The study is unique in that it is based on the direct analysis of state assessment policy documents and state guidelines for including and accommodating ELLs in state assessments rather than on self-reported surveys of state practices. Direct analysis of documents is important for a couple of reasons. First, primary sources allow for verification and therefore have greater credibility than self-reported data. Second, using state policies minimizes the likelihood that the existence of certain practices within a state are confused

---

[1]This chapter uses the term *English language learner (ELL)* rather than *limited English proficient (LEP)* throughout in order to avoid the negative emphasis of the latter on the student's deficiencies (LaCelle-Peterson & Rivera, 1994). Readers should be aware, however, that *LEP* is still the legal term used in legislation and by government agencies.

[2]We gratefully acknowledge the contributions of Lew Scialdone and Peggy Sharkey to the study on which this chapter is based.

with formally established policies, which are much more likely to be implemented in a relatively uniform way as compared to established practices not formally documented.

At our request, Title VII bilingual and English as a second language (ESL) directors and state assessment directors in state education agencies provided the following types of state policy documents:

- State assessment handbooks that include policies for exempting, assessing, and accommodating ELLs
- State assessment policy memoranda applicable to the inclusion of ELLs in state assessment programs and not included in the state assessment handbook
- Guidelines regarding the implementation of policies for exempting, including, or accommodating ELLs that the state provides to districts, schools, or test administrators
- Documents the state has produced to help districts and schools implement state assessment policies for ELLs

Forty-nine states with statewide assessment programs[3] submitted policy documents. These documents were first classified by document type, the most common of which included guides, guidelines, manuals, and handbooks. Next, the documents were classified by the degree of relevance to the study. The relevant documents served as the basis for the policy analysis. The documents were examined and interpreted, and information in them was entered into a database, from which a report for each state was generated and sent to the Title VII and state assessment director for review and verification. Following corrections in the data, a report for the entire country was generated. The findings provide a nationwide description of accommodation and score reporting policies for the 1998–99 school year.

Results

History of ELL Accommodations

The recent practice of providing accommodations to ELLs is an extension of similar policies to accommodate students with physical, developmental, or cognitive limitations that have existed for some time in the field of special education. For example, states' lists of accommodations available to ELLs often include the following: Braille versions of tests, use of a magnifying glass, use of sign language interpreters, use of special recording equipment for student responses, test administration in a student's home, the use of masks or markers to maintain place, and extending the testing time to a point where the student seems no longer able to remain on task. Because it is evident that the state policies that contain these accommodations were developed for students with disabilities and simply transferred to documents concerning the testing of ELLs, these accommodations are not discussed in this chapter. Accommodations carried over from special education more

[3]Iowa and Nebraska do not have state assessment programs; however, the District of Columbia does, and it was treated as a state in this study.

likely to be of benefit to ELLs are considered. These include individual or group administration, extended testing time, and allowing the student to dictate answers.

As shown in Figure 7.1, the analysis of state policies indicates a range of policies across the states for accommodating ELLs on statewide assessments. Although 40 states have accommodations policies for ELLs, only 37 states allow accommodations. Of the 37 states allowing accommodations, 13 prohibit at least one type of accommodation, and 3 states prohibit all accommodations. Following is a description of the various types of accommodations traditionally offered by states.

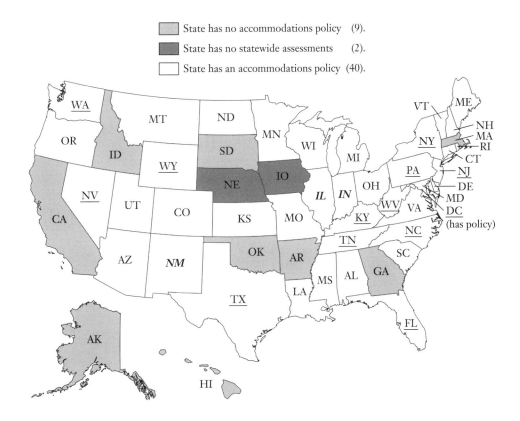

- States in bold allow no accommodations; $N = 3$ (IL, IN and NM).
- Remaining states with a policy allow accommodations; $N = 37$.
- Underlined states prohibit at least one (but not all) accommodation(s); $N = 13$ (DC, FL, KY, NC, NJ, NV, NY, PA, TN, TX, WA, WV, and WY).
- New Mexico and Massachusetts translate tests, although New Mexico does not allow accommodations and Massachusetts has no accommodation policy. Massachusetts also has untimed tests.

FIGURE 7.1 Accommodation Policy Overview

Types of Accommodations

Accommodations offered by states are traditionally classified into four types:

1. Setting
2. Timing/scheduling
3. Presentation
4. Response

Setting accommodations include practices that affect the environment in which the test is given. Examples of setting accommodations include individual or small-group administration and administration in a separate location. *Timing/scheduling accommodations* include extended testing time and extra breaks during a test administration. *Presentation accommodations* affect the manner in which the assessment instrument is presented to the student. Presentation accommodations include explanation, repetition, or oral reading of the test directions, bilingual or translated versions of the test, and administration of the test by a person familiar to the student. *Response accommodations* affect how a student is allowed to respond to test items. Response accommodations include allowing a student to dictate answers, allowing a student to mark answers in the test booklet instead of on the answer sheet, and allowing a student to respond in native language. However, because these four categories do not account for all accommodations allowed by states, we established an *other accommodations* category. This category includes accommodations such as the use of bilingual dictionaries and word lists and a variety of other accommodations.

The results of our analysis of allowable accommodations are depicted in Figure 7.2, which shows the accommodations allowed by number and percent of states.

Setting Accommodations.   Setting accommodations are the type most frequently allowed for ELLs. States that permit setting accommodations usually allow them on all components of a state assessment program. Of the 37 states that allow accommodations, none prohibit any setting accommodations.

As shown in Figure 7.2, the majority of states allow three setting accommodations: (1) small-group administration (allowed by 29 states on some or all components of the assessment program, (2) individual administration (allowed by 26 states on some or all components), and (3) testing in a separate location (allowed by 23 states). Another setting accommodation, preferential seating, is allowed by 17 states. This accommodation permits a student to sit in the front of the room and is intended to provide the student with the best opportunity for understanding oral directions given by the test administrator. For similar reasons, one state, New Hampshire, identifies one setting accommodation as "making sure that the teacher is facing the student."

Timing/Scheduling Accommodations.   Like setting accommodations, timing/scheduling accommodations are offered by many states, and no state prohibits their use. By far, the most popular timing/scheduling accommodation is extending the test time on the same day. As shown in Figure 7.2, extra time is allowed by 26 states on all components, and by 6 states on some components of a state testing program. Regarding restrictions to the

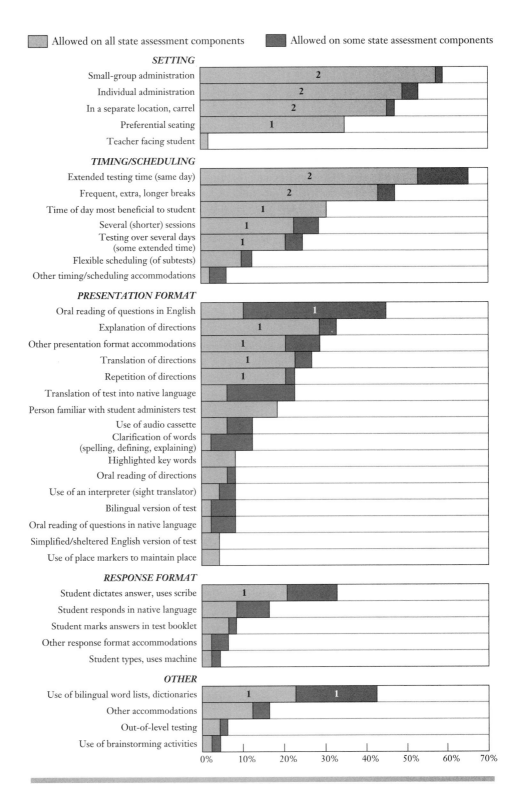

Allowed on all state assessment components   **Allowed on some state assessment components**

SETTING
- Small-group administration — 2
- Individual administration — 2
- In a separate location, carrel — 2
- Preferential seating — 1
- Teacher facing student

TIMING/SCHEDULING
- Extended testing time (same day) — 2
- Frequent, extra, longer breaks — 2
- Time of day most beneficial to student — 1
- Several (shorter) sessions — 1
- Testing over several days (some extended time) — 1
- Flexible scheduling (of subtests)
- Other timing/scheduling accommodations

PRESENTATION FORMAT
- Oral reading of questions in English — 1
- Explanation of directions — 1
- Other presentation format accommodations — 1
- Translation of directions — 1
- Repetition of directions — 1
- Translation of test into native language
- Person familiar with student administers test
- Use of audio cassette
- Clarification of words (spelling, defining, explaining)
- Highlighted key words
- Oral reading of directions
- Use of an interpreter (sight translator)
- Bilingual version of test
- Oral reading of questions in native language
- Simplified/sheltered English version of test
- Use of place markers to maintain place

RESPONSE FORMAT
- Student dictates answer, uses scribe — 1
- Student responds in native language
- Student marks answers in test booklet
- Other response format accommodations
- Student types, uses machine

OTHER
- Use of bilingual word lists, dictionaries — 1   1
- Other accommodations
- Out-of-level testing
- Use of brainstorming activities

0%   10%   20%   30%   40%   50%   60%   70%

FIGURE 7.2 Traditional Classification of Individual Accommodations Allowed by Number and Percent of States (*N* = 49 states with statewide assessments)

amount of extra time an ELL may be allowed, only Alabama, Nevada, and New Jersey specify a maximum amount of allowable time.

Four timing/scheduling accommodations are fairly popular: (1) offering frequent, extra, or longer breaks, which is allowed on some or all components by 23 states; (2) choosing the time of day most beneficial to the student, which is allowed by 15 states on all components; (3) offering several (often shorter) sessions, which is allowed by 13 states on some or all components; and (4) allowing testing over several days, which is allowed by 12 states on some or all components. One timing/scheduling accommodation, flexible scheduling of subtests, is less popular. It is offered on all components in 5 states and on some components in 1 state.

There appears to be less of a consensus regarding the use of the remaining accommodation types (*presentation format* and *response format)* in the traditional classification. This is evidenced by the fact that fewer states allow these accommodations; conversely, some states explicitly prohibit their use. These prohibitions will be discussed in more detail in the following section.

Presentation Format Accommodations.   Although presentation format accommodations are less frequently acceptable to the states than setting or timing accommodations, they are more numerous, accounting for nearly half of the approved ELL accommodations.

- The most popular presentation format accommodation is oral reading of questions in English. As shown in Figure 7.2, 5 states allow this on all assessment components and 17 states allow it on some assessment components.
- The next most commonly used presentation accommodations all involve test directions. Explanation of directions is allowed on some or all components by 16 states. It is noteworthy that, in Minnesota, the explanation of directions is allowable before, but not the day of, the actual administration of the test. Repetition of directions is allowed on some or all components by 11 states. Translation of directions is allowed on some or all components by 13 states.
- Nine states allow a person familiar with the student to administer the test on all components.
- Translation of the test into the native language is allowed by 3 states on all components of the state assessment (Delaware, Kentucky, and Maine) and by 8 states on some components (Minnesota, New Mexico, New York, Oregon, Rhode Island, Texas, Utah, and Vermont).
- Similarly, few states allow either bilingual versions of tests or simplified/sheltered English versions. Bilingual versions of tests are available in Spanish in 4 states (Colorado, Massachusetts, Oregon, and Wyoming). Wyoming allows the use of bilingual tests on all components; the other states allow bilingual tests on some components. Simplified/sheltered English versions of tests are available in 2 states (Kansas and Maine), where they are allowed on all tests.
- The least-used presentation format accommodations are those related to use of the native language. Oral reading of questions in the native language is allowed on all tests by New York, and on some tests by Oregon, Rhode Island, and Wyoming.

- Use of an interpreter or sight translator[4] is allowed on all components by Delaware and New Hampshire; it is allowed on some components by Ohio and Vermont.

A handful of states allow other presentation format accommodations related to making English more accessible. Clarification of words in English is allowed by 1 state, Montana, on all components; it is allowed on some components by 5 states: Arizona, Colorado, Florida, Nevada, and Wyoming. Use of audiocassettes is allowed on all components by 3 states—Montana, North Dakota, and Vermont—and on some components by 3 states—Maryland, Minnesota, and Rhode Island. Oral reading of directions is allowed on all components by 3 states—Colorado, Virginia, and West Virginia—and on some components by Wisconsin. Highlighting key words on the test to focus the student's attention on main ideas is allowed by 4 states, Kansas, North Dakota, Oregon, and Virginia.

Response Format Accommodations.   Response format accommodations affect how a student is allowed to respond to test items. Like presentation format accommodations, they are less frequently used than setting and timing/scheduling accommodations. This category is different from presentation format accommodations in that it consists of fewer accommodations, and these accommodations are less popular.

The most significant accommodation in this category is permitting the student to dictate answers and/or to use a scribe. Ten states allow this accommodation on all components, and 6 states allow it on some components. Other response format accommodations include allowing the student to respond in the native language, which is allowed by four states on all components and by 4 states on some components; allowing the student to mark answers in the test booklet, which is allowed by 4 states on at least one component (Alabama, Minnesota, North Carolina, and South Carolina); and allowing the student to type or use a machine, which is allowed on all components by Maryland and on some state assessment components in Alabama.

Other Accommodations.   Since the four traditional accommodations categories do not account for all accommodations allowed by states, we have included a fifth category, other accommodations. The most significant accommodation in this category is allowing the use of bilingual dictionaries or word lists. This accommodation is allowed on all tests by 21 states on some or all components. One policy of note is that of Louisiana, which stipulates that an "English/Native Language dictionary (no definitions)" is allowed for all tests, while an "English/Native Language dictionary" (apparently with definitions) is allowed only for the written composition test. Other accommodations in this category include the use of out-of-level testing (administering a test designed for a lower grade level) and the use of brainstorming activities such as creating solution maps and discussing in pairs. The former is allowed by Kansas, Montana, and Vermont; the latter is allowed by Delaware and Vermont.

---

[4]Sight translation is the act of orally rendering a document written in language A to language B. In the context of state assessment, sight translation involves rendering orally all or part of a test written in English into the student's native language. While *sight translation* is the correct technical term used by professional translators and interpreters, in most state assessment policy documents it is referred to as *oral translation*.

Considering the number of possible accommodations and the choices involved in determining the extent to which they should be offered, it is no surprise that state policies regarding which accommodations are allowable are so varied. Just as much (and perhaps more) can be learned about states' attitudes toward ELL accommodations by considering the accommodations that are prohibited.

Prohibited Accommodations.   When discussing the use of accommodations, most state policies enumerate the accommodations that are allowed. Some state's policies also identify accommodations that are explicitly prohibited. The policies of 3 states (Illinois, Indiana, and New Mexico) prohibit the use of all accommodations, and the policies of 13 states prohibit the use of at least one accommodation, but not all (District of Columbia, Florida, Kentucky, North Carolina, New Jersey, Nevada, New York, Pennsylvania, Tennessee, Texas, Washington, West Virginia, and Wyoming). In the previous section, we explained that presentation format accommodations, response format accommodations, and other accommodations are not used as frequently as setting and timing/scheduling accommodations. The first three categories are the accommodations that some states explicitly prohibit.

The most popular presentation format accommodation, oral reading of questions in English, is prohibited by 2 states (Pennsylvania and Tennessee). Less popular presentation format accommodations, those related to native language use, are also prohibited by some states. Translation of the test into the native language is explicitly prohibited by 6 states (District of Columbia, Illinois, Indiana, New Jersey, Pennsylvania, and West Virginia). Pennsylvania explicitly prohibits bilingual tests and the oral reading of questions in the native language. Two presentation format accommodations related to making English more accessible, oral reading of directions and paraphrasing test items, are also prohibited by 2 states. Tennessee prohibits the former; Wyoming, the latter. One response format accommodation, allowing the student to respond in the native language, is prohibited by two states (Kentucky and Pennsylvania).

Under the category of other accommodations, the use of bilingual dictionaries or word lists is prohibited on all components by Nevada, Tennessee, and Texas. Allowing the use of English language dictionaries is prohibited on all components by 3 states (Florida, North Carolina, and New York). Similarly, the use of student-created word lists is prohibited by the state of Washington. Finally, the use of out-of-level testing and the use of accommodations that are not in the students' regular classroom or testing situations are prohibited by North Carolina.

To better understand the extent to which allowed and prohibited accommodations directly address the language development needs of ELLs, we next analyze accommodations from a linguistic perspective.

A Linguistic Classification of Accommodations

Since an ELL's primary disadvantage in a standardized testing situation is related to the development of English language proficiency skills, it is useful to reclassify the traditional set of accommodations according to linguistic factors. Using a linguistic approach, we have reclassified accommodations into two broad categories, *linguistic* and *nonlinguistic accommodations*. This classification is shown in Figure 7.3.

The first category includes *native language accommodations*, which are any accommodations used to make the content information accessible to the student in the native language (e.g., allowing the use of bilingual dictionaries, translating the test's directions), and *English language accommodations*, which are any accommodations used to help the student better understand test information presented in English (e.g., allowing questions to be read orally in English, explaining directions, etc.). The remaining accommodations can be classified as *nonlinguistic accommodations* (e.g., extending the test time, allowing the test to be administered in a small-group setting). The data in Figure 7.3 suggest that nonlinguistic accommodations are used by states far more than either native language or English language accommodations. The least utilized and perhaps more controversial group of accommodations appears to be native language accommodations, because they are also the most often prohibited accommodations cited in state policy documents.

Native Language Accommodations. The most common native language accommodation is allowing the use of bilingual word lists and dictionaries. Eleven states allow their use on all state assessment components (Florida, Kentucky, Louisiana, Maryland, Maine, Michigan, Montana, North Carolina, New Jersey, Ohio, and Wyoming), and 10 states allow them on at least one component (Alabama, Arizona, Colorado, Delaware, Mississippi, New York, Rhode Island, South Carolina, Virginia, and Washington). Some states have gone a step further in addressing the language needs of ELLs by producing translated directions and tests. Eleven states translate directions on all test components (Michigan, Minnesota, Montana, New Jersey, Nevada, Ohio, Oregon, Pennsylvania, South Carolina, Texas, and Washington), and 2 states translate directions on at least one component (Alabama and Arizona).

Combining the two categories, translated tests and bilingual tests, 14 states allow the use of translated tests (Colorado, Delaware, Kentucky, Massachusetts, Maine, Minnesota, New Mexico, New York, Oregon, Rhode Island, Texas, Utah, Vermont, and Wyoming). Nine of these states specify that the translation be available in Spanish (Colorado, Massachusetts, Minnesota, New Mexico, New York, Oregon, Rhode Island, Texas, and Wyoming); 5 states do not specify the target language (Delaware, Kentucky, Maine, Utah, and Vermont). In addition to offering Spanish versions, Minnesota translates tests into Vietnamese and White Hmong; New York has translated versions in Chinese, Haitian Creole, Korean, and Russian. It is interesting to note that there are 2 states that provide translated tests although they have not specified accommodation policies related to translation (Massachusetts and New Mexico). Massachusetts has a bilingual test in Spanish. Similarly, Texas allows Spanish language tests for some components. New Mexico offers a Spanish version of its High School Competency Examination. For its other tests, instead of offering translated versions, the state recommends using commercially published Spanish language tests as alternate tests.

Other native language accommodations are allowed by few states. Figure 7.3 shows that 8 states allow students to respond in their native language (Delaware, Kansas, Massachusetts, Montana, North Dakota, Oregon, Rhode Island, and Texas). Four states allow the student to use an interpreter or sight translator (Delaware, New Hampshire, Ohio, and Vermont). Four states permit oral reading of questions in the student's native language (New York, Oregon, Rhode Island, and Wyoming).

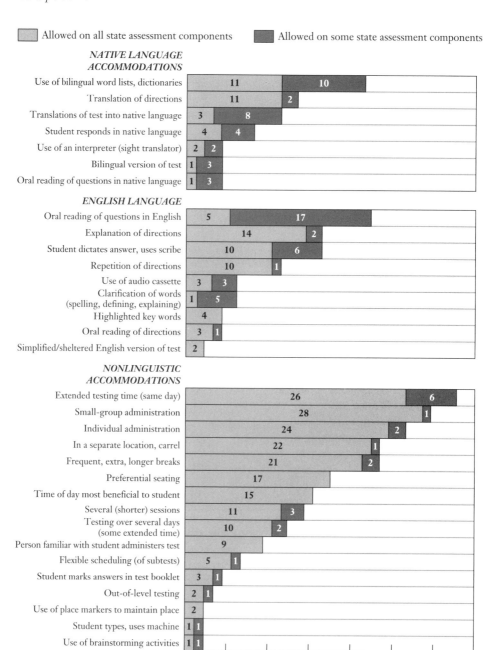

FIGURE 7.3   Linguistic Classification of Individual Accommodations Allowed by Number and Percent of States (*N* = 49 states with statewide assessments)

English Language Accommodations.   Figure 7.3 shows that English language accommodations are offered by more states than native language accommodations. These accommodations most often affect the manner in which the test is presented. Most English language accommodations focus on lessening the reading/writing burden of assessments. The most common English language accommodation is oral reading of questions in English. A total of 22 states allow this accommodation on at least one test component (Alabama, Colorado, Delaware, Florida, Kansas, Kentucky, Maryland, Maine, Michigan, Missouri, Mississippi, North Carolina, North Dakota, New Hampshire, Oregon, Rhode Island, South Carolina, Virginia, Washington, Wisconsin, West Virginia, and Wyoming). Six states allow the use of an audiocassette to present the test (Maryland, Minnesota, Montana, North Dakota, Rhode Island, and Vermont). One of these states (Vermont) allows the use of a videotape.

In addition to accommodations that apply to the presentation of the entire test, there are English language accommodations that apply solely to the directions. Explanation of directions[5] is offered on at least one component by 16 states (Arizona, Connecticut, District of Columbia, Delaware, Florida, Kentucky, Maine, Minnesota, Montana, Nevada, Oregon, South Carolina, Texas, Virginia, Washington, and West Virginia), and repetition of directions is offered on at least one component by 11 states (Arizona, Colorado, District of Columbia, Delaware, Louisiana, Maryland, Oregon, South Carolina, Texas, Washington, and Wyoming). Oral reading of directions is less popular; it is allowed in 4 states (Colorado, Virginia, West Virginia, and Wisconsin).

Beyond modifying the presentation of the test and directions, 6 states attempt to lessen the language demands of their tests by allowing the clarification of words through spelling, defining, and explaining vocabulary (Arizona, Colorado, Florida, Montana, Nevada, and Wyoming). Four states attempt to provide clarification by highlighting key words (Kansas, North Dakota, Oregon, and Virginia). Two states, Kansas and Maine, go beyond offering limited modifications to either the questions or directions. They have developed simplified/sheltered versions of their assessments.

One English language accommodation addressed by the states does not affect the presentation of the assessment: allowing the student to dictate answers. This accommodation is allowed on at least one component by 16 states (Colorado, Delaware, Kansas, Maryland, Maine, Michigan, Missouri, Montana, North Dakota, New Hampshire, Oregon, Rhode Island, Virginia, Vermont, Wisconsin, and Wyoming). Figure 7.3 illustrates that the remaining accommodations, those that account for the majority of accommodations addressed in state policies, are nonlinguistic.[6]

Prohibited Accommodations.   By reclassifying allowable accommodations based on a linguistic classification scheme, it is apparent that both native language and English language accommodations are offered less frequently by the states than nonlinguistic accommodations. Similarly, if we apply the linguistic classification scheme to prohibited

---

[5]Explanation of directions includes the paraphrasing of directions. In at least one state, Minnesota, this is allowed as early as days before the test, but not at the testing time.

[6]For a detailed description of the results regarding nonlinguistic accommodations, please refer to Figure 7.1 and the corresponding discussion in the previous section.

accommodations, we find that nearly all prohibited accommodations are linguistic. The only nonlinguistic accommodations that are prohibited are out-of-level testing and accommodations that are not used in daily classroom and testing situations, both of which are prohibited by North Carolina. All other prohibited accommodations are linguistic accommodations.

The most frequently prohibited accommodation is test translation, which is explicitly prohibited by 6 states (District of Columbia, Illinois, Indiana, New Jersey, Pennsylvania, and West Virginia). Pennsylvania also prohibits bilingual tests. (In contrast, as discussed earlier, 15 states allow some type of test translation.) Other prohibited native language accommodations are the use of bilingual word lists or dictionaries, prohibited by 3 states (Nevada, Tennessee, and Texas), allowing the student to respond in the native language (Kentucky and Pennsylvania), and oral reading of questions in the native language (Pennsylvania).

Prohibited English language accommodations are use of English language dictionaries (Florida, North Carolina, and New York), oral reading of questions in English (Pennsylvania and Tennessee), oral reading of directions (Tennessee), paraphrasing of test items (Wyoming), and the use of student-created word lists (Washington).

Accommodations Decision Makers

In a previous publication (Rivera & Stansfield, 1998), we recommended that school districts establish district committees on accommodations to plan the implementation of state policies and guidelines, and we recommended that individual schools do the same. We further specified the need to create a subcommittee tailored to each student in order to determine the most appropriate accommodations for that student.

In our analysis of state policies, we found that of the 37 states that allow accommodations, 23 states have policies that identify those individuals who should be involved in the decision-making process. In 14 states, the accommodations decision-making team most frequently includes the student's classroom teacher(s). Parents or guardians may be included in 9 states. Twelve states mention a local committee without specifying its members. Likewise, school officials, who form a relatively broad category, are included in 11 states. Six states' policies recommend the involvement of ESL or bilingual education professionals in the accommodations decision-making process. Only 3 states explicitly specify that the student may be involved in the process.

Score Reporting

Once a state has decided to allow accommodations, it must also decide if the accommodated students' scores will be reported. The state may establish a policy of including or excluding the scores in state, district, and/or school totals that are released to the public and the press. In some states, use of a particular accommodation on any component does not affect score reporting; in others, the use of an accommodation on one or more components does affect score reporting.

Nine of the 37 states that allow accommodations for ELLs indicate that when specific accommodations are used, scores are *not* to be included in state, district, and/or school totals (Delaware, Kansas, Maryland, Mississippi, North Dakota, Oregon, Virginia, West Virginia, and Vermont). Eight states have a policy requiring the scores of ELLs who have received accommodations to be included in state, district, and school totals (Kentucky, Louisiana, Maine, Michigan, North Carolina, Nevada, Texas, and Washington). These numbers account for only 17 states. The remaining 20 states that allow accommodations do not address score reporting in their policy documents.

Policies on score reporting vary by the category of accommodation used. No states exclude scores that are obtained through any setting accommodations. However, some states exclude scores from group totals for students who receive timing/scheduling, presentation, response, and other accommodations. The accommodation that most frequently results in excluded scores is the provision of extended testing time. In 4 states (Delaware, Maryland, Mississippi, and Virginia) this accommodation on at least one component results in excluded scores, and in 2 states (North Dakota and West Virginia) it results in the exclusion of scores on all components. Thus, while this accommodation is allowed in 32 states (see Figure 7.2), it nonetheless results in the exclusion of scores from the state and district totals in 4 of these states. The oral reading of questions in English, a linguistic accommodation involving the presentation format allowed in 22 states, results in the exclusion of scores on at least one specific component in 4 states (Maryland, Mississippi, Oregon, and Virginia) and on all components in 3 states (Delaware, North Dakota, and West Virginia).

The following accommodations, when used, result in excluded scores on at least one component but not on all components: the use of bilingual dictionaries (Virginia); allowing the student to dictate the answer (Maryland and Oregon); oral reading of questions in the student's native language (Oregon); student responding in native language (Oregon); translation of the test into the student's native language (Oregon); the provision of frequent, extra, or longer breaks (Virginia); the use of an audio cassette recorder either to present the test to students who have difficulty with printed words and numbers or to allow students to respond to test questions orally (Maryland); and the oral reading of directions (Virginia). All of these accommodations can be classified as linguistic accommodations.

Use of the following accommodations on any component of the assessment program results in exclusion of scores on that component: several shorter sessions (Delaware); breaks during a subtest (West Virginia); explanation of directions (Delaware); use of an interpreter (Delaware); use of brainstorming activities (Delaware); the provision of frequent, extra, or longer breaks (Delaware); the use of an audio cassette recorder either to present the test to students who have difficulty with printed words and numbers or to allow students to respond to test questions orally (North Dakota); the oral reading of directions (West Virginia); translation of the test into the student's native language (Delaware); the use of a linguistically simplified version of the test (Kansas); out-of-level testing (Kansas); and use of a scribe to record student response to a writing prompt (Delaware).[7] Seven of these 12 accommodations can be classified as linguistic accommodations.

[7]Both Virginia and West Virginia have determined that oral reading of directions does not maintain standardized conditions, and therefore they do not include the scores of students who receive this accommodation.

Summary and Analysis

Accommodations are offered to minimize the effects of disadvantage. As applied to ELLs in testing situations, disadvantages generally fall into one of two categories: *linguistic* and *other*. Linguistic disadvantages are related to the student's limited English proficiency. This is a temporary condition, which can be corrected in time through exposure to and training in English. The use of certain linguistic accommodations can help to minimize the impact of these limitations. Other disadvantages include lack of familiarity with American culture, particularly its education system and the system of standards-based assessments. Such obstacles include a student's inexperience and unfamiliarity with the testing process. Some students from diverse cultural and educational backgrounds may lack experience with the test-taking process familiar to American students. Such students would likely be lacking in testwiseness and may also lack confidence in their test-taking abilities. These limitations may affect their interest in and motivation to perform on a standardized test. There was no evidence in any state document of accommodations that address these features of cultural background. These features can be appropriately addressed by a test preparation program, such as that described in Rivera and Stansfield (1998).

Two notable patterns about the specific use of accommodations emerged from this study: (1) The types of accommodations most frequently allowed are setting and timing/scheduling accommodations. (2) The types of accommodations least frequently offered and most frequently prohibited are those that are designed to lighten the language load of the test, that is, accommodations that directly address the linguistic needs of ELLs.

As enumerated earlier, the most frequently allowed accommodations fall into the setting and timing/scheduling classifications. Although any one of these accommodations might be of coincidental benefit to any one student, close examination reveals that none of these accommodations is designed to meet the linguistic or cultural disadvantages of ELLs. This raises two critical issues:

- For which students were the accommodations developed?
- What student needs do the accommodations appropriately address?

Let us consider the following two accommodations, both of which are among the most frequently allowed accommodations for ELLs: (1)Administering the test to one individual (setting). (2) Administering the test at a time of day most beneficial to the student (timing/scheduling). An initial impression might be that these accommodations seem appropriate and may be beneficial to some students. However, it is not easy to identify which specific needs of the ELL these accommodations are intended to meet or which specific limitations of the ELL these accommodations are intended to minimize. Both of these accommodations are designed to reduce test anxiety. As such, they would be beneficial to *any* student, not just an ELL. In fact, it could be argued, albeit weakly, that the provision of these presentation accommodations to any one student provides an unfair advantage to that student. If this is not an effective accommodation for meeting students' needs in general, it is not an effective accommodation for meeting the needs of ELLs, either. Although these accommodations might not do any harm, and might ultimately provide some positive psychological or attitudinal benefit to the ELL, they do not address the ELL's principal limitation, which is lack of English proficiency, or the ELL's lack of familiarity or readiness for formal assessment situations.

It should be expected that the allowance or prohibition of any one accommodation should include examination of the underlying assumptions that serve as a basis for that accommodation. Let us consider the possible assumptions that underlie the allowance of oral reading of questions in English, one of the most popular accommodations for ELLs. This accommodation assumes that spoken questions are more comprehensible than written questions. This is a questionable assumption, because spoken questions require retention of what is heard, and both decoding and retention are affected by lack of proficiency in a language. The accommodation also assumes illiteracy in English and that this can be offset by a student's aural comprehension. Although such a configuration of second language skills is frequently found in adult immigrants, migrants, and native second language learners working in this country, immigrant children in school situations normally acquire literacy and oral language skills more or less contiguously. The assumption of illiteracy also means that a student with limited literacy in English would not be able to provide written answers in English to constructed-response questions. Therefore, this accommodation should not be considered particularly helpful for students who have limited English proficiency. This accommodation thus does not seem to be designed to address the linguistic needs of an ELL.

Finally, a look at the list of presentation accommodations indicates a strong tendency toward ensuring that the student understands test directions. Following the oral reading of questions in English, four accommodations intended to help the student understand test directions—the explanation, repetition, translation, and oral reading of test directions—represent nearly 50% of all presentation accommodations allowed. Because the understanding of test directions is essential, accommodations involving test directions are appropriate for ELLs. Yet, one would think that test directions would be explained to students well before the test administration. Making sure that the test directions are understood is not really an accommodation; it is an essential task of the test administrator and the examinee.

To facilitate discussion of the infrequency of accommodations designed to lighten the language load of the test, we again use the linguistic framework for classifying accommodations proposed earlier in this chapter that more appropriately addresses the needs of English language learners. This framework divides accommodations into two broad types: linguistic and nonlinguistic accommodations. Linguistic accommodations include English language accommodations and native language accommodations. Nonlinguistic accommodations consist of all those that are designed to address other (nonlinguistic) characteristics of the ELL.

Analysis of policy documents across the states indicates that states allow a disproportionate number of nonlinguistic to linguistic accommodations for ELLs. This finding may be explained as the logical result of a combination of factors. One factor may be the history of how accommodations came to be available to ELLs. Another may be the controversial nature—both pedagogical and political—of some linguistic accommodations. A third factor may be the challenge, in terms of cost and human resources, of appropriately providing and administering some linguistic accommodations.

Linguistic Accommodations

A contributing factor to the infrequent availability of linguistic accommodations may be the practical, political, and financial implications of offering them. Native language accommodations, specifically the use of an interpreter and the translation of tests, can be of particular concern. The use of interpreters and translated assessments in the native language incur practical problems. Interpreters with appropriate language and interpreting skills must be identified and trained in appropriate assessment practices. The creation of assessments in the native language can also be complicated. If the assessment is to be a substantially or completely different assessment, the time and effort required are equivalent to the time and effort required to develop assessments in English. If the assessment is to be essentially a translation of the standard assessment, the task is simpler, but the translation must be competently done, reviewed, and revised, perhaps several times. Test translation requires a competent professional translator who is also trained in item-writing procedures, and currently there are few individual who fit this profile. The political atmosphere prevalent in any one state can inhibit a state from providing native language accommodations. For example, in states that have declared English as the official language of the state, it may be neither possible nor politic to devote substantial amounts of energy and money to the development of native language accommodations. From a financial perspective, the cost of hiring interpreters and the development of translated versions of tests can be prohibitive, particularly if the number of students to be served is small.

Accommodation Considerations

Additional factors that must be considered when assessing the appropriate use of accommodations for ELLs include (1) whether an accommodation should be applied on an individual basis or broadly applied and (2) who should be making accommodation decisions for ELLs.

Over the last several years, researchers (Lara & August, 1996; Rivera & Vincent, 1997; Rivera & Stansfield, 1998) have called attention to the need to consider the use of accommodations on an individual basis rather than applying them broadly to ELLs. However, state policies do not generally delineate which accommodations best address the requirements of individual and groups of English language learners. Reclassifying accommodations offered to ELLs based on linguistic factors might be a step toward providing educators with a useful framework to assess which accommodations actually help ELLs and which do not.

A look at decision-making policies reveals a tendency to suggest use of a team approach in making accommodation decisions, along the lines recommended by Rivera and Stansfield (1998). Team members typically include the student's classroom teacher, a school official, the student's parent(s) or guardian(s), and one or two other members, often unspecified. Accommodation policies frequently specify that a student's classroom teacher take part in the decision-making process. This policy is appropriate, particularly in light of the tendency to specify classroom accommodations as those to be allowed in a testing situation. Less praiseworthy is the absence of a team member with professional knowledge of language learning processes, for example, a bilingual educator or ESL teacher. This is most unfortunate, because this type of individual is in the best position to understand the special needs of the ELL.

An individual notably absent from most state lists of accommodation decision makers is the student. Rivera and Stansfield (1998) recommend asking students which accommodations they believe they need. Considering the lack of research in the area of accommodations, and the widely varying policies that exist, it is possible that student input would provide quite useful information regarding choice of accommodation(s). A student could be given a practice test, with the opportunity to try out different accommodations. The student could then decide which accommodation(s) would be of benefit. In addition to providing valuable information from the student perspective, this practice would also provide another means of involving the student in the educational program.

In light of the practical, political, financial, and other concerns surrounding the provision or prohibition of linguistic accommodations, we suggest that states identify allowable accommodations only after having sufficiently answered the following questions:

1. Is the accommodation appropriate for ELLs? What specific need or disadvantage is it intended to address, and can it address the need or disadvantage appropriately?
2. Will use of the accommodation give the accommodated student an unfair advantage?
3. Is use of the accommodation likely to provide more accurate information on the student's knowledge and skills than would otherwise be provided?
4. Can proper provision of the accommodation be ensured, given the pedagogical and practical resources available?

In summary, it seems that the recommendations outlined in Title I, and highlighted by Stancavage and Quick (1999, p. 7) are worth repeating:

> . . . assessments used for Title I must provide for inclusion of LEP students, who shall be assessed, to the extent practicable, in the language and form most likely to yield accurate and reliable information on what they know and can do to determine their mastery of skills in subjects other than English. (To meet this requirement, the State shall make every effort to use or develop linguistically accessible assessment measures, and may request assistance from the Secretary if those measures are needed.)

Score Reporting

Our analysis indicates that current state policies typically do not address the issue of reporting ELL scores. In addition, policy documents from the 17 states that do address score reporting often lack detailed evidence of a comprehensive policy. For these reasons, the description of score reporting practices is limited. Since IASA requires states to implement comprehensive policies regarding the participation of ELLs in state assessments by the 2000–2001 school year, states need to address the issue of score reporting. States that have minimally addressed the issue need to analyze where their policies fall with regard to ELLs and the extent to which the policies are appropriate and adequate.

Recommendations to States

In light of efforts to provide equitable educational opportunities for *all* students, state accommodation policies generally need to be more fully developed. Consideration of the following recommendations can be useful to states that wish to review existing policies and revise them so that they are aligned with current legislation and good practice. To equip local districts and schools with the tools necessary for making appropriate decisions regarding the participation of ELLs in state assessments, states need to continue to develop assessment policies that offer specific guidance and guidelines in the following areas:

1. *The definition and identification of ELLs.* A definition of an ELL or LEP student should be included in state assessment policy documents. Similarly, guidance in the form of procedures for identifying such students and assessing their English language skills should be included in the documents.
2. *The process.* States should describe in their policy documents a process for implementing the accommodations policy at the district level and for making decisions on including and accommodating ELLs at the building level and at the level of the individual student.
3. *Criteria.* States should enumerate the criteria that can or should be used in making decisions on the inclusion or accommodation of ELLs. Multiple criteria (e.g., English language proficiency, time in US schools, prior academic background, etc.) should be used.
4. *Decision makers.* States should identify the kinds of individuals who should be involved in deciding who should receive accommodations and which accommodations students should receive. These decision makers should include, where possible, a person knowledgeable about second language learning (e.g., an ESL or bilingual education teacher).
5. *Appropriate accommodations.* Accommodations allowed for ELLs should be designed to address the specific needs of ELLs. The primary need of ELLs is for linguistic accommodations.
6. *Score reporting.* States need to develop and include in their assessment documents policies on the reporting of scores for students who have received specific kinds of accommodations. This will involve deciding which accommodations will, and which will not, affect score reporting. Similarly, the state's policy should address the aggregation and disaggregation of the test scores of ELLs in state, district, and school totals. Except where accommodations have been determined to provide an unfair advantage, ELLs scores should be included in totals (aggregated). At the same time, the scores of ELLs should be reported separately as a group (disaggregated). This will enhance the accountability of schools vis-à-vis ELLs.
7. *Tracking and research.* States and LEAs should work with their test development contractor and with local districts to develop mechanisms for tracking which accommodations are provided to each ELL. The record of accommodations provided, along with other background information on the child, can add to a database on the child's performance in the assessment system. The record can also

be used to research the appropriateness and validity of the different types of accommodations.

8. *Separation from SD*. Because ELLs are inherently different from students with disabilities (SD), they should be treated differently in state policies. Each group merits a separate policy within the relevant policy document.

Recommended Research

As IASA implementation deadlines arrive, the development of new state policies is a major focus in many states. Therefore, it is advisable that descriptive and experimental research be conducted at the national and state levels. At the national level, there is a need to gather and analyze state policy documents every two years in order to keep pace with the constant changes in the ways that states address the assessment needs of ELLs. The regular gathering of policies would identify new polices and provide an updated picture of ongoing efforts of states to accommodate ELLs in state assessment programs. At the state and district level, research should focus on both policy and implementation studies regarding inclusion and accommodation policies for ELLs. The following topics of study should be pursued:

- Regarding accommodation policies, research in districts and schools is needed to examine accommodations used and their utility and effect on ELL scores and on school and district test scores. The goal of this research should be to identify the accommodations that enable ELLs to demonstrate content knowledge by minimizing interference caused by limited English proficiency, without providing them with an unfair advantage over students who do not receive the accommodation. It would be an ideal situation if all accommodations were studied in terms of their appropriateness and impact before being allowed, but in many cases, this is far from practical. Like other worthwhile educational innovations, the provision of accommodations cannot wait until a research base for them has been compiled. Instead, educators should use good judgment and then study the effects and adequacy of the policies they have set.
- At the national level, reviews of the literature should be carried out periodically to aggregate the research literature on accommodations emanating from states. This will allow educators to determine which accommodations are effective and appropriate and enhance the validity of ELL test scores.
- In this study, only 17 of the 37 states that allow accommodations addressed score reporting in their policy documents. Thus, research is needed to determine how scores of ELLs, whether tested under standard or nonstandard conditions, are treated at the state, district, and school levels. In addition, it is important to analyze the effects of score reporting policies on the students and on their education.

The findings from these kinds of studies should provide information about best practices that can help states improve their ELL accommodation policies.

references

LaCelle Peterson, M., & Rivera, C. (1994). Is it real for all kids?: A framework for equitable assessment policies for English language learners. *Harvard Educational Review, 64*(1), 55–75.

Lara, J., & August, D. (1966). *Systemic reform and limited English proficient students.* Washington, D.C.: Council of Chief State School Officers.

Rivera, C., & Stansfield, C. W. (1998). Leveling the playing field for English language learners: Increasing participation in state and local assessments through accommodations. In *Assessing student learning: New rules, new realities,* ed. R. Brandt, pp. 65–92. Arlington, Va.: Educational Research Service.

Rivera, C., Stansfield, C. W., Scialdone, L., & Sharkey, P. (2000). *An analysis of state policies for the inclusion and accommodation of English language learners in state assessment programs during 1998–99.* Arlington, Va.: Center for Equity and Excellence in Education, George Washington University.

Rivera, C., & Vincent, C. (1997). High school graduation testing: Policies and practices in the assessment of English language learners. *Educational Assessment, 4*(4), 335–355.

Stancavage, F., & Quick, H. (1999). Laws and regulations, current practice, and research relevant to inclusion and accommodations for students with limited English proficiency in the voluntary national tests. Paper presented at the meeting of the American Education Research Association, Montreal, Canada.

United States Congress (1994). Improving America's Schools Act. PL 103-382. (Section 1111(b)(3); subsections 200.1(b)(2) and 200.4.) Washington, D.C.: U.S. Government Printing Office.

United States Department of Education (1999). *Peer review guidance for evaluating evidence of final assessments under Title I of the Elementary and Secondary Education Act.* Washington, D.C.: U.S. Government Printing Office.

8

How Will Assessment Data Be Used to Document the Impact of Educational Reform?

LAURESS L. WISE

Human Resources Research Organization (HumRRO)

R. GENE HOFFMAN

Human Resources Research Organization (HumRRO)

This paper was prepared for the conference on Assessment in Educational Reform: Both Means and Ends sponsored by the Maryland Assessment Research Center and the Maryland State Department of Education. We were asked to envision how assessment data might be used in documenting the impact of educational reform. Our focus is on assessment. We will leave it to others to delineate the scope of interventions that constitute educational reform.

We want to describe the ideal assessment of the future as it might be used for program evaluation. Our thesis, however, is that to know where we want to go with assessment, we need to understand both where we have been and what is wrong with where we are now. Consequently, we spend considerable time on the past and present and only toward the end of the paper do we begin make future projections.

Trends in the Use of Assessment Data

We start with a March 8, 2000 *Education Week* article that was disturbing for many of us. David Hoff begins the article as follows:

> The federal testing program has been a tool akin to a ruler for 30 years, measuring students' knowledge of basic subjects. Now, President Clinton and two leading presidential contenders want to turn it into a lever, giving states financial incentives to improve performance and close the gap between high and low achievers.

Another way of stating the theme of this paper is "What would it take for the above proposal to be a good idea?"

Linn (1998, 2000) provides a good description of the progression in our use of assessment from measuring student progress to accountability. Most of us who are over 40 remember when assessments were used to measure individual student growth. We spent a day or so taking a battery of tests and received back a profile showing our relative strengths and weaknesses. (For example, some of us were pretty good at math and terrible at spelling.) Typically, the results were reported in grade-equivalent units so that we could see how our scores compared to the median scores for different grades. Teachers could use this information to provide remedial instruction for students scoring below their current grade level and more advanced material to challenge students who scored well above their grade level. Figure 8.1 illustrates this traditional use of assessment.

Although as far back as the ancient Greeks we have experienced countless waves of efforts to reform schools, it is only recently that the idea of using assessments as a lever of curriculum change emerged. Resnick (Resnick & Resnick, 1992) talked passionately about building the type of tests we would want teachers to teach to. She and Mark Tucker led the development of the New Standards tests to implement this idea (Tucker and Codding, 1998). Figure 8.2 reflects this different use of student assessments.

The National Assessment Governing Board, in developing the National Assessment of Educational Progress (NAEP), has also sought to strike a balance between "leading" the curriculum with forward-looking frameworks and reflecting the curriculum presently enacted. Many state assessments, including particularly those in Maryland and Kentucky,

Evolution in Assessment Use: **Measuring Student Growth**

In earlier years, assessments were used to measure
individual student progress

**FIGURE 8.1   Using Assessment to Measure
Individual Student Growth**

have been intentionally designed to lead instruction. Many states have also begun to attach
consequences to the results from statewide student assessments. The Kentucky Educational Reform Act (KERA) of 1990, for example, included provisions for rewarding
schools showing significant progress toward 20-year goals while "helping" other schools
that were "in decline" (Kentucky Department of Education, 1996). This has not always
worked as intended (Abelmann & Kenyon, 1996), but Kentucky is continuing to hold
schools accountable for student performance, albeit with some refinement in the measures
used.

Evolution in Assessment Use:
Assessments Became a Lever for Reform

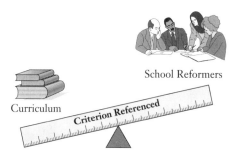

If you test it, they will teach. (School of Dreams)

**FIGURE 8.2   Using Assessment as a
Lever for Reform**

For better or worse, education is receiving a great deal of attention in current political debates at both the national and state levels. There is talk of adding funds for training, hiring, and compensating good teachers. Many policy makers are not convinced that this is enough, however, and there are increased calls for accountability at all levels. More states and districts are adding high school exit examinations and, in some cases, the Title II legislation currently being debated in Congress calls for use of outcome measures to hold teacher training institutions accountable for the performance of their graduates. States are continuing to hold districts and schools accountable for student outcomes and many districts and schools are, in turn, looking to shift their accountability to individual teachers (see Figure 8.3). In the recent presidential campaign, the candidates talked about using NAEP to hold states accountable for the use of educational funds provided by the federal government.

Somehow, assessments have changed from a yardstick into a lever and now into a beating stick. The next section of this paper discusses why this could be a problem.

Issues in Using Assessments to Measure Program Impact

There are several possible problems with the current use of assessments to leverage educational reform and also measure its impact. First, the assessments may or may not have much to do with the goals educational reformers are trying to achieve. There needs to be an explicit link between the changes advocated by reformers and the types of measures used in assessing the outcomes of these reforms. Further, we must be sensitive to factors that lead to inaccurate results, either overstating or understating student gains associated

Evolution in Assessment Use:
Assessments Now Used for Accountability

Teachers

Achievement Standards

Novice | Basic | Proficient | Advanced

Policy-makers

Hold them accountable and they will teach better (or else!)

FIGURE 8.3 Using Assessment for Teacher Accountability

with educational changes. Finally, we must be sensitive to the possible and even probable unintended consequences that might flow from using assessments for accountability.

Establishing an Evidentiary Link

Many attempts to use the assessment of student outcomes to evaluate the students, their teachers, or their schools, districts, and even states are not well grounded in the theory and practice of evaluation. (See, for example, Shadish, Cook, & Leviton for a standard discussion of approaches to program evaluation.) It is not sufficient to determine whether the ultimate outcome is achieved. We must also look at whether the program was implemented as intended and, if so, whether it led to the immediate consequences that were intended (Snyder, Raben, & Farr, 1980). A failure to find gains in the ultimate outcome (i.e., student achievement) may result from (1) improper or nonexistent implementation of the reform, (2) a failure to achieve the near-term outcomes intended for the program (e.g., curriculum-specific knowledge and skill), or (3) incorrect assumptions about the relationship of the near-term outcomes to ultimate program goals (e.g., more general knowledge and skill). Similarly, without carefully constructed control groups, outcome gains do not prove that the reform is working, particularly if there are flaws in program implementation or a lack of gain on near-term measures.

Haertel (1999) described the need to tease out assumed links between what you are trying to evaluate and the measures you are using for the evaluation. His example of using student outcome measures to evaluate school quality is quite relevant. He suggested that all of the following assumptions, and perhaps several more, need to be investigated and confirmed:

1. Tests scores show how much students know and can do.
    a. The test items require skills included in the curriculum.
    b. Skills demonstrated on the test can also be used on other tasks.
    c. Proficiency on tested skills shows proficiency on untested skills as well.

2. The more a student knows and can do, the better the school is performing.
    a. The purpose of schooling is to impart the skills being assessed.
    b. Students' skill levels depend directly on the quality of their schooling.

In evaluating California's new High School Exit Examination (Wise, Hoffman, & Harris, 2000), we focused on several intermediate outcomes that may lead to improved student achievement. These include changes in courses and special programs offered and in the way these are taught, changes in the number and types of students taking these courses, and changes in student effort in the courses they take. These are intervening variables, but so is passing the exit exam itself. The more ultimate outcomes include scores on a wide array of important achievement measures (e.g., SAT/ACT scores, the STAR exam) and indicators of success after high school (e.g., college attendance, career success).

The need to study intervening measures in some depth cannot be overstated. The TIMSS video study (Stigler & Heibert, 1997) illustrates the richness and diversity of classroom activities that we seek to reform. Suzanne Lane and her colleagues (Lane, Stone, & Parke, 2000) have analyzed "classroom artifacts" (textbooks, lesson plans, examinations, and examples of student work) in examining instructional changes in response to the Maryland assessment. Gene Hoffman and staff at HumRRO (Hoffman et al., 1997; Harris, et al., 1998) have spent considerable time over the past four years visiting schools throughout Kentucky to examine firsthand how Kentucky's assessment has changed classroom practices.

As we model the ways in which reform efforts may lead to improved student achievement (and/or other important outcomes), we must be ever mindful of the difference between correlation and causality. If education could be evaluated in a laboratory, we would have random assignment of students to programs and it would be reasonable to infer that differences in student outcomes across programs were in some way attributable to elements of the program. In the real world, many factors influence student outcomes, only some of which are related to the classroom or to schooling at all. One obvious factor is that students come to school with different levels of preparation, different resources, different expectations, and different levels of motivation to succeed. Almost any program implemented in a district of advantaged students will appear to work better than the best of programs in districts of disadvantaged students.

As researchers, we must measure and analyze the many moderators that may magnify or mask true program effects. The Tennessee Value-Added Assessment System (Sanders and Horn, 1994) is gaining popularity in many states as a more equitable way to assess schools' contributions to student achievement. The basic idea is to control for differences in prior student development by looking at gain scores for all students rather than at their absolute level of achievement.

One additional reason that it is important to understand the whole context within which assessment is being used to evaluate the effects of reform is that assessments are imperfect and can significantly overstate or understate true gains in student achievement. Figure 8.4, from Linn's 1998 career-achievement address (1998) shows conflicting information on achievement gains from two different assessments. In the next sections of this paper, we discuss potential biases in assessment results. Our point here is that, because of what we have seen in classrooms and heard from teachers during our visits to Kentucky schools, we have some basis for understanding the differences reflected in the figure.

The open-response questions of the Kentucky Instructional Results Information System (KIRIS, now KCCT) assessment has had an enormous impact on classroom practices, as illustrated by the extensive displays of "power verbs" and "four-column method" posters on the walls of Kentucky classrooms (Harris et al., 1998). Power verbs refer to higher-order thinking skills and include words like *compare* and *contrast*, but also some simpler words like *identify*. When KIRIS first hit, students apparently did not recognize the importance of these words or know how to respond to these words when they appeared in test items. Similarly, students apparently did not know how to begin to think about answering the open-ended KIRIS questions. In addition to the power verb, the four-column method sprang up to help teachers teach students how to systematically decode, recall, organize, and then write a complete, coherent response to an open-response question. The power verb and the four-column method charts were created by "Distinguished Educators" in Kentucky (who were assigned to "sanctioned" schools). Teachers, from "distinguished" on down, instinctively knew that KIRIS measured different skills than the bubble-response tests students were used to taking. In a very real sense, Kentucky's

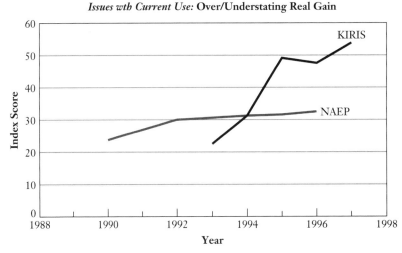

Issues wth Current Use: Over/Understating Real Gain

**KIRIS and NAEP Math Scores for Kentucky Middle Schools:
Does KIRIS Overstate or NAEP Understate Real Gains?**
(from Linn, 1998)

**FIGURE 8.4   Illustration of Divergent Information on
Achievement Gains**

teachers and classrooms have provided us with an ongoing cognitive laboratory—one in which we have watched teachers struggle with a problem (teaching students to answer open-ended questions) and then develop and refine approaches to solving the problems posed by these questions. Untold thousands of hours and agony had been spent by teachers adapting their instruction to the new item format. It is not surprising, therefore, that students are now better able to answer open-ended questions requiring not just factual knowledge, but thinking and an organized response. It is also not surprising that student scores on NAEP, which has relatively few such questions, did not reflect any of these improvements.

Why Assessment Results May Overstate Real Gains

It is ironic that it was not an educational researcher, but a physician, who most dramatically called our attention to the fact that assessments can overstate student performance levels. Cannell (1987) noted that all states appeared to have average scores above the publishers' estimates of the national mean. Labeled the "Lake Wobegon effect" (after Garrison Keillor's mythical town where all students are above average), this result stimulated an extensive reexamination of our assumptions about normative results from assessments. In the fall of 1990, a special issue of *Educational Measurement: Issues and Practice* (Phillips, 1990) was devoted to a discussion of this phenomenon. As assessments have become used for accountability, with higher stakes attached to assessment results, concerns about potential inflation of score results have been expanded to include intentional as well as unintentional factors. We offer here a brief description of four leading concerns about ways in which assessment results may improve over true student achievement.

Measuring Student Performance Too Narrowly. One consistent finding described in the 1990 *EM:IP* issue just mentioned is that scores tend to rise for several years after a particular test is adopted and then fall back down when a new test is introduced (Linn, Graue, & Sanders, 1990). Figure 8.5, adapted by Linn (1998) from that article illustrates this point. The explanations for this phenomena range from benign factors (e.g., general shifts in content emphasis) to more sinister assumptions about the motives of teachers and administrators (e.g., explicit efforts to identify and teach specific test items).

Tests may measure content too narrowly if it is possible to improve test scores by teaching to details of the test specifications (Shepard, 1990). Even when tests measure the same general frameworks, there may be important differences in test specifications that can lead to a narrowing of the content that is measured. For example, under the objective of graphical display of data, specifications for one test may include stem-and-leaf plots as a topic to be measured, while specifications for another test do not (Koretz, personal communication). In this case, emphasizing stem-and-leaf plots in instruction will lead to score improvements on the first test that may not generalize well to the second test. When test results matter, we must expect that decisions about areas of the curriculum to emphasize or use as illustration will reflect the universal student question, "will it be on the test?"

A more specific problem is teaching to specific test items. Security breaks, where test items are reproduced and incorporated in instruction, get headlines, but are not necessarily common. There are, however, subtler forms of teaching to specific test items. A

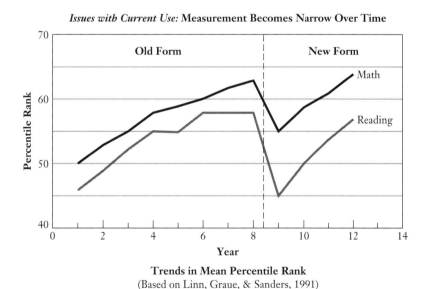

Trends in Mean Percentile Rank
(Based on Linn, Graue, & Sanders, 1991)

FIGURE 8.5   Illustration of Score Gains from Reuse of Test Forms

teacher recently recounted to us how several students came to her after a recent statewide assessment to ask how they should have responded to some of the specific questions. Although she may not use those specific questions in instruction next year, it is only natural to want to be sure that students can demonstrate the specific skills required by those questions. Performance-based items are more memorable, leading to greater potential for discussions among students and with teachers after the examination. They are also expensive to develop, increasing pressure to use them again on subsequent examinations.

Inappropriate Proctoring and Scoring. Given the high costs of test administration and scoring, there is a natural tendency to use local teachers to administer, and sometimes even score, assessments. Teachers are available at little or no additional cost while their students are being tested. In high-stakes settings, this practice gives at least the appearance of conflicting interests, and it only takes one or two incidents, such as recent problems in Montgomery County, Kentucky, to create concern. Subtle factors, from relaxed timing to more specific ways to encourage students to do their best and check their work, could influence results. In Kentucky, where portfolio assessment has been part of the school accountability scores, districts were asked to score their own students. Audits conducted the first year showed some score inflation; improved training (or increased threats) in subsequent years eliminated most or all of the inflation detected by audits (Kentucky Department of Education, 1996).

Problems in Year-to-Year Linking. Another possible source of error in estimating achievement gains is problems with the equating of forms used in different years. Equating problems may, of course, lead to underestimating as well as overestimating true gains, but some sources of equating error lead specifically to overestimates. For example, year-to-year linking is typically based on reuse of a set of items from the prior or base year. To the extent that specific items are memorable and there is increased teaching of specific skills measured by these items, performance on the linking items will improve to a greater degree than would performance on other items leading to overestimates of score gain. Koretz (personal communication) found some evidence that scores on Kentucky performance items were correlated with number of prior uses of the items.

Another potentially biasing source of equating error is item position effect. It is sometimes the case that linking items are administered toward the end of a form (possibly in "matrixed" positions to reduce exposure) during the first year and then earlier in the form on the following year. There is reason to believe that students give more attention to and perform better on items earlier in the test (e.g., Wise, 1996; Wise, Chia, & Park, 1989), leading to artificial score gains in the second year.

Inappropriate Exclusion of Low-Performing Students. As many states move to include all students in school accountability measures, there is increased attention to the appropriate and valid assessment of students with disabilities or limited proficiency in English. After the 1998 NAEP state-by-state reading results were released, it was noted in the press that the proportion of students excluded from the assessment due to limitations in available accommodation had risen in many states and that, across states, increases in exclusions were correlated with the score gains that were reported.

Why Assessment Results
May Understate Real Gains

While critics focus on ways in which assessment results may overstate achievement gains, there are also many ways in which the results may understate true gains. Three such factors are discussed here: (1) poor measurement of the targeted skills, (2) low student motivation on the assessment, and (3) insufficient time for changes at lower grade levels to have impact. Some other factors, such as errors in year-to-year linking, were discussed earlier.

Targeted Skills Not Measured by the Assessment.   First, lack of perfect reliability will lead to an understatement of achievement gains when gains are expressed in standard deviation units. To the extent that assessment results contain error, the observed standard deviation is inflated and the ratio of any true gains to this standard deviation is reduced. Put another way, error components in the assessment scores are not likely to be related to what is being taught, and so that portion of the score variance is less responsive to instruction. Measurement error (other than main effects due to sampling items from a larger universe) is reduced significantly for large sample means in comparison to individual student scores. Measurement error can still be a problem for moderate-sized schools where the number of students assessed is not large. Note that some critics have expressed particular concerns about performance items where performance tends to be context-specific, leading to smaller interitem correlations and thus smaller estimates of test reliability (Catterall et al., 1998).

Paradoxically, there is also a real danger in giving too much emphasis to reliability, to the extent that it leads us to measure the wrong things. For example, open-response items cost more to implement, take longer to administer, and take longer to process than multiple-choice items. As a result, per dollar and test minute, reliability is higher with multiple-choice items alone. In response to the concern of Caterall and his colleagues (1998), the Kentucky legislature voted to increase the use of multiple-choice items in accountability assessment. Florida is similarly considering banning open-response items from the FCAT. No one is asking whether open-response items measure important aspects of performance not covered by current multiple-choice items. Efforts in Kentucky to help students "compare, contrast, and identify" (see earlier) are not likely to lead to much gain on a multiple-choice-item-only assessment.

Apart from format differences, inappropriate content emphases can mask true gains. Figure 8.6 shows trends in different parts of the Iowa Test of Basic Skills (ITBS) for grade 8 mathematics. Clearly, a test that emphasized computation items (which, after all, are easy to construct and may lead to greater estimates of reliability) would show little gain over this period. Changes in curriculum to help students with estimation or data interpretation would not be appropriately evaluated by such a test. Another example of how test content might matter is provided by a story told by Alan Ginsberg of the U.S. Department of Education at a 1990 conference on assessment. In the early days of Head Start, the department was looking for a measure to use in assessing the impact of the Head Start program. Researchers told them it would take several years to develop an assessment tailored to the specific skills the program was designed to impart. The evaluators did not have years and had to settle on what was essentially an IQ measure. Was it any wonder that initial estimates of gain were modest?

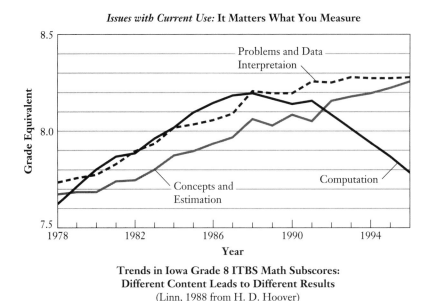

FIGURE 8.6   Illustration of Divergent Trends across Content Areas

Low Student Motivation on the Assessment.   Clearly, if students do not try their best to show what they know and can do, assessments will understate what they have learned. Concern about the motivation of grade 12 students in the second semester of their final year was one factor cited by a National Academy of Sciences committee to recommend alternatives to the NAEP grade 12 assessment (National Research Council, 1999). At all grade levels, there are concerns that assessments that are long, have items that are difficult for some students, or require significant effort may lead to underestimates of student performance (Wise, McCloy, & Quartetti, 1998; Wolfe, Smith, & Birnbaum, 1995).

Insufficient Time for Changes at Lower Grade Levels to Have Impact.   In the current climate of accountability, policy makers (some of whom may move to reelection cycles) want to see significant short-term gains. Reform efforts, however, must be systemic if they are to have significant impact. Improvements in eighth-grade mathematics will result from changes in the curriculum for first through seventh grade as much or more as from changes in the eighth-grade curriculum. It will take at least eight years, however, before the full effects of such changes will be seen in the eighth-grade assessment.

Unintended Consequences of Attaching Stakes to the Assessment of Outcomes

As we attach higher stakes to assessment results, we must be increasingly alert to unintended consequences resulting from this use of assessment. HumRRO is at the beginning of an evaluation of a new High School Exit Exam (HSEE) being developed in California. We have had recent opportunities to ask educators and policy makers both what they wanted to happen as a result of this new graduation requirement and also what other impact the requirement might have besides these intended consequences. In this section, we describe some of the main concerns that were identified as potentially negative consequences.

Narrowing the Curriculum.　　In most states, assessments focus on the core curriculum. The California HSEE covers just English language arts and mathematics. If student achievement in these areas is given all the weight for determining school accountability results, will there be motivation to put less time and resources into the teaching of other subjects? Within a specific subject, the assessment may cover only certain topics. Will these topics be taught to the exclusion of others? Although we don't have specific examples of instances where curriculum narrowing has occurred, we are concerned by instances in Kentucky, where teaching assignments were shifted to put the best teachers on accountability grade subjects.

Demotivating High-Performing Students.　　A persistent concern with minimum competency testing is that it could reduce time and resources spent on helping students achieve higher levels of proficiency as well as reduce the motivation of the students themselves. If students pass a high school exit examination in the 10th grade, will they be motivated to work hard over their remaining two years of high school? (Or over the next year-and-a-half, if you believe that few students work hard during their last semester.) Efforts to raise the performance of low-scoring students should not restrict opportunities or motivation for other students to progress above minimum levels.

Demotivating Low-Performing Students.　　An opposite concern is that if standards are perceived to be high, low-performing students may give up altogether. In California, we will be monitoring dropout rates. Students who drop out before or after initially failing the exit exam will lose whatever benefit they may have received from further schooling.

In evaluating the Voluntary National Tests of fourth-grade reading and eighth-grade math (Wise, Hauser, Mitchell, & Feuer, 1999; Wise, Noeth, & Koenig, 1999), we encountered repeated concerns that the use of the NAEP achievement standards would provide little information for disadvantaged students and schools. What good would it do to tell these students, yet again, that they were below the relatively high level that defines basic performance?

Demotivating Teachers.　　Another area of potentially negative consequences is the impact of assessments on teachers. State and national assessments often demand that they take considerable time away from their classrooms, without providing specific results on individual student strengths and weaknesses. When high stakes are attached to the assessments, the potential for impropriety can lower the esteem in which they are held and create significant tension between what they think would be most enriching for students and what students need to do to pass the exam.

Potential Improvements

So how can we improve assessments to provide more complete information while minimizing factors that lead to biased results and avoiding unintended negative consequences? Obviously, if we had the answer to this question, we would be running a testing company or a state assessment agency. Nevertheless, here are several suggestions for improving the use of assessments for accountability and program evaluation.

Keep Assessment Results in Perspective

First, we need to keep some perspective on the role of assessment results. Should results from a half-day event, no matter how "objective," be given more weight than a teacher's opportunity to observe a student's performance across a wide variety of settings for a whole year? The AERA/APA/NCME test standards (AERA, APA, NCME, 1999) caution against the use of a single measure for any high-stakes decision. Unfortunately, although some efforts to report on school quality cover a wide range of indicators and describe educational programs in more depth (e.g., Toch, 1999), most results are typically summarized by the press in terms of a single school (or district or state) score.

Our first suggestion is to use a broad array of outcome measures that include indicators of different valued outcomes. Student and school evaluations should include supplemental subjects (e.g., arts and humanities, vocational studies) as well as core subjects, and all subjects should be covered widely. Using a broad array of measures will reduce pressure to narrow the curriculum and also allow for profiles of the relative strengths and weakness of each student.

Another important part of maintaining perspective on assessment results is providing as much information as possible about the conditions under which those results occur. This includes identifying and reporting important moderating information and providing student and school result comparisons that take these moderating influences into account. The development of "value-added" models represents a potentially useful step in this direction.

Alignment, Alignment, Alignment

Another significant opportunity for improving on current practice is to improve the ways we conceive of and evaluate alignment issues. The American Institutes for Research has worked on the use of cognitive laboratories (AIR, 1998) to determine the extent to which items measure their intended content. Porter (2000) reports ways of displaying alignment information that show promise. We also need improvements in the way we determine the alignment of the curriculum to both test content standards and the test items themselves. Improved alignment will solve two different problems with current assessment efforts. First, alignment to test specifications will prevent inappropriate estimates (either over or under) of achievement gains that can result from measuring the wrong thing. Second, indicators of alignment with the curriculum will prevent inappropriate attribution of achievement failures.

Reduce Chances for the Appearance of Cheating.   Another important problem to solve is the appearance of cheating. One clear way to reduce the potential for teaching to the test would be to change the test more often. Unlike most commercial tests, the Voluntary National Tests were (are) being developed with the idea of releasing all of the items after each use. This means one or more new forms every year, which is, of course, costly (and why commercial testing companies shy away from this idea). Although it is unlikely that individual states and districts could afford to develop new forms each year, collaborative or national efforts might make this feasible.

Proctoring is another issue that must be addressed more systematically. It is, of course, expensive to train and pay outside test administrators for a single test. Perhaps if there were a network of such test administrators, who could work on a variety of programs, the cost would be less daunting. The costs of risking public confidence in the teaching profession through a few well-publicized compromises, while less tangible, are equally considerable.

Provide Diagnostic Value for Students.   A final issue that we believe will be better addressed in the future is the problem of student motivation. We must find some compromise between providing no individually useful information on student performance and high-stakes uses that place inappropriate value on individual student results (see our earlier comments on keeping results in perspective). Students will be more motivated if they know they and their teachers and, possibly, their parents will receive useful feedback on their performance.

Further, even though it may not be meaningful to test publishers, student and classroom time is precious. We must strive to maximize the diagnostic value of the information that is returned. Simply telling students that they have failed to pass an exit exam leaves them with little information on what they need to do to pass it the next time. Students should know, over time, how much closer they are coming to meeting the standard and, insofar as possible, the areas within a subject where improvement is most needed. Even if testing time is too short to support reliable subscores, release of individual item results could provide rich examples of what a student at any level can do and some examples of areas where further improvement is possible.

r e f e r e n c e s

Abelmann, C. H., & Kenyon, S. B. (1996). Distractions from teaching and learning: Lessons from Kentucky's use of rewards. Paper presented at the Annual Meeting of the American Educational Research Association, New York.

AERA, APA, & NCME. (1999). *Standards for educational and psychological testing*. Washington, D.C.: American Educational Research Association.

American Institutes for Research. (1998). Cognitive lab report. Prepared for the National Assessment Governing Board. Washington, D.C.: author.

Cannell, J. J. (1987). *Nationally normed elementary achievement testing in America's public schools: How all 50 states are above the national average*, 2d ed. Daniels, W.V.: Friends of Education.

Catterall, J. S., Mehrens, W. A., Ryan, J. M., Flores, E. J., & Rubin, P. M. (1998). *Kentucky instructional results information system: A review*. Frankford, Ky.: Office of Educational Accountability.

Haertel, E. H. (1999). Validity arguments for high-stakes testing: In search of the evidence. *Educational Measurement: Issues and Practice, 18*(4), 5–9.

Harris, C. D., Hoffman, R. G., Koger, L. E., & Thacker, A. A. (1998). *The relationship between school gains in 7th and 8th grade KIRIS scores and instructional practices in mathematics, science, and social studies for 1997*. (HumRRO Report FR-WATSD-98-05). Alexandria, Va.: Human Resources Research Organization.

Hoff, David J. (8 March 2000). NAEP weighed as measure of accountability. *Education Week.*

Hoffman, R. G., Harris, C. D., Koger, L., & Thacker, A. (1997). *The relationship between school gains in 8th grade KIRIS scores and instructional practices in mathematics, and social studies*. (LRS97-3). Frankfort, Ky.: Bureau of Learning Results Services, Kentucky Department of Education.

Kentucky Department of Education (1996). *KIRIS accountability cycle 2 technical manual*. Frankfort, Ky.: Author.

Lane, S., Stone, C. A., & Parke, C. S. (2000). Consequential evidence for MSPAP from the teacher, principal, and student perspective. Paper presented at the Annual Meeting of the National Council on Measurement in Education, New Orleans, La.

Linn, M. C., Lewis, C., Tsuchida, I., & Songer, N. B. (2000). Beyond fourth-grade science: Why do U.S. and Japanese students diverge? *Educational Researcher, 29*(3), 4–14.

Linn, R. L. (1998). Assessments and accountability. Paper presented at the Annual Meeting of the American Educational Research Association, San Diego, Calif.

———. (2000). Assessments and accountability. *Educational Researcher, 29*(2), 4–16.

Linn, R. L., Graue, M. E., & Sanders, N. M. (1990). Comparing state and district results to national norms: The validity of the claims that "everyone is above average." *Educational Measurement: Issues and Practice, 9*(3), 5–14.

National Research Council. (1999). *Grading the nation's report card*. Eds. James W. Pellegrino, Lee R. Jones, & Karen J. Mitchell. Washington, D.C.: National Academy Press.

Phillips, G. W. (1990). The Lake Wobegon effect. *Educational Measurement: Issues and Practice, 9*(3), 3, 14.

Porter, A. (2000). Alignment of state testing programs with NAEP in math and science at grades 4 and 8. Paper presented at the Annual Meeting of the American Educational Research Association, New Orleans, La.

Resnick, L. B., & Resnick, D. P. (1992). Assessing the thinking curriculum: New tools for educational reform. In *Changing assessments: Alternative views of aptitude, achievement and instruction*, B. G. Gifford & M. C. O'Conner, eds. Boston: Kluwer Academic Publishers.

Sanders, W. L., & Horn, S. P. (1994). The Tennessee value-added assessment system (TVASS): Mixed-model methodology in educational assessment. *Journal of Personal Evaluation, 8*, 299–311.

Shadish, W. R., Cook, T. D., & Leviton, L. C. (1991). *Foundations of program evaluation*. Newberry Park, Calif.: Sage Publications.

Shepard, L. A. (1990). Inflated test score gains: Is the problem old norms or teaching to the test? *Educational Measurement: Issues and Practice, 9*(3), 15–22.

Snyder, R. A., Raben, C. S., & Farr, J. L. (1980). A model for the systematic evaluation of human resource development programs. *Academy of Management Review, 5*(3), 431–444.

Stigler, J. W., & Hiebert, J. (1997). Understanding and improving classroom mathematics instruction: An overview of the TIMSS video study. *Phi Delta Kappan, 79*(1), 14–21.

Toch, T. (18 Jan. 1999). Outstanding high schools. *U.S. News & World Report*, 1–5.

Tucker, M. S., & Codding, J. B. (1998). *Standards for our schools: How to set them, measure them, and reach them*. San Francisco, Calif.: Jossey-Bass.

Wise, L. L. (1996). A persistence model of motivation and test performance. Paper presented at the annual meeting of the American Educational Research Association, New York.

Wise, L. L., Chia, W. J., & Park, R. K. (1989). Effects of item position on IRT parameter estimates and item statistics. Paper presented at the Annual Meeting of the American Educational Research Association, San Francisco, Calif.

Wise, L. L., Hauser, R. M., Mitchell, K. J., & Feuer, M. J. (1999). *Evaluation of the Voluntary National Tests, phase 1*. Washington, D.C.: National Academy Press.

Wise, L. L., Hoffman, R. G., & Harris, C. D. (2000). *Evaluation of the California High School Exit Examination: Evaluation plan*. Alexandria, Va.: Human Resources Research Organization.

Wise, L. L., McCloy, R. A., & Quartetti, D. A. (1998). *Indicators of student effort on the National Assessment of Educational Progress*. (HumRRO Draft Final Report DFR-EADD-98-58). Alexandria, Va.: Human Resources Research Organization.

Wise, L. L., Noeth, R. J., & Koenig, J. A., eds. (1999). *Evaluation of the Voluntary National Tests, year 2*. Washington, D.C.: National Academy Press.

Wolfe, L. F., Smith, J. K., & Birnbaum, M. E. (1995). The consequence of performance, test motivation, and mentally taxing items. *Applied Measurement in Education, 8*, 227–242.

9

How Will We Gather the Data We Need to Inform Policy Makers?

EDWARD D. ROEBER

Advanced Systems in Measurement and Evaluation

At the present time, almost every state has developed content and performance standards, and virtually every state has some form of statewide assessment program. Several states have multiple assessment programs, and it is not unheard of for students to participate in a state-run assessment program every year of their schooling. These efforts are in addition to local assessments that districts choose to administer. These statewide assessment programs serve several purposes, not the least of which is to satisfy the needs of policy makers for data that they need for decision making and to satisfy the policy makers' desires to supply others, such as parents and educators, with information they need in order to improve student learning. The amount of large-scale assessment activity at the state level has expanded rapidly over the past two decades, but local assessment has not diminished.

The impetus for developing standards and assessments came from standards developed at the national level by national curriculum groups, but the development of standards became a movement as a result of policy makers at the national and state levels realizing the power of standards-based educational reform. These policy makers realized that the standards provide the benchmarks for schools to strive to achieve and that assessments provide information on how close schools are coming to achieving the targets, as well as how far schools need to go to achieve success. Assessment has become the means of notifying schools about what is considered important, where they currently stand relative to the standards, and whether school reform efforts are paying off in terms of higher student achievement. The relative low cost (at least in comparison to serious attempts to achieve school reform through intensive, statewide professional development for educators, for example) makes testing the inexpensive approach to school reform. This is why testing has grown in popularity among policy makers.

Unfortunately, local school systems have by and large been left out of this work, so that as the state assessments have been developed and implemented, they come in conflict with the standards being addressed (which range from the standards addressed in textbooks, off-the-shelf tests, local curricula, or teacher preferences) and the tests that are given to students (whether district-level testing programs or classroom-based tests) at the local level. However, local educators ignore the state-assessed standards at their own peril, teach to multiple sets of standards (at the students' peril), or teach to the state's test (at the educators' and the students' peril). None of these are constructive approaches. The tool intended by policy makers to promote school reform may instead become a barrier to of constructive, long-term improvement of schools and student learning.

The interest in standards-based reform driven by assessment resulted in the adoption of legislation at the state level calling for new or revised standards and assessments, as well as federal legislation such as Goals 2000 and the reauthorization of Title I. These efforts provide a unique opportunity for states and local districts to work together to develop assessments for different levels of the educational system that provide a more complete picture of student performance and that can be used to help students learn at high levels.

This paper discusses an approach to gathering the data that policy makers *will* need in the future. It is an approach that states and local districts might use to develop an assessment system coordinated so that the information collected at the state and local levels is complementary, not redundant nor unintentionally conflicting. The purpose is not to show how to collect more data, or more sophisticated information (since policy makers have shown considerable skill on their own at placing increasing assessments and other data collection requirements on states and local school systems), but to suggest ways in which the data needs of policy makers and their requirements for collection of data to be used by others can be met in constructive ways that will better serve to improve schools. Coordinated assessment systems will be defined, some reasons why such coordination is both feasible and desirable will be described, and ways in which coordinated assessment systems could be created will be suggested. Strategies with which states could work to create such systems from the outset will also be suggested. Of course, many states and local districts have systems already in place that were not created in the manner described here, so this paper will also describe how to retrofit coordination of state and local standards and assessments to existing state and local standards and assessment systems. The suggestions made here can serve as a model for states and their local districts to strive for while using their existing standards and assessments.

The Data Policy Makers Are Presently Getting

Policy makers at the state level (governors, chief state school officers, state boards of education, and state legislators and their staffs) or local level (local boards of education) want information on the effectiveness of schooling and the steps educators are taking to improve the quality of education overall and for subgroups of students. Discussions with these policy makers often reveal that they are less concerned about receiving this information directly and more interested in persons in positions to affect the quality of education (i.e., superintendents, principals, and teachers) receiving it so that they can make the necessary changes to bring about improved student learning.

Policy makers believe in student assessment for several reasons. First, student assessment identifies the important targets for educators and the public. Assessments by definition assess something, and that something (such as content standards) needs to be publicly identified so that schools can be encouraged to teach it and students can be encouraged to learn it.

Second, policy makers see that the state assessment gathers information that can help inform them and others about the quality of schooling. Which schools or districts do the best? The worst? Which schools are improving (or declining) in performance? Why? What can be done to improve the quality and quantity of student learning? Assessments, and the performance standards needed to interpret the assessment information, help to define "how good is good enough" so that everyone can judge the effectiveness of schools.

Third, policy makers see student assessment as the stick or the carrot to encourage/force schools to change and to improve. The stakes associated with the state assessment program help to define the extent of the "encouragement" and who the recipients of this "encouragement" are. Not only do state assessment programs gather and report data that pressures students and educators but, increasingly, states are adopting school accountability systems that include this student achievement data and other information about schools that may have either positive and/or negative consequences for local educators as well. Pressure has been ratcheted up. Indeed, in one recent action, a major city's school board declined to hire a candidate for the position of superintendent due to the failure of that candidate to bring about improvements in test scores in his current position. Of course, failure to bring about improved test scores can also be the grounds for dismissing administrators.

Finally, policy makers see that the annual information collected in the assessment program provides them with a convenient method for monitoring the efforts of local school systems to improve. The programs help them answer the questions about where schools have improved substantially, where improvement has not occurred, and which schools are doing worse today than in the past.

With all of these "advantages" to statewide assessment programs, is it no wonder that states continue to add new components to their overall assessment efforts, and that the added or revised assessments carry increased stakes or use more rigorous assessments of higher-level content standards? Surveys of state assessment programs such as the annual surveys conducted by the Council of Chief State School Officers reveal that more and more student assessment is taking place, that the stakes associated with these programs continue to be raised (with many other states exploring whether to do so), that the public is increasingly interested in the quality of schools, and that the number of subject areas and grade levels assessed continues to grow. "If the process works, lets have more" seems to be the philosophy.

However, all is not rosy with this scenario.

What's Wrong with This Picture?

Unfortunately, the proliferation of assessments at the state level has also had several negative consequences. As noted earlier, the number of states that have a state assessment program has been growing over the past 20 years. By 2000, only two states did not have statewide programs, but one of those was working on it and the other was using a collaborative local school approach to develop local assessments in place of a state-run program. Over the same period, the stakes for students have risen slowly but surely each year. Over 22 states use state tests to award, deny, or endorse high school diplomas. Questions continue to be raised about the adequacy of students' opportunities to learn, particularly those of poor and minority students. Basic fairness has been challenged.

A growing movement among states is the annual assessment of students for use in promotion decisions. Students are pressured to pass exams so that they can be promoted from one grade to another, sometimes without having received an adequate opportunity to learn the material covered by the assessments. At the high school level, end-of-course exams used in several states may determine grades achieved in school. The results of these assessments are also used to hold teachers accountable for improvements in achievement.

As mentioned earlier, both the increasing number of state assessment components and the tendency to use the results (either directly or through state accountability systems) to place pressure on schools to improve has increased pressure on educators even more than on students. The administration of state assessments is an important time in the life of a school, because the performance of the students can mean public favor or disfavor, whether school leaders keep their jobs, and whether schools receive the financial and other support they need to provide education to students. The stakes have increased dramatically! The pressure of assessments on educators may skew the instructional program so that an inordinate amount of time is spent in preparing students to take the assessments rather than in teaching material that would have a more enduring value than passing an assessment. The threat of doing poorly on the assessment may cause some educators to implement programs of dubious quality to prepare students to do well. These same pressures may also lead less ethical educators to cheat in order to artificially raise test scores. The result is that students are cheated out of opportunities for learning so that the school can look good publicly. Local educators complain that state assessments are imposed on top of the standards they consider to be important, and, as a result, they are forced to stop teaching the content they believe students need and teach to the test, at least long enough so that students pass the assessments. Or, they must teach what the state considers to be important as well as what they value, thereby risking an uncoordinated approach to instruction.

Backlash against state efforts to define and enforce a set of standards external to the school system through state assessment programs has grown in recent years. In fact, at this time there is a strong and rising chorus of protest against state testing programs. Students, parents, educators, and other citizens are uniting to protest against assessment programs and some particular uses of them in states such as Michigan, Minnesota, Massachusetts, and Texas. It is too soon to say whether these largely unorganized protests will amount to much, or whether they will cause changes in the states' assessment programs. However, these protests highlight problems with current accountability and assessment models, problems that need to be addressed if the positive power of assessment is to be realized. The goals of policy makers in establishing state assessment programs will be lost unless the causes of this growing backlash are addressed.

Why Are There Problems?

The reality of local curricula and instructional programs is that instruction provided locally is too often a patchwork of what the textbook, the off-the-shelf tests, the local curriculum committee, the building principal, and, mainly, individual classroom teachers feel are important. The pressures to standardize teaching that the state content standards and state assessments might bring are imposed on this crazy quilt of a disjointed, uncoordinated system of providing instruction to students. Local educators often do not seek to provide a consistent, articulated program of instruction to students based on standards important to their continued intellectual growth. Rarely are teachers encouraged to coordinate among themselves what is taught to students across grade levels within a school, much less across different levels of schooling. This is most evident when local educators examine why students did poorly on state (or local) assessments. The most frequent reason why students do poorly is that they have not been taught the skills assessed (or the precursor skills needed), in spite of the fact that teachers report that the skills are important and should be learned. In this situation, the potential power or opportunity for standards created by the state to set a common agenda for teaching is lost, both because of the decentralized process of determining what is taught and a general perception by local educators that they are being forced or coerced into teaching what they do not value.

Although states have used committees of local educators and content specialists to develop the content standards that are the basis of the state assessment programs, these committees are not truly representative of local school systems. A process of building local support and buy-in is rarely engaged in, so that most local educators do not support the imposition of external standards. Indeed, the content-area committees, which may be made up of zealots in the content area, may create standards as an impetus for setting high, even unattainable goals for schools with the aim of using the state assessment program to force local educators to change. They, just like the policy makers, see the power of state assessment programs to create change. They want to "force" schools to teach what they value, and they create "challenging" content standards so that the assessments will bring this about.

Questions also continue to be raised about whether increases in test scores reflect true changes in student achievement or whether they represent merely more sophisticated test taking or the impact of efforts to artificially raise test scores without changing underlying student achievement. Some parents, some educators, and even some policy makers have raised questions about the impacts of the state assessment programs and whether these programs cause more harm than good. These critics imply that rather than causing improvements in the educational system, assessments may cause inferior instruction and lower student achievement (at least on outcomes of schooling they deem more important than those assessed in the tests), as well as increase pressure on students to perform on assessments for which they have not been adequately prepared.

In sum, what is wrong with this picture is that state assessments are increasingly being imposed on local educators, who resent the pressures that such examinations bring yet bow to the pressures to prepare students and avoid negative consequences. Although many disdain the types of assessments being used and the ways they feel these programs distort the system, they are pragmatic (or fearful) enough to stop doing what they consider to be important and teach to the skills assessed if not the assessment itself. The goals that policy makers set when creating these assessment programs, however, are not being met. Although they have caused the setting of public targets for schools, these targets are not embraced by local educators. In many schools, they have not brought about a systematic improvement in schooling, and questions have even been raised about the nature of the gains in student performance that such assessments have yielded.

Now is an opportune time to stop and ask the question: How *will* we *better* gather the information we need to inform policy makers? Can we design a better system that not only meets the information needs of policy makers (and their desire to provide others with the information needed to improve the instructional system and increase student learning) but also provides a more appropriate school improvement model for educators, another important need for policy makers? The answer is yes. A coordinated, comprehensive assessment system is needed at the state and the local level.

The Coordinated, Comprehensive Assessment System

Several basic elements of a coordinated assessment plan need explanation. First, what is meant by a "coordinated" assessment system? Second, what are the purposes for assessment, and can these be met with one assessment program? What are the information needs at different levels? Are the purposes of assessment the same at the state and local levels? How do the types of assessment exercises used fit into the coordinated assessment system? States and local districts will have different options when starting from scratch than when one or both levels has already developed standards and assessments and coordination of the results is desired. How can such coordination be retrofitted?

An essential element in designing state and local student assessments is how the assessment program(s) at one level "fit" together with other assessments in use or development to make up an overall *coordinated*, comprehensive system of assessments. This is important because it is usually difficult or impossible to use one assessment instrument for multiple purposes (whether it is one program at the state level or a program implemented by local school districts). None of the intended purposes may be well served if it is not considered. What is meant by the terms *coordinated* and *system?* A coordinated set of assessments is defined as assessments used at different levels of the educational system that are designed or selected to fit together to provide a more complete picture of student achievement than any one assessment could provide alone. They are intentionally selected to work together to provide a multiple-measures approach to assessing students, looking at students' performance from several perspectives in order to gain a better understanding of what they know and can do and providing more assurance that their level of performance is real. The assessments "fit" because they measure the same set(s) of skills. That is, somehow the state has developed content standards that both the state and local school systems agree are important and should be taught to. Ideally, this agreement is made before the assessment is developed, so that the "agreement" is not based on fear of the consequences of failing to agree about the common standards (e.g., my students will perform poorly and I will lose my job), but on a consensus that the standards represent what is important for students.

A system of assessments means a group of assessments of a *different nature or type*, that are selected to complement one another and that measure the same skills but from different perspectives. This helps to meet the "multiple-measures" provision of Title I, but more important, assesses students from more than one perspective. The assessment system may be more messy, but it is more accurate, not in the sense that there is absolute agreement (redundancy) among the different measures, but that the picture the combined set of assessments provides is more complete.

Under a coordinated system, duplicative data collection (e.g., the collection of the same information using the same type of assessments, such as the use of two norm-referenced assessments, one at the state level and another at the local level) is also eliminated even though multiple sources of information are used (e.g., a test at the state level and a portfolio assessment process locally, which includes the test score as one measure). Different formats for assessment are used to create a composite of student and school information to better inform the decision being made, especially important decisions about students, schools, or instructional programs. For example, a high school graduation decision might be based on the combination of a state test, a local assessment that utilizes portfolios, and grade-point average.

State and local assessment systems built in tandem, based on a common set of content standards so that the skills assessed are related, with different assessment tools used at different levels (each well suited for its intended purpose), could work together to provide a more complete and coordinated picture of student and school program performance. When assessment systems have already been developed at the state and/or local levels, coordination could occur in one of two ways. The assessment system at one level (e.g., the state level) could be used by the other level (e.g., local school districts) as the basis for revision. Alternatively, the two levels could look for commonalties among the standards and assessments and strive to report information derived from assessments of these common standards. Either approach begins the process of coordination, which can be furthered once the standards at one or both levels are revised.

Rationale for a Coordinated Assessment System

Coordinated assessment *systems* make sense because they may reduce the collection of unintentionally redundant information, use resources available for assessment to collect information most useful for decisions at each educational level, and serve to reduce the number of "mixed messages" that policy makers and the public receive about "what is important." When retrofitting state and local-level assessments, the participants could identify existing commonalties among the standards at all levels so that common assessment information and instruction can be emphasized. By developing one set of content standards agreed upon by educators across the state at all levels, along with appropriate curricula and instructional strategies, the likelihood that students are taught the important skills is also increased. Because states and even local school districts have little ability to dictate what gets taught or learned in individual classrooms, a system of uncoordinated standards and assessments increases the probability that different students will learn different knowledge and skills and that, perhaps, the students with the greatest educational needs, the students being served by compensatory education programs, will not be taught under content standards as rigorous as those used for other students.

Purposes for Assessment

There are several purposes for large-scale assessment at the state or local levels. For example, student assessment is viewed as the means of setting higher, more rigorous standards for student learning, focusing staff development efforts for teachers, encouraging curriculum reform, and improving instruction and instructional materials in a variety of subject matters and disciplines. Assessment may also serve to hold schools accountable for whether these reforms have occurred and have been effective. Large-scale assessment has been a key policy tool in the attempt to effect change in the nation's schools. However, what we have learned over the past decade is that assessment programs that feature accountability for performance as a key purpose are often unable to fulfill the equally popular purpose of improving instruction. This is because accountability measures administered at the state level tend not to provide detailed information to teachers on a timely basis nor to assess students in a fashion most related to day-to-day instruction.

One response to these issues regarding statewide assessments has been to develop teacher-based assessments in the hope that while providing more valuable information to teachers, they could also be used to provide system accountability information at the school, district, and state levels. This upward aggregation is possible, and there have been a couple of instances where it has been planned or has taken place, but the types of assessments that are most useful to teachers do not often produce the public credibility demanded of accountability assessments, because they are often developed, administered, and scored by individual classroom teachers. There are concerns about whether the pressure of accountability would corrupt the trustworthiness and value of such information to teachers. Clearly, the purposes for assessment may differ at different levels of the educational system, and trying to fulfill multiple purposes with one measure may compromise all uses of the instrument.

Another way to view this is depicted in Table 9.1, which shows purposes for assessment that are much more likely to occur at the national or state levels than at the classroom or school levels. Monitoring school and district performance is a purpose often ascribed to state assessment programs. Another equally valued purpose is the improvement of individual student's educational programs. Because state assessment programs can efficiently collect information across all students at a grade level, they are ideally suited to fulfill the accountability or monitoring purpose. Yet, while any data set *could* be used to help individual students learn, it is less likely that such information will be helpful to classroom teachers than information collected much closer to the classroom.

Hence, if the purpose for assessment is to help improve individual student learning, some type of assessment established at the local level is needed; if the purpose is to hold schools accountable for improving all students' performance, then some form of statewide assessment is needed. One practical implication of this idea is that a statewide assessment program may not be the most efficient or effective means of accomplishing all assessment information needs. Nor is it likely that classroom assessment, as valuable as it is for accomplishing certain needs, will be effective in meeting all assessment purposes. For the assessment system not to send disjointed, conflicting messages, however, the assessments used at these different levels ought to be measuring the same or related content standards. A more complete description of the various purposes for assessment is contained in Appendix A.

TABLE 9.1   Assessment Purposes at Different Levels of Education

			Purposes for Assessment				
Education Level	*Monitor*	*Accountability*	*Improve Student Performance*	*Allocate Resources*	*Selection/ Placement*	*Certification*	*Program Evaluation*
National	XXX	X		X		X	
State	XXX	XXX	X	XX		XXX	X
District	XX	XXX	XX	XX	XX	XX	XX
School	X	XX	XXX	X	XXX	X	XX
Classroom		X	XXX		XX	X	X
Student		X	XXX		X	X	X

Note: Each X indicates the levels at which each type of assessment might be used most efficiently. Multiple Xs indicate the strength of appropriateness of the assessment purpose at each educational level.

Achievement Information Needed at Different Levels

It is important to consider the information about student achievement needed by different individuals. Certainly, the information needs of the parent are different from those of the teacher. The parent wants to know what the student can and cannot do and whether this is comparable to other students, while the teacher is more concerned with what the student's strengths are (what aspects of the learning task has the student accomplished) and what additional work is needed. These information needs are different from those of the building principal, who needs to know if achievement in the school is comparable to that elsewhere and, more broadly, whether students are learning what they need to learn. The principal also wants to know whether student achievement is improving. At the district level, the concern may be whether achievement needs are greater in mathematics than in reading, to decide whether to allocate additional resources (extra staff and additional instructional materials) for mathematics instruction. At the state level, the concern is often whether there is equity in school programs and whether differences in student performance are due to the lack of resources in some schools. Issues of funding, incentive programs for improving in key areas such as mathematics, staff training, and so forth are discussed on a statewide level. Underlying these discussions is a concern about whether the students in the state are economically competitive in a manner comparable with other states and other nations. This competitive concern also permeates discussions at the national level. Although national policy makers are concerned about differences among states, as well as among types of school systems, the underlying worry is about how much American students are learning in comparison to their peers in other countries, particularly those who are our trading partners.

These information needs, which may be very different at each level from the classroom to the national level, often form the basis for assessment design. In top-down models of assessment systems, assessments that meet the needs of policy makers at the state or national levels are developed and implemented. We presume that such data may be useful for other purposes, so we try to convince others, such as building principals, teachers, and parents, that the information will meet their needs as well. An alternative is to build the assessment system that teachers, parents, and students need and presume that the concerns of users at the district, state, and national levels can be answered just by aggregating the types of assessments used in the classroom. In a coordinated assessment system, both the top-down and bottom-up approaches are used, thereby meeting the informational needs of policy makers at the state and national levels as well as the instruction-related needs of local school administrators, teachers, and parents.

Assessment Formats

During the past several years, as the nation has become increasingly concerned about the skills that the nation's students possess or should acquire, an essential element of the discussion of the standards which students should meet is the format for assessment used in this country. Unlike other countries, the United States relies almost exclusively on the multiple-choice test as the means of assessing student performance. Critics indicate that such assessments tend to stress basic knowledge types of skills and so encourage teachers to stress memorization of content rather than the use of content to solve meaningful problems.

Various content-area groups have defined what they view as important and how schools should be teaching these outcomes. An element common to these subject-matter groups is their deemphasis of content knowledge and growing emphasis on application and use of content, even to the point of advocating not teaching certain content. This, of course, has caused heated public debate, such as recently occurred in mathematics (i.e., just how much attention should be paid to arithmetical operations versus problem solving). It is this growing shift in student outcomes that leads some at the national, state, and local levels to urge new means of assessing student performance. Emerging techniques for assessing students, such as the use of portfolios, performance tasks (projects, exhibitions, demonstrations), performance events (individual or group performance assessments and hands-on assessments), and constructed-response exercises are increasingly viewed as more appropriate and more directly tied to instruction. It is ironic that these techniques plus others (such as use of anecdotal records, observation, structured interviews, and others) that are widely viewed as more suited for classroom-level assessment, are emerging as potential strategies to be used in large-scale assessment programs. In recent years, however, questions have been raised about the feasibility of using such innovative assessment strategies on a widespread basis. Issues of assessment time, generalizability, quality and breadth of resulting information, and financial cost have emerged as major impediments to the adoption of performance assessment in many large-scale assessment programs. Policy makers and others have come to view these instructional-related assessment strategies as the ones to use for assessment programs tied to instructional improvement.

Each of these types of assessment may be more useful or may be more feasible (due to cost, time, and the availability of the information) at different levels of the educational system. Table 9.2 illustrates this point. More information about assessment formats is provided in Appendix B.

TABLE 9.2   Effective Use of Assessment Strategies at Different Education Levels

	Types of Assessment Exercises					
Education Level	*Selected Response*	*Short Constructed Response*	*Extended Constructed Response*	*Performance Events*	*Performance Tasks*	*Portfolio*
National	XXX	XX	X			
State	XXX	XX	XX	X		X
District	XXX	XXX	XX	XX	X	XX
School	XX	XXX	XXX	XX	XX	XXX
Classroom	XX	XXX	XXX	XXX	XXX	XXX

Note: Each X indicates the levels at which each type of assessment might be used most efficiently. Multiple Xs indicate the strength of the utility/practicality of the assessment method at each level.

Summary

As policy makers, assessment specialists, and curriculum specialists look to design the rational and comprehensive assessment system needed by this country at the state and local levels, important elements of this discussion should include what skills are most critical, how these will be learned, and what assessments will most inform and lead students to this learning. What are the assessment designs most appropriate for the states and for local districts, and should these designs focus on assessment procedures traditionally used in large-scale programs or assessment strategies that have been used predominantly at the classroom and school level or both? Finally, the discussion should also focus on what a coordinated assessment system might look like and how we could achieve such a system.

An Example of a Coordinated Assessment System

This section will present the ideal, start-from-scratch model of a coordinated assessment system as well as suggestions for how this ideal model can be approximated when retrofitting the ideal onto existing standards and assessments.

Each of the 48 states that have some form of large-scale assessment program have a different configuration of grades and subject areas assessed, different forms of assessment, and, in some cases, multiple forms of assessment. Therefore, the manner in which each state could develop a coordinated assessment system would undoubtedly be different. The following example illustrates what such a system could look like and how it could be developed; it is *not* intended to serve as the only model of a coordinated assessment system.

A. First, the state selects a state coordination team to democratically represent the state. The large-city school is automatically represented by three persons, the middle-sized school districts receive four slots, and the rural districts are represented by five persons. This twelve-member committee determines the content standards to be addressed by the statewide and district assessment program. The state coordination team also determines the types of assessments to be developed at the state level and the local level, in the overall assessment development project.

B. The state, working through the state coordination teams, develops a set of content standards in several content areas: mathematics, reading/writing, science, social studies (with particular emphasis on history, geography, and civics), health education, physical education, the arts, and world languages. The coordination teams help to ensure local district input into the development of the state content standards. Because they have had input into the state's standards, many school districts adopt the state standards as their own.

Each time the state coordination team completes a meeting, the draft standards are shared among the constituent school systems. The rural representatives, for example, are responsible for sharing the draft standards with the local school systems they represent and obtaining school-level input on the standards. These representatives then compile the feedback from local schools, reconcile (or simply represent) conflicting testimony, and present this information at subsequent meetings of the state coordination team.

C. In each content area, the state coordination team develops an assessment blueprint that describes the manner in which the content standards are to be assessed, at the state, local district, and classroom levels. The assessment blueprint is also developed with local school districts so that the types of assessments created will be effective at both the local and state levels and will provide a coordinated picture of student achievement.

Each time the state coordination team completes a meeting, the draft blueprint is shared among the constituent school systems. That is, the representatives are responsible for sharing the draft standards with the local school systems they represent and obtaining school-level input on the blueprint. These representatives then compile the feedback from local schools, reconcile (or simply represent) conflicting testimony, and present this information at subsequent meetings of the state coordination team.

D. The state selects the areas of mathematics, reading/writing, and science for statewide assessment. The assessments are to be administered in grades 4, 8, and 10. The purpose of the assessments is primarily to hold schools accountable for student performance. The results are reported to parents, teachers, schools, and school districts shortly following the assessments, which are conducted in the fall.

E. The state creates the assessments that will be used for the grade 4, 8, and 10 statewide assessment program. The state chooses multiple-choice and constructed-response formats for the statewide assessment. The state coordination team oversees the work of the education department and the assessment contractor to ensure that the assessments match the content standards and fulfill the purposes of the overall state assessment system.

F. The state also creates assessments (portfolio assessments, performance events, performance tasks, plus more conventional selected-response and open-ended assessments) for use in grades 4, 8, and 10, as well in the "off-grades," throughout the school year. The purpose of these assessments is to provide information to teachers to improve the learning of individual students as well as group information to improve the instructional program at the school and classroom levels.

Although these assessments are to be used by local school districts, the state takes the responsibility of seeing that the assessments are created, validated, and distributed across the state. As part of this process, the state administers the assessments to a sample of students statewide at each grade level, K–12, develops scoring rubrics and training materials for each open-ended or performance measure, and prepares the materials for distribution to school districts.

G. Once the assessments are created, they are tried out in a representative set of classrooms around the state. The results of the assessment are used in several ways: to refine the assessments themselves, to refine the assessment administration directions, to revise and expand the scoring rubrics using actual samples of student work, and to revise the tentative performance standards.

H. For each area in which the state has created content standards, the state coordination team also creates performance standards. These performance standards are created so that the assessments at the local and state levels can be used to judge the performance of students and schools.

I. For each area in which the state has created content standards, the state coordination team also develops a comprehensive professional development program (the strategies and the materials) to ensure that all local educators are able to address the content standards to help students achieve a high level. This professional development effort consists of awareness-level information about the content standards in each subject area as well as guided practice in teaching the content standards in a standards-based classroom. This program assists teachers in addressing the standards in a manner that maximizes the likelihood they will use the assessment strategies created for use at the local level.

J. The state provides ongoing information and professional development opportunities to all local school districts. The assessment information collected by classroom teachers is summarized at the building level. In addition, the district and school summaries from the state assessment information are added to the classroom-level information to provide a more complete picture of student achievement.

At every step along the way in developing the coordinated assessment system, the state coordination team guides the development, pilot testing, and implementation of the state–local assessment programs. They not only advise the state but gather input from local schools and inform local schools about the emerging consensus on standards, assessment, instruction, and professional development. The goal of the state coordination team is to ensure that as many actual classroom teachers in the content area across the state as possible are involved in the development and refinement of the assessment system. The more individuals involved, the greater the acceptance of the system once it is fully developed.

Developing the Coordinated Assessment System

How Should the Assessment System Be Developed? Top-Down or Bottom-Up?

How the assessment system should be developed, top-down from the state to local school district or bottom-up from the school or district level to the state, should be determined. Information gathered at the classroom level can be aggregated upwards, but is it the most cost-effective instrumentation to answer the questions posed by state-level policy makers concerned about the performance of school systems within the state? The portfolio of work that would be much more effective for a classroom teacher may not be cost-effective or credible in answering state-level questions. Assessment that answers the questions of policy makers at the state level probably won't to inform classroom teachers effectively about the learning of individual students. Given the different information needs at different levels of the educational system, plus the variety of reasons why assessment takes place and the various tools available, is it any wonder that one instrument imposed at all levels will not meet all the needs and purposes for assessment?

What is needed is both a top-down and bottom-up approach to assessment development, with parties from each level involved in the assessment design, as mentioned earlier.

Within the ideal assessment system, some data will be collected at the national and state levels, some at the state and school district levels, some at the school district and building levels, some at the school and classroom levels, some at the classroom and student levels, and some only at the student level so it is important that representatives of the different levels in the assessment system be involved in the assessment system design process. The ideal coordinated assessment system is one that has identified the various audiences for assessment information, the types of information that each audience needs (keeping in mind that each audience may need more than one type of information), the type(s) of instrument that best meets the assessment needs, the impact of the use of the instrument on the educational system, and the levels at which to use the instruments.

The discussion of a coordinated, comprehensive assessment system, as described in this paper, has been somewhat theoretical up to this point. This section describes the process of developing the standards and assessments in a coordinated manner. The implication that the reader might draw from this discussion is that unless this process is followed precisely, coordination of state and local assessments is impossible. This is not the intent of this paper, nor is it the intent to imply that current efforts to reform teaching or assessment are not adequate. Obviously, states and local districts already have testing or assessment programs in place, and many have created standards or frameworks to guide instruction or assessment. Some local districts have built standards to amplify and extend state standards and have constructed assessments to complement those used at the state level. In this fashion, useful coordination has been achieved, although it did not occur simultaneously. Other states have delegated the development of standards or assessments to local districts, and districts are well along in creating the rigorous standards and assessments needed to improve education. States and local districts that have carried out these activities should receive recognition for their efforts. The ideas presented here are meant to suggest ways in which states and local school districts could *better* coordinate their standards and assessment efforts. There is no implication that all assessments developed without coordinated effort are inappropriate nor that such assessments need to be scrapped. By presenting the information from a more theoretical point of view, it is hoped that as such assessment systems are revised in the future, some of the ideas presented here can be implemented.

Process of Coordination

To develop a coordinated, comprehensive assessment system, several steps must be taken. The *process* by which these are accomplished is important. For the system to be coordinated across levels of the educational system, the individuals responsible for education at the different levels must be adequately represented in the decision-making process to be described next. This means that policy makers, curriculum and assessment experts, and practitioners from each level will need to be actively involved in each step of the development process.

The first step in the process is to determine at which levels coordination is desired. Is state and local district coordination to be accomplished, or are individual school or national efforts to be coordinated as well? Will the state take the lead in developing standards and assessments with local districts expected to expand upon these for local use, or are local districts expected to take the lead and the state serve to coordinate the standards and assessments developed within individual school districts? If the state takes the lead, school districts will also have to attend to inclusive procedures for the development of standards and assessments at the district and school levels.

The second step is to establish teams that will encourage the types of buy-in that this process is set up to encourage. Although states typically include local educators on teams that develop standards or assessments, the inclusion of individual teachers or curriculum specialists in these efforts does not encourage the school districts or schools they are employed by to value the state frameworks or assessments they help to create. Instead, a process of inclusion of teams from districts and schools (if school-level coordination is desired) is needed. However, there are usually so many school districts within a state that any team made up of even one person per school district would be overwhelmingly large in size. How could such a team be set up to function effectively? The process to be described shows what states should do, but local school districts will also need to attend to the manner in which the district organizes to include school-level representation on district teams.

One way to ensure representation, yet keep the working groups' size manageable, is to use representative committees and to encourage iterative reviews to be carried out by the representatives at the state level and the individuals they represent at the district level. At the state level, a *state coordination team* is needed, with representatives either drawn directly from individual school districts (perhaps more appropriate for the largest school districts in the state) or selected to represent groups of school districts (selected either by size of school district or region of the state).

At the district level, a *district coordination team* should be established. For smaller districts, such coordination teams could be made up out of multiple school districts. For example, it is not necessary to have every suburban district represented on a state committee to know what such school districts think an assessment framework should contain. A few representatives to the state committee, selected by the suburban districts, could represent the suburban districts, particularly if given the opportunity and encouragement to share drafts with all of the districts that they represent. If school-level coordination is desired, then the district-level representatives could be encouraged to share the drafts with school-level representatives. In either case, feedback from the districts or schools could be brought back to the state coordination team from the local level.

The model described here will work whether the expectation is for the state to take the lead and local districts to coordinate their efforts with the state, or local districts to take the lead (working independently of one another) and the state serve to coordinate these independent developmental projects. The difference will be in the flow of information (from the state to local districts, with feedback returned to the state, or from local school districts to the state, with feedback flowing back to the local districts). When attempting to retrofit locally developed systems with one another and with the state's, the flow of information may be in both directions. The suggestions that follow describe an ideal system, but they can also apply to these two other models of developing an assessment system.

As documents are completed in draft form (and subsequently revised), they could be transmitted to all school districts (which, in turn, could be encouraged to copy them and send them to all school buildings) for a formal review by district-level (and school-level) teams. The result will be comments from these teams that can be used in reshaping the documents being examined, be they assessment frameworks, assessment blueprints, draft assessments, and so forth. In the case of secure materials, such reviews could be carried out through regional meetings run by the state for the local districts in each region. In an ideal process, after drafts had been sent to local school districts for review at both the district and school levels, the representatives on the state coordination team would convene a meeting of these school systems to hear in person what the reactions are to the draft material. Such a meeting would assist the representatives to understand the advice of local educators and allow them to pose and attempt to reconcile differences in their advice.

If this process is carried out in a thoughtful manner, and the resulting ideas are used to redraft the materials, then it should be possible for coordination to begin to occur, since educators at each level will have the opportunity to determine similarity of assessment purposes, design, and instrumentation and to provide feedback to one another to reduce redundancy and increase the collection of complementary information.

Developmental Steps

If the mechanism for coordination can be implemented, how will the coordinated assessment system be developed? The process may not be too dissimilar from that used in the development of a statewide assessment system. For example, the content standards may be developed first. Second, the assessment blueprint could be written, including assessment purpose(s), types of assessments to be used, and the development, review, tryout, and revision process to be implemented. Finally, the performance standards might be written for how individual student and system performance (at the school, district, and state levels) will be measured. In other models, the performance standards might be developed first along with the content standards, with the design of the assessment instrument following both of these (with the performance standards "verified" once the assessment is piloted). In any case, each of these activities needs to be carried out in a coordinated manner, regardless of which is developed first, second, or last.

A. State and Local Content Standards Coordination.   The development of a coordinated, comprehensive assessment system, combining assessments at the state and local levels, or retrofitting existing assessments and standards at the state and local levels, begins with the development of a coordinated set of content standards that is suitable for use at both the state and local levels (or identification of the commonalities among existing sets of standards). At the state level, content standards set an overall direction for education within the state as well as serve as the framework for holding schools accountable for student performance. At the local level, content standards serve as the framework for curriculum and instruction that should be implemented at the classroom level. The two purposes can be met with one set of standards. Even in states where local districts are expected to develop standards that meet or exceed those of the state, it may be useful and necessary for the state to create a set of standards to be used for district-to-district coordination. Or one set of local districts' standards might be selected to serve as the set around which to seek coordination, or the state and local districts could develop a consensus framework drawn from common standards at both levels. A third alternative is to develop a consensus about what the important concepts are across the local school systems.

Where state content standards already exist, local districts can amplify and extend them for use at the local level. State standards may be few in number, and local districts may need to expand upon these to provide a curriculum framework for guiding instruction (and assessment) at every grade level. Districts can do this work either alone or with other districts.

In any case, it is possible to develop a set of consistent standards with different levels of specificity. Typically, at the state level a set of content standards are quite general. At the district level, each of these general standards may be broken down into several subskills or benchmarks useful in curriculum planning. At the classroom level, each of these may be further broken down into additional subskills for use in planning instruction. Hence, it is feasible to develop an assessment program that draws on the overall standards document and simultaneously to create curriculum and instructional frameworks based on the same overall set of standards but identifying the specific subskills necessary. In addition, the bases for assessment at each level could be the different levels of skill definitions contained within the same set of content standards.

The process of development needs to include local school districts in the fashion described earlier in order to achieve "buy-in" to the resulting standards (regardless of which level takes the lead). As the development process unfolds, the state–local committees can foster a two-way communication process, providing input from local districts into the format and content of the standards as well as ongoing feedback to work under development. Once the final draft of the standards has been completed at the state level, two types of reviews could be invited. First, the draft content standards could be shared with professional organizations for *organizational* input. Second, the draft standards could be shared with all, or a representative sample of, school districts within the state, which would elicit *district* input to the standards (and, secondarily, build even stronger district commitment to the standards).

An additional way to strengthen district commitment to the overall content standards is by providing state incentive monies to local school districts to construct instructional programs based on the content standards. By funding several groups of local school districts, carefully selected to be representative geographically and by size and type, the state can further encourage individual local school districts to use the content standards as the basis for instruction. Using the same model to develop, for example, instructional materials, professional training programs for educators, and public information materials can build further support for the content standards. The goal is to use the coordinated set of content standards to develop resource materials and strategies for local school districts, to provide incentives for local districts to use them, and, overall, to develop multiple ways in which local school systems can implement quality instructional programs that address the content standards.

B. The Assessment Blueprint. The typical assessment blueprint has several purposes. The first of these is to serve as a living, working document that describes how the assessment program was developed, what types of measures will be used, how these assessments are to be administered and scored, and how the results will be reported. The reporting should include what performance standards for student or system performance are to be created and, eventually, the definitions of each level of performance. To aid the reader of the document, the blueprint should eventually contain sample exercises (of each type to be used in the program), extensive exercise specifications and criteria, and sample report formats. At the outset of the development process, the document may contain only outlines of these sections, to be filled in as the assessment development process unfolds.

In cases where the state and local school districts seek to coordinate existing standards and assessments, it still may be useful to construct an assessment blueprint with the elements discussed here; this will help the participants in the process look for commonalties in assessment purpose, format, reporting, and so on. Such a document can also serve as the basis for future development work and increase the likelihood of coordination from the start.

1. Purposes for Assessment.   The state coordination team first needs to determine the purposes for assessment. Actually, at some levels (such as the state level), this decision may have already been made in the legislation that enabled the program. In this case, the purpose may have most importance for the state coordination team.

It is important to consider what the purposes of student assessment are at the student, school, district, state, and national levels because too often, the purposes are not well thought out, particularly in advance of the development of the instruments that will be used in the assessment system. (Appendix A provides a list of common purposes for assessment.) More often than not, the program is implemented for one purpose, using instruments that are well suited to that purpose, and then additional purposes or uses are added to the program that may fit less well with the assessment formats and purpose. It would be better to consider all of the intended purposes up front and to decide which of these will be addressed at the state and local levels. For example, an assessment program may be implemented to hold schools accountable, and the individual student results it provides may be thought by some to provide the information that teachers need to improve instruction. However, the pressures of accountability may distort the instructional value of the individual student results. A program effective for one purpose may not be so for another. Unfortunately, these conflicts are rarely thought through. It is important, therefore, that the policy makers who create the assessment system think through and prioritize the purposes of assessment, so that the instruments used can be matched to them.

2. Formats for Student Assessment.   Next, the types of assessments must be selected. As described in Appendix B, there is a wide variety of assessments from which to select. Until recently, most assessment programs used primarily multiple-choice tests, with constructed-response exercises used occasionally where needed, such as in writing examinations. Although programs like the National Assessment of Educational Progress pioneered the use of a broader array of assessment formats, much of that innovation was dropped for budget reasons 20 years ago and, hence, no longer serve as models for other possible designs.

Educators will also need to decide whether to use criterion-referenced or norm-referenced measures. Criterion-referenced assessments describe whether students have achieved certain knowledge and skills; norm-referenced assessments express student performance in comparison to a comparison or norm group. Examples of each type of assessment can be obtained commercially, or they may be developed within each state. It is important not to confuse the manner in which results are reported (relative to norms or standards) with the *types* of exercises such assessments typically contain.

Because the nature of the skills that educators consider important may be changing, the manner in which the skills are assessed may need to change as well. Alternatives are increasingly being used in large-scale assessment programs. Such alternatives as the use of essays or extended-response formats in assessing entire areas like mathematics or reading, interview questions, hands-on performance exercises, and group performance exercises, which are scored both for end result and group process, are some of the "on-demand" types of exercises now finding their way into large-scale assessment programs. Some programs now use a few of these types of exercises, while several state programs are based solely on these alternatives. In addition to the on-demand exercises, other assessment formats that break out of the time constraints and allow students to develop a response over time are currently being used in a few large-scale programs. Such assessment formats include portfolios, demonstrations, exhibitions, and projects.

As the large-scale assessment program is being designed, both the purpose(s) for assessment, as discussed in the previous section, and the types of assessment formats must be considered. The measures should be selected based primarily on which strategies are needed to effectively, accurately, and efficiently assess the content standards. By dividing up the assessment load among levels, it is possible to use assessments that are more costly and time-consuming where they will do the most instructional/learning good—at the classroom level—while using measures at the district and state levels that are supportive and complementary.

C. Performance Standards.   Performance standards determine how well students or schools need to do in order to reach different, predefined levels of performance. Once the content standards across levels are developed (or the standards developed at different levels are conceptually mapped together) and the assessment design has been determined, the next step may be to determine the desired levels of student and school performance. Performance standards may also be developed in concert with the content standards, or, in other systems, performance standards may not be developed until student information is collected. One advantage of setting performance standards in advance of creating the assessments, at least in draft form, is that the standards can help determine at what levels the assessments should be developed as well as the content of specific assessment exercises. Once the assessments have been created and validated, these verbal definitions can be refined using the assessment information collected during tryouts.

The first step is to review the range of student performance(s) elicited by the content standards and/or assessments and then to decide how many levels of student performance are desired or needed. The most basic level, of course, is "pass–fail," but this is generally too broad for most intended uses of the information. Therefore, there is generally a more advanced level of passing and another more basic level of not passing. For IASA (Improving America's Schools Act) Title I purposes and where initially many students are expected to do poorly on the assessments, it may be desirable to have three or more levels of not passing. This will allow smaller increments of improved student performance to be noted in future reports of assessment results. Some may choose not to set multiple levels of not passing, however, because that might send the unintended message of being satisfied with lower, unacceptable levels of improvement in performance.

Typically, the next step is to further define what students should know and be able to do at each performance level. These descriptions should be as specific and as behavioral as possible so that persons unfamiliar with the content standards or the assessment to be used can understand them without reference to the definition of "proficient," "advanced," or other labels. Stating performance descriptions in specific terms means that the developers of the assessment will have a good idea of the types of assessment exercises that must be created. These descriptions also guide the development of the assessment blueprint and, more important, are used to ensure sufficient numbers of exercises at or about each performance level in order to classify students accurately. If student work is available, through informal or formal field tests, it can be used in both the development of the performance standards and the validation of the levels and standards once the assessments are formally field-tested on students.

Next, decisions will need to be made about what levels and procedures are to be followed in categorizing *school-level* performance. How will group performance in any year be described? How will improvement over time be determined? How much change and of what kinds is needed to describe a school as "improving"? Additionally, will the determination of performance level be restricted to the assessment created for each level of the educational system or will the assessment data collected at different levels by multiple assessments be used to make the overall determination? Under a coordinated assessment system, it may be possible to establish cross-level performance determinations that draw on information collected at the state and the local levels. For example, judgments could be based on the performance of students on the state assessment program (comprised of selected-response and open-ended exercises) plus their performance on portfolios collected and rated by classroom teachers. This would require, of course, substantial coordination not only of the content standards used at different levels but also of the assessment strategies at each level to ensure that they really measure the same sorts of standards. Such a multilevel determination of performance has yet to be accomplished, in large part due to the lack of coordinated assessment systems that span state and local levels; and it is an area that needs fruitful developmental research.

The next step in the process is to develop the assessments that will follow the assessment blueprint and be based on the content standards. During the assessment development process, during the tryout phase, data from students will be collected. This data, or the data from the initial live use of the assessment instruments, should be used to establish the final performance standards for both students and schools. There are several established procedures for setting student performance standards, such as the modified Angoff method, the contrasting groups method, and other emerging strategies for setting cut scores. One or more of these strategies can be used to set the final levels of desired performance as well as to revise the descriptions of these levels to match actual performance.

Finally, the projected school performance standards will need to be reviewed for realism once either tryout or live data are available. Did students perform as anticipated or were the a priori judgments too high or too low? Policy makers, parents, business leaders, and others can help educators judge the realism of the standards.

D. Professional Development Programs on Assessment and Instruction.   Too often, the presumption is made that all educators need in order to understand and effectively use the information that the statewide assessments produce is an understanding of the forms used to report the information. Then they will know how to use the assessment results to meet individual student needs, review and improve the school's instructional programs, and report the results to the parents of individual students, to all parents of students in the school, to the community, and to the local board of education. This assumption is clearly incorrect. Few local educators have been taught how to use and report assessment results effectively. Assessment literacy among educators is low; it is lower still among policy makers and the general public. Thus, we have a system in which data are routinely provided that potential users do not understand how to use. In addition, local educators may not be aware of how to create and use assessments for the classroom, which does not increase the likelihood that assessments either at the state or local levels will help improve student performance!

What is needed is a comprehensive approach to professional development that addresses these problems in several ways. First, local educators (and policy makers and the public) need to be provided with basic assessment literacy to better understand different types of assessments, their strengths and weaknesses, and how they could be used to improve student learning. Second, local educators need to be shown effective ways of using assessment results. Third, they need to be shown how to report the assessment results to students, parents, local boards of education, and the general public. Finally, local educators need to be made aware through in-depth training opportunities that teaching in a standards-based environment is different. This type of instruction calls for educators to teach in such a manner that they are constantly collecting evidence of student performance. Teaching to the standards is not simply changing the content of instruction but also the manner in which instruction takes place. Educators need practice in teaching in a more student-centered manner, as well as in using and developing further the assessment tools made available to them through the state/local coordinated assessment system.

Issues in Developing Coordinated Assessment Systems

There are a number of issues inherent in developing coordinated assessment systems. Some are inherent in any attempt to develop an assessment system, while others are related to the goal of coordination. Regardless of where a state and its local districts are in developing a coordinated assessment system, these issues are important to consider.

Alignment of Standards

As the development process unfolds, the state coordination committee will need to wrestle with what constitutes "alignment" of content standards. Both whether a particular local district's content standards are aligned with the state's content standards and whether the content standards developed in one school district match those developed in another district are important issues to consider. One strategy is to use the state's standards for examining the match to local districts' standards and to encourage each district to maintain its unique standards.

Even if the standards at the district and state level are developed at the same time and even if there is overlap in the committees that develop them, there may be different interpretations of similar standards and there may well be different levels of specificity in the standards. One way to respond to both problems is to conceptually map the different sets of standards together.

How is conceptual mapping done? One strategy is to have the developers of the different sets of standards examine first their structure and then their content at comparable levels of specificity.

- Does one framework contain more specific examples of the standards than the other?
- Have different districts developed different sets of specific examples of the state standards?
- Are the sets of specific examples of state standards related to one another?
- Are there important differences that should be maintained for an overall set of standards or are apparent differences simply different ways of describing the same thing?

By carefully considering questions such as these, one set of standards representing a complete set of the different standards drawn from state and local districts and that contains all of the important standards valued at the different levels of the system can be compiled by the group charged with doing so. The group carrying out the conceptual mapping can by addressing these questions determine the extent of similarity or difference among the different sets of content standards and therefore whether different sets of standards are aligned.

Alignment of Assessments

In a comprehensive assessment system, some attention will need to be paid to whether the different assessment formats used will actually measure the same standards. For example, if the state is assessing state standards using a mixed assessment model comprised of selected-response and constructed-response exercises and the district is conducting assessment using constructed-response exercises and performance-type assessments and classrooms teachers are assessing student performance using a combination of selected-response, constructed-response, and portfolio assessments, do the different assessments used at the various levels measure the same standards? Assuming that there is planned redundancy in assessment types, will the assessment results from various levels be related to one another?

Each assessment needs to be compared to the content standards that it is measuring to determine whether the assessments do match the content standards. There are several key questions that assessment system designers need to answer.

- Does each assessment measure an important aspect of one or more content standards?

Quality assessments measure important content standards. They should also measure one or more standards in each assessment exercise.

- Are the content standards well measured by the assessment (that is, does the assessment assess the breadth and depth of the content standards)?

This question is the reverse of the first one. The alignment of assessment to standards needs to be examined from the perspective of the standards as well. How well are the content standards assessed by the assessment(s)?

- Do the formats used in the assessment convey a sense of the importance of the balance between content and skills?

The nature of the assessments used conveys a sense of the meaning of the standards. For example, if the standards indicate that students are to design innovative approaches to studying a scientific concept, yet students are simply asked to select answers to multiple-choice questions regarding science content, the format of the assessment may not be well aligned with the standards to be assessed.

- Will the assessment reports convey a sense of what is important in the content standards by emphasizing content and skills contained in the content standards?

Regardless of the types of assessment exercises used, how will the reports of results match the types of standards assessed? Will student performance on the most important standards be reported? Will such a report carry greater weight than reports of student performance on other standards?

Can One Assessment Meet Multiple Purposes?

The issue of whether it is *really* necessary to have a different test for every assessment purpose is one that always arises, because each assessment costs time and money. The evidence suggests that multiple assessments are needed; trying to fulfill too many purposes may lead to fulfilling none of them well. However, the state coordination team will want to ask itself this question periodically, in order to avoid adding redundant measures to the system or encouraging their use locally.

Do Some Assessments Work Better for Some Assessment Purposes?

Some assessment purposes are best achieved by particular types of assessment. The match of assessment type to purpose is important. The state coordination team will want to make sure that the assessment formats selected match well the intended purposes for assessment.

Do Local Schools Really Desire Coordination?

Too often, local school districts have either waited for the state to develop its system or have tried to minimize the impact of the state system on classroom instruction. Through working together, states and local districts will, it is hoped, establish the pattern of trust necessary for the coordination of standards and assessments to occur. In the short run in some states, it may be difficult to establish this trust and working relationship. The state can still offer to work with and provide resources and incentives for local schools, with the hope that the materials and resources will be so compelling local districts will choose to work with the state.

Does the State Desire Coordination?

The answer to this question is not as simple as it may seem. Even though some personnel at the state level may strongly desire to provide technical assistance to local districts and to work on assessments for local districts that coordinate with state assessments, they may not be given the resources or the opportunity/mandate to do so. In some cases, working with local schools might be viewed suspiciously. In other instances, state-level staff is actually prohibited from working to influence what is taught or assessed locally. For those who do not understand it is important to clarify why it is important to work together. Such coordinated work should not be viewed as diminishing the value of accountability assessments.

Are There Professional Development Implications of Coordinated Assessment Systems?

For coordination in the development and use of assessment systems to truly occur, all participants in the system (policy makers, administrators, teachers, parents, and students) will need information about assessment that is suitable to their backgrounds and interests. This means that substantial training in assessment will be needed. Given the current, relatively low levels of assessment literacy, a concerted effort to improve assessment literacy among educators and noneducators alike, and at all levels of the educational system, will have to be made. How well do educators understand the content standards to be addressed and the ways to address them effectively. Without a deep understanding of both the conceptual basis for the standards and the most effective methods for addressing them, all of the effort to coordinate the development and implementation of a standards-based system may be for naught.

Summary

A variety of reasons and purposes for assessment exist, and there are a variety of audiences for assessment information at the student, school, district, state, and national levels. There are also many assessment strategies, each with advantages and disadvantages. Designing the ideal assessment program, the one that meets the needs of people at these various levels, consists of matching the purposes with appropriate types of assessment instrumentation. The full variety of measures should be considered when designing the system because some types are better suited to some purposes than are others. An example of a school coordination team was used here to convey that there is a strong advantage in using multiple measures at the building level to collect information on the success of the school in meeting the objectives that the staff has developed.

Generalizing from this, the ideal assessment system would attempt as much as possible to capture information from the bottom up while adding measures from the top down, so that users at all levels may have more than one assessment approach to use when reporting the status of the system at that level. This has the advantage of demonstrating that different approaches to assessment may yield different results and that these differences help to inform the debate on what skills students should be able to perform and whether students are currently able to perform them.

If such a coordinated assessment system can be created, the advantage for policy makers is that more information about the performance of students will be more readily available, which will serve to ensure that students are being held to the high standards. It can also help ensure that the assessments used for monitoring programs or for accountability purposes do not distort educational programs by emphasizing only less important aspects of the standards being assessed. A coordinated assessment design will help to ensure that the assessments used at different levels are well suited to the purposes for which they are being used and are not being used in ways for which they were not designed.

When the steps outlined in this paper are followed, the end product will be a cross-level coordinated assessment system that uses different modes of assessment to assess a common or conceptually linked set of content standards and that reports the results via performance standards established at each level or across levels. The result of using multiple measures to accomplish different assessment purposes and reducing the amount of redundant information as well as the number of mixed messages sent by uncoordinated assessments based on different standards will be a more coherent picture of student performance at the individual and group levels.

appendix a

Purposes for Assessment

The major purposes for assessment can be summarized as follows:

Monitoring

- *Student Level:* Provide periodic measurements of student progress in order to determine the educational "growth" of a student from year to year.
- *System Performance:* Provide a periodic measure of the performance of groups of students to track performance over time.

Information/Accountability

- *Parents and Students:* Inform parents/student about student performance so as to encourage student or teachers to improve performance.
- *Public:* Provide the public with information about the performance of groups of students so as to encourage schools to improve the system.

Improving Student Performance

- *Student Level:* Provide data to teachers and students that encourages instruction geared to the needs of individual students to help them achieve at high levels.
- *System Level:* Provide information to educators on groups of students, such as at the school level, that can be used to review current instructional strategies and materials at one or more grade levels and to make improvements where needed. This will promote articulation of instruction across grades and school levels.

Allocation of Resources

- *Human:* Use information to determine where additional staff are needed.
- *Financial:* Determine where financial resources are most needed or should be used.

Selection/Placement of Students

- *Selection:* Help determine the eligibility of students for various educational programs or services
- *Placement:* Determine the program or service most appropriate for the instructional level of the student.

Certification

- *Student Level:* Provide a means of determining the competence level of individual students.
- *Program Level:* Provide data to certify the adequacy of an educational program, such as advanced placement courses.
- *System:* Provide data to certify the acceptability of an educational system, such as in accreditation programs.

Program Evaluation

- Provide the information needed to determine the effectiveness of an educational program or intervention.

a p p e n d i x   b

Formats for Assessment

Some formats for assessment are listed and defined below.

On-Demand Assessments

- *Selected-Response (Multiple-Choice, Matching, True–False) Exercises:* In these types of exercises, students select one or more answers from a list of suggested responses. These exercises have the advantage of not taking much time to complete, which may make them well suited for assessments of broad content standards. However, because students select a response, it is more difficult to assess student thinking with such items.
- *Short Constructed-Response Exercises:* In these types of exercises, students write in an answer to a question. The response is typically a phrase, a sentence, or a quick drawing or sketch. Response time is generally limited to 10 minutes or less. Less guessing is involved than in selected-response exercises, but these exercises do not tap much student thinking either.
- *Extended Constructed-Response Exercises:* These exercises require students to compose a response that may be several pages in length and require 15 minutes or more for a complete response. They require much thought on the part of the student. Still, this is only first-draft student work, so it may not represent what students could do given additional time and encouragement in which to compose a final draft.
- *Individually Administered Interview:* In these exercises, an assessment administrator administers the exercise individually to students. This format permits the interviewer to ask each student questions about the topic being assessed, which may be needed in order to judge the performance of the student on other parts of the exercise. It has the advantage of tapping important skills often desired of students, although it is quite expensive both to administer and to score.
- *Individually Administered Performance Events:* These are exercises that are completed by individual students within a class period and involve some type of performance on the part of the student. This may be because the exercise requires special equipment (as in a science experiment), requires an individual student to perform (such as playing a musical instrument), or because we may wish to observe the process that a student used to respond to the question (such as in a mathematics problem-solving activity).
- *Group-Administered Performance Events:* These are exercises that groups of students respond to. The groups may be existing groups (e.g., a band or orchestra) or groups made up just for assessment purposes (a group of six students assessed for teamwork skills). The students typically perform in some fashion, and the group interaction and/or performance is scored as a whole (and, perhaps, individually).

Extended-Time Assessments

- *Individual Performance Tasks:* These exercises are ones on which students may work for several days, weeks, or months to produce an individual student response. They could be, for example, a science experiment (e.g., design and plan a garden and make observations about it over time) or other projects that students will need time to complete.
- *Group Performance Tasks:* These exercises are ones on which groups of students may work for several days, weeks, or months to produce either a group and/or individual student response. They could be, for example, a health education task (e.g., design a school lunch menu for a month that is nutritious, affordable, and appealing to students) or other projects that students will need time to complete.
- *Portfolio Assessment:* There are several reasons why portfolios of student work may be kept. First, they can serve to document the changes that students are making in a work (e.g., different iterations of an essay). Second, the portfolio can be used to assemble a collection of students' best or most polished pieces (e.g., a collection of musical performances). Third, and perhaps most important, students can use their portfolios to document their ability to achieve important outcomes, such as those contained in state or national content standards. In this case, the portfolio provides the evidence that the student needs to demonstrate competence on the standards, with the demonstration being provided by a persuasive piece that the student provides to the scorer.
- *Observations:* Other important types of information that teachers can collect over time come from structured and unstructured observations of students. Structured observations, for example, might be made in a prearranged classroom setup in which students are given several choices of free-time activities and observed as to which ones they engage in and for how long. Unstructured observations are the events that occur within the day-to-day classroom that teachers may wish to record for the future. For example, if a student is having difficulty in mathematics, the teacher may observe that the student is not listening during instruction and therefore not picking up the knowledge needed to take tests.
- *Anecdotal Records:* There are other sources of information about students, such as notes from other educational professionals, parents, and others. These records may also provide useful information about individual students.

10

How Can We Make NAEP and State Test Score Reporting Scales and Reports More Understandable?*

RONALD K. HAMBLETON

University of Massachusetts at Amherst

Laboratory of Psychometric and Evaluative Research Report No. 384. Amherst, Mass.: University of Massachusetts, School of Education.

The National Assessment of Educational Progress (NAEP) provides policy makers, educators, and the public with information about the reading, mathematics, science, geography, history, and writing skills of elementary, middle, and high school students and monitors changes in student achievement over time. NAEP has been producing achievement test results for over 30 years. Considerable statistical and psychometric sophistication is used in test design, data collection, test data analysis, and scaling (see, for example, Beaton & Johnson, 1992; Johnson, 1992; Mislevy, Johnson, & Muraki, 1992). A similar situation exists with many state testing programs. Substantial time and money is spent in overcoming technical problems associated with these state testing programs. Most state departments of education have technical advisory committees and hire technical consultants, and all of the large test contractors have substantial technical expertise.

Less attention, however, is given to ways in which the complex array of test results is organized and reported. Over the years, I have been struck by the contrast between the efforts and successes in producing sound technical assessments, drawing samples, administering the assessments, and analyzing the assessment data and the efforts and success in disseminating the assessment results.

Concerns about NAEP and state data reporting have become an issue in recent years and have been documented by Hambleton and Slater (1995), Jaeger (1992, 1999), Koretz and Deibert (1993), Linn (1998), Linn and Dunbar (1992), Wainer (1996, 1997a, 1997b, 1997c), and Wainer, Hambleton, and Meara (1999). A body of results has now been compiled that shows confusion among policy makers, educators, and the public over the meaning of national and state test results.

This chapter was prepared to address the issues and methods associated with reporting national and state test results. Three topics will be considered:

1. Background on NAEP score reporting with performance standards (since 1990)

2. The results of a small-scale study that addressed the understandability of NAEP score reports among policy makers

3. Several promising new directions in score reporting with implications for NAEP and state reports:
   a. Redesign of NAEP displays (Wainer, Hambleton, & Meara, 1999)
   b. Guidelines for preparing displays (Hambleton, Slater, & Allalouf, in progress)
   c. Marketbasket reporting (Mislevy, 1998)

Background on NAEP Score Reporting

"What is the meaning of a NAEP mathematics score of 220?" "Is a national average in mathematics of 245 at grade 8 good or bad?" These were two questions from policy makers and educators in a study by Hambleton and Slater (1995) using the executive summary of the 1992 NAEP national and state mathematics results (Mullis, Dossey, Owen, & Phillips, 1993). Questions about the meaning of scores are common from persons attempting to make sense of IQ, SAT, ACT, and standardized achievement test scores as well. The fact is that people are more familiar with popular ratio scales, such as those used in measuring distance, time, and weight, than they are with educational and psychological test score scales.

Test scores are elusive. Even the popular percent score scale that many persons think they understand cannot be understood unless (1) the domain of content to which percent scores are referenced is clear and (2) the method used for selecting assessment items is known. Few persons seem to realize the importance of these two critical pieces of information in interpreting percent scores. Another example of the problem occurs when state legislation is written that establishes a passing score on an important statewide test, without any knowledge of the contents of the test or its difficulty!

One solution to the score interpretation problem is simply to interpret the scores in a normative way, that is, scores gain meaning or interpretability by being referenced to a well-defined norm group. All of the popular norm-referenced tests use norms to assist in test score interpretations. But normative statements are not always valued. Sometimes the question important to policy makers concerns level of accomplishment—what percent of students has reached (say) a Basic level of performance on the assessment? Many policy makers want to choose points such as 250 to represent well-defined levels of accomplishment (these points might be called Basic, Proficient, and Advanced) and then determine the numbers of students in groups of interest (e.g., regions of the country) who achieve these levels of accomplishment. This is known as criterion-referenced assessment. NAEP and most state assessments are examples of criterion-referenced assessments, and with these assessments, scores need to be interpreted in relation to content domains and performance standards (Hambleton, 1994).

With NAEP, an arbitrary reporting scale was constructed with scores ranging from 0 to 500 for each subject area. (In 1996, the scale was changed to place scores on a scale from 0 to 300; placing scores from assessments at grades 4, 8, and 12 on a common reporting scale was discontinued.) The original scale was obtained in, basically, the following way: The distributions of scores from nationally representative samples of grade 4, 8, and 12 students were combined and scaled to a mean of 250 and a standard deviation of about 50 (Beaton & Johnson, 1992). The task then was to facilitate criterion-referenced score interpretations on this scale (see Phillips et al., 1993). Establishing benchmarks such as grade-level means, state means, and performance of various subgroups of students (such as males, females, Blacks, Hispanics, etc.) is helpful in bringing meaning to the scale, but these benchmarks provide only a norm-referenced basis for score interpretations.

One of the ways of making statistical results more meaningful to intended audiences is to report the results by connecting them to numbers that may be better understood than test scores and test score scales. For example, to relieve the concern many persons had about flying after the TWA crash a few years ago, the airlines reported that there is a single plane crash every 2,000,000 flights. In case the safety of air travel was still not clear, the airlines reported that a person could expect to fly every day for the next 700 years without an accident. Probably some people felt more confident after hearing these statistics reported in this way. Knowing that the probability of being in a plane crash is less than .0000005 may not be so meaningful.

Concerning the reporting of NAEP results, what, for example, is the meaning of a single point? It was noted (Hambleton & Slater, 1995) that the typical student (the student at the 50th percentile) between fourth and eighth grade in mathematics gained about 48 points, which converts to about 1.2 points per month of instruction (a gain of 48 points over 40 months of instruction). Recognizing that the growth over four years is not necessarily linear (see, for example, grade-equivalent scores on standardized achievement tests), it might be said that one point is at least roughly equivalent to about one month of regular classroom instruction. United States Secretary of Education Richard Riley used this approach to communicate findings about the 1996 science assessment, and the connection between NAEP score points and instructional time appeared to be a valuable way to enhance the meaning of points on the NAEP scale.

Other possibilities of considerable promise for criterion-referenced interpretations of scores include item mapping, anchor points, performance standards (called "achievement levels" in the NAEP context), and benchmarking (see Phillips et al., 1993). All of these approaches capitalize on the fact that IRT-based scales locate both the assessment material and the examinees on the same reporting scale. Thus, at any particular point (i.e., ability or proficiency level) of interest on the reporting scale, the sorts of tasks that examinees at that ability level can successfully complete can be described. And, if of interest, tasks that these examinees cannot complete with some stated degree of accuracy (e.g., 50% probability of successful completion) can be identified. Descriptions at these points of interest can be developed, and exemplary items could also be selected—that is, items can be selected to highlight what examinees at these points of interest might be expected to be able to do (see Bourque, Champagne, & Crissman, 1997; Mullis, 1991).

Figure 10.1 shows "item characteristic curves" for three dichotomously scored test items (see Hambleton, Swaminathan, & Rogers, 1991). At any point on the achievement (or proficiency) scale, the probability of a correct response (i.e., a correct answer) to an item can be determined. Item 16 is the most difficult of the three items because, for all proficiency levels, the probability of a correct response to item 16 is lower than that for

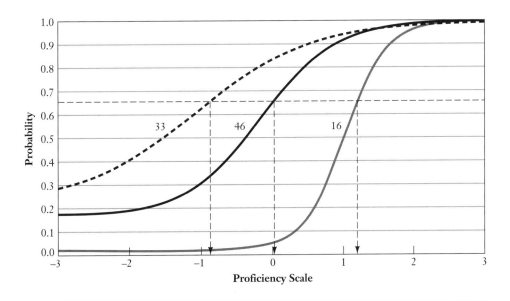

FIGURE 10.1   RP$_{65}$ Item Mappings

items 33 and 46. The location on the proficiency scale where an examinee has a 65% probability of success on the item is called the "RP_{65}" for the item. In Figure 10.1, it can be estimated that the RP_{65} for item 33 is about –0.90. For item 46, the item RP_{65} value is 0.00; and for item 16, the RP value is 1.2. (On a reporting scale with a mean of 250 and a standard deviation of 50, the RP_{65} values for items 33, 46, and 16 are 205, 250, and 310, respectively.) This is known as "item mapping." Each item in the assessment can be located on the proficiency scale according to RP_{65} values. If 65% probability is defined as the probability at which an examinee can reasonably be expected to know something or be able to do something (and other probabilities have often been used, such as 80%) then an examinee with a proficiency score of (say) 205, could be expected to answer items like item 33 and other items with RP_{65} values around 205 on a fairly consistent basis (i.e., about 65% of the time). In this way, then, a limited type of criterion-referenced interpretation can be made even though examinees with scores around 205 may never have actually been administered item 33 or other items like it as part of their assessment.

The validity of criterion-referenced interpretations of the kind just described depends on the extent to which a unidimensional reporting scale fits the data to which it is applied. Any score on the proficiency scale can be made more meaningful—for example, the average score of students—by describing the content of items with RP_{65} values near the score. The item-mapping method is one way to facilitate criterion-referenced interpretations of proficiency scores. Cautions to take with this approach have been clearly outlined by Forsyth (1991). One of the main concerns has to do with the content domain to which inferences about student performance can be made from a small number of test items.

With NAEP currently, RP_{65} values are used to enhance the meaning of score points on the proficiency scale. For more details on current practices, readers are referred to Mullis (1991), Phillips et al. (1993), and Beaton and Allen (1992). Note, too, that a similar process for item mapping of polytomously scored tasks is readily available. The method is not limited to dichotomously scored response data.

Some policy makers and educators were not happy with the proficiency scale for reporting NAEP results. They wanted to interpret student performance in terms of performance categories. Figure 10.2 shows the proficiency scale with the performance standards for Basic, Proficient, and Advanced indicated. The items that might be used to describe student performance at each performance standard are clear (item 33 for Basic, item 16 for Proficient, and item 30 for Advanced). Here, the concept of item mapping is used to enhance the meaning of the performance standards. Also, the performance standards permit the classification of students into performance categories and provide another way for interpreting student performance.

Small-Scale Study of the Understandability of NAEP Score Reports

The design of tables, figures, and charts for transmitting statistical data to enhance their meaningfulness and the understandability of test scores is a new area of concern in education and psychology (Wainer, 1992, 1997c; Wainer & Thissen, 1981). There is, however, an extensive literature that appears relevant to the topic of data reporting in the fields of

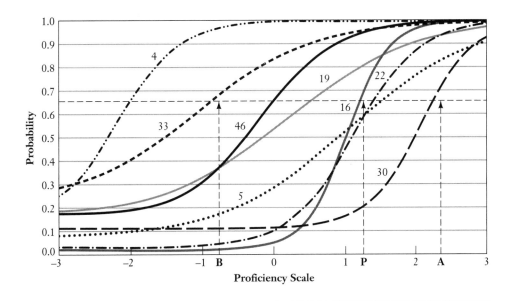

FIGURE 10.2   Item Mappings to the Proficiency Scale

statistics and graphic design (see, for example, Cleveland, 1985; Henry, 1995; Wainer, 1997c).

But how bad (or good) is the current situation? Do policy makers and educators understand what they are reading about student achievement and changes over time? Do they make reasonable inferences and avoid inappropriate ones? And what do they think about the information they are being given? Is it important to them? What do they understand and where are their deficiencies and strengths when it comes to NAEP score reports? In view of the shortage of available evidence about the extent to which intended NAEP audiences understand and can use the reports provided by NAEP, a small research study was carried out by Hambleton and Slater (1995) (1) to investigate the extent to which NAEP Executive Summary Reports were understandable to policy makers and educators and, to the extent that problems were identified, (2) to offer a set of recommendations for improving reporting practices. The project was initiated by the Technical Review Panel that was funded by the National Center for Education Statistics and carried out by Sharon Slater and me.

The 59 participants in the interviews comprised a broad audience, similar to the intended audience of the NAEP Executive Summary Reports. We spoke with persons at state departments of education, attorneys, directors of companies, state politicians and legislative assistants, school superintendents, education reporters, and directors of public relations. The interviews were designed around the *Executive Summary of the NAEP 1992 Mathematics Report Card for the Nation and the States* (Mullis et al., 1993). This particular report was chosen because it was relatively brief and was intended to stand alone for policy makers and educators. Also, the NAEP Executive Summary Reports are well known and widely distributed (over 100,000 copies of each Executive Summary are produced) to many people working in education or interested in education. Further, we thought that the NAEP Executive Summary Report results, which included both national and state results, would be of interest to the interviewees, who were from different areas of the country. Our goal in the interviews was to determine just how much of the information reported in the Executive Summary Report was understandable. We attempted to pinpoint the aspects of reporting that were confusing to readers and to identify changes in the reporting that the interviewees felt would improve their understanding of the results.

The 1992 NAEP Mathematics Executive Summary Report consists of six sections that highlight the findings from different aspects of the assessment. For each section, interview questions were designed to ascertain the kind of information interviewees were obtaining from the report. Interviewees were asked to read a brief section of the report, and then they were questioned on the general meaning of the text or on the specific meaning of certain phrases. Interviewees also examined tables and charts and were asked to interpret some of the numbers and symbols. Interviewees were encouraged to volunteer their opinions and suggestions.

Our sample of interviewees was mainly white and included more females than males (64% to 36%). The interviewees were from various areas of education, and we were able to locate two education reporters for the study. All interviewees indicated that they had medium-to-high interest in national student achievement results. Most interviewees (90%) were familiar with NAEP in a general way at least, and 64% had read NAEP publications prior to the interview. Approximately half the sample had taken more than one course in testing and/or statistics (46%); one-fourth had only one course; and one-fourth had none.

Nearly all of the interviewees (92%) demonstrated a general understanding of the main points of the text summarizing the major findings of the report, though several interviewees commented that they would have liked more descriptive information (e.g., concrete examples). One of the problems in understanding the text was due to the use of some statistical jargon (e.g., *statistical significance*, *variance*). This confused and intimidated a number of the interviewees. Several interviewees suggested that a glossary of basic terms would have been very helpful. Terms such as *Basic*, *Proficient*, *Advanced*, *standard errors*, *the NAEP scale*, and so on could be included in a glossary.

Here is one example: The meaning of the phrase "statistically significant" was unclear to many interviewees (42%). We expected that interviewees would know that "statistically significant increases" are not just increases resulting from chance events. We discovered that 58% of the interviewees had an idea, or thought that they knew the meaning, but many of the interviewees in this group could not explain what the term meant or why it was used. This was surprising because more than half the interviewees had taken statistics courses. Typical responses to the question, "What does statistically significant mean?" were:

"more than a couple of percentage points"

"10 percentage points"

"at least a 5 point increase"

"more than a handful—you have enough numbers"

"statisticians decide it is significant due to certain criteria"

"the results are important"

"I wish you hadn't asked me that. I used to know."

The common mistake was to assume "statistically significant differences" were "big and important differences."

Several interviewees mentioned that although they realized that certain terms (e.g., *standard error, estimation, confidence level*) were important to statisticians, these terms were meaningless to them. They tended to "glaze over" technical terms when they were used in reports or form their own "working" definitions such as those just listed for significance levels.

Many interviewees offered helpful and insightful opinions about the report. One common suggestion was the need to try to make the reports accessible to nonstatisticians. A comment made by a couple of interviewees was that the report appeared to be "written by statisticians, for statisticians." To remedy this, many interviewees suggested removing the statistical jargon. Phrases like "statistically significant" did not hold much meaning for the policy makers and educators we interviewed.

The conclusions and recommendations from a study like this one by Hambleton and Slater must be limited because of (1) the modest nature of the study (only 59 interviews were conducted), (2) the nonrepresentativeness of the persons interviewed (though it was an interesting and important group of policy makers and educators), and (3) the use of only one NAEP report in the study. Note, too, that the research was conducted on a 1992 NAEP report; reports in 1994, 1996, and 1998 appear to be better designed and more responsive to the needs of intended audiences.

Despite the limitations of the study, several conclusions and recommendations seemed to follow from the research: (1) There was a considerable amount of misunderstanding about the results reported in the 1992 NAEP Mathematics Assessment Executive Summary Report, (2) improvements would need to include the preparation of a substantially more user-friendly report with simplified figures and tables, and (3) reports ought to be kept straightforward, short, and clear because of the brief time persons are likely to spend with these executive summaries.

On the basis of the findings from their study, Hambleton and Slater (1995) offered several reporting guidelines for NAEP and state assessments:

1. Charts, figures, and tables should be understandable without reference to the text. (Readers didn't seem willing to search around the text for interpretations.)
2. Graphs, figures, and tables should be tried out on focus groups representing the intended audiences prior to their use in score reporting.
3. Charts, figures, and tables should be reproducible and reducible without loss of quality. (This is important because interesting and important results will be copied and distributed and these copies must be legible.)
4. Graphs, figures, and tables should be kept relatively simple and straightforward to minimize confusion and shorten the time required by readers to identify the main trends in the data.

5. With respect to NAEP executive summaries, an introduction to NAEP and NAEP scales is needed. Also, a glossary of statistical terms is needed; statistical jargon should be minimized, and tables, charts, and graphs should be simplified.

6. Specially designed reports may be needed for each intended audience. For example, with policy makers, reports might need to be short and use bullets to highlight main points such as conclusions.

A broad program of research involving measurement specialists, graphic design specialists (see, for example, Cleveland, 1985), and focus groups representing intended audiences for reports is very much in order to build on some of the successes in reporting represented in the reports of Kirsch et al. (1993) and Bourque et al. (1997) and some of the findings of Jaeger (1992, 1999), Koretz and Deibert (1993), Wainer (1996, 1997a, 1997b), and others. Ways need to be found to balance statistical rigor in reporting with the informational needs, time constraints, and quantitative literacy of intended audiences. Some of this emerging research will be described in the next section.

Three Current Advances in Score Reporting

Wainer, Hambleton, and Meara Study

The National Center for Education Statistics (NCES), through the Council of Chief State School Officers (CCSSO) and the National Science Foundation (NSF), recently funded a small project (Wainer, Hambleton, & Meara, 1999) to extend the earlier work of Wainer (1996, 1997a, 1997b) and Hambleton and Slater (1995). The purpose of this new study was to take a diverse mix of the current NAEP data displays that seemed to be problematic, revise them along the lines of emerging data reporting principles, and field-test the original and revised displays with educators and policy makers. The data displays for the study were selected from the 1994 NAEP Reading Study (Williams et al., 1995). Questions were generated that were believed to be the sorts of questions that policy makers and educators might want to answer with the data displays. Sample questions follow:

1. What was the general direction of results between 1992 and 1994?
2. Which region showed the greatest decline in performance for 12th graders from 1992 to 1994?
3. In 1994, which region of the country had the lowest average reading proficiency at all three grade levels?
4. What is the ranking of the regions from *best to worst* in terms of *average reading proficiency* for grade 12 in 1994?
5. Which of the four regions is most typical of the U.S. results?
6. Which regions for eighth graders in 1994 performed better than the average for all of the United States?

The performance of educators and policy makers on the six questions and many more with the two versions of the data displays was of central interest. In addition, on some questions, the researchers kept track of time to respond. The results were very interesting.

For three of the five displays that were studied, the revisions made little difference to the speed or accuracy of responses. For the other two, respondents were often faster in giving responses and substantially more accurate when they were using the revised displays of data. Also, we discovered that respondents' preferences for displays were not always associated with those that led to the most accurate interpretations. Clearly, for serious evaluations of the presentations of displays, respondent preferences should not be the sole basis for selection.

Wainer, Hambleton, and Meara concluded that (1) policy makers and educators had considerable difficulty with a number of the score report displays and (2) many of the problems associated with the data displays might be overcome with more careful consideration during the design phase and with field tests to identify strengths and weaknesses.

Hambleton, Slater, and Allalouf
Instructional Module on Score Reporting

In recognition of the need for steps and guidelines for preparing data displays, and as a follow-up to the work of Hambleton and Slater (1995), Hambleton, Slater, and Allalouf (in progress) are producing an instructional module with a six-step model for the design of figures and tables and specific guidelines for preparing tables and figures. A draft of their guidelines for preparing data displays, most of which can be supported by research findings, follows:

1. Keep presentation clear, simple, and uncluttered.
   * Frame the graph on all four sides.
   * Use no more ticks than necessary and place ticks on all four sides of the graph frame.
   * Use scales on the vertical and horizontal axes that include a slightly larger range than the data range.
   * Do not be place tick marks or numbers at the corners of the graph frame.
   * Clearly label the left and lower axes.
   * Avoid the use of scale breaks.
   * Use symbols that are visually distinguishable. Avoid placing isolated data points too close to the frame, where they are likely to be hidden. Ensure that overlapping data points are identified.
   * Consider using visual summaries, such as regression lines or smoothing, if the amount of data is large or important trends are unclear because of outliers and other problems in the data presentation.
   * The elements of bars and graphs should be labeled directly rather than indirectly by key or grid. Horizontal bars give room for labels and figures on or near the elements; this is the main reason for preferring them to vertical bars.
   * If memory of specific amounts is required, use a table with round numbers in numerical form (5000 not 5422 or five thousand).

2. Ensure that the graph is able to stand alone.
   * A graph should be able to be interpreted in isolation from the main text.

- Highlight data, not extraneous material.
- Minimize noninformative material in the data region.
- Ensure that the entire graph is capable of being reduced and reproduced without loss of clarity.

3. Ensure that the text complements and supports the graph.
   - Never present numerical data in text form if there are more than one or two items to be presented.
   - Use questions after the table or chart to emphasize its chief features.
   - Include text to support and improve interpretations of charts and tables.

4. Plan the graphical presentation.
   - Proofread and pilot the completed graph with a sample from the intended audience.
   - Be prepared to use more than one graph to communicate an idea or concept.

5. No form of graph is more effective in all respects than all other forms. However, the following suggestions have been found in the literature:
   - Comparisons based on bar charts were more accurate than comparisons based upon circles or squares.
   - Comparisons based on circles or squares were more accurate than comparisons based on cubes.
   - Bar charts were easier to read than line graphs.
   - In general, color coding improved interpretations over black-and-white code.

Our expectation is that this instructional module, which includes the preceding guidelines (with explanations and examples), will be valuable to district, state, and national agencies who want to design data displays and communicate test results more clearly.

Market Basket Reporting

Bob Mislevy (1998) created the concept of a "market basket" for score reporting. An excellent explanation of market basket reporting and some of the variations are provided in a report by Mislevy et al. (1996) and a paper by Mislevy (1998).

The idea apparently came from the use of market basket reporting to explain economic changes over time as reflected by the Consumer Price Index. The price of a market basket of food (with known and fixed grocery items) is reported each month to provide the public with a single, easy-to-understand measure of economic change. The extension to education is as follows: One might imagine a collection of test items and performance tasks that measure important outcomes of education. The collection of assessment material would reflect diverse item formats, difficulty levels, and cognitive levels within a subject area (and any other dimensions that are of interest). The quality of education might be monitored by reporting performance of a national sample of students on the market basket of items each year. Certainly, many policy makers seem to desire a single, clear index about the quality of education, much like the Consumer Price Index.

The market basket items would be clearly explained to the public to enhance the meaning of statements such as, "In 2000, the average American grade 4 student obtained

37 out of 50 points on the assessment. This is 3 points higher than the results reported in 1999." Alternatively or in addition, standards could be used in reporting: "An advanced student would need to score 45 points on the assessment. Approximately 5% of the students in the national sample were judged as advanced. In 1999, only 3% of the students met the standard for being advanced. Thus, there is evidence of improvement."

Figure 10.3 shows how performance standards (B-basic, P-proficient, and A-advanced) might be mapped onto the percent score scale (or test score scale) associated with the "market basket assessment." The monotonically increasing curve involved in the mapping is the "test characteristic curve" (TCC) for the assessment material in the market basket (see, for example, Hambleton, Swaminathan, & Rogers, 1991). The TCC links the proficiency scale and the performance standards to the more meaningful percent score scale (or test score scale) for the particular items and tasks (i.e., the assessment material) in the market basket assessment. The student score distribution for the student population of interest can be mapped onto the more meaningful percent score scale (for many audiences) along with the performance standards and used in score reporting. There are many problems to overcome, but the basic concept of market basket reporting appears to be one that will be attractive to many audiences.

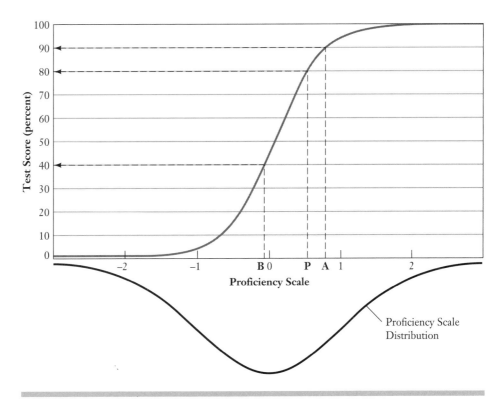

FIGURE 10.3   Market Basket Assessment

One example of a problem is that if the market basket items and tasks are administered or released to the public in reports (as seems desirable to fully communicate the meaning of the results), then these items and tasks are compromised and cannot be used in future assessments. Students may perform better on them in the future not because the quality of education has improved, but because the assessment material has become known and taught to them. For the market basket concept to work, then, an equivalent set of items and tasks must be found for each administration. But the construction of strictly equivalent forms of a test is a very difficult task, and even minor errors may distort the interpretation of the results. Perhaps part of the market basket of assessment material could be released after each administration, but which parts, and how big would the market basket need to be to be able to release a suitable amount for review by the public?

Another problem is that the released items and tasks might have unintended effects on curricula and assessment, such as a narrowing of the curricula to match the released assessment material and elimination of assessment formats that are not used in the market basket items and tasks. These and other problems have reasonable solutions, but research will be needed to address them before the concept is ready for implementation.

Conclusions

There is now substantial evidence in the measurement literature to suggest that NAEP and state reporting scales for proficiency and score reports are not fully understood by intended audiences. At the same time, there are many signs that the problems associated with misunderstanding these scales and reports are being addressed: (1) A review of NAEP reports from 1990 to 1998 shows clear improvements in the clarity of displays; (2) anchor points, performance standards, benchmarking, market basket displays, and so on, which were considered in this chapter, appear to be useful approaches for improving national and state reporting and ongoing research on these and other innovations will further enhance the reporting scales and score reports; and (3) the emerging guidelines for data displays from Hambleton, Slater, and Allalouf (in progress) address a pressing need and should contribute to improved data displays. At the same time, a considerable amount of research is needed if national and state reporting scales and reports are going to achieve their desired purposes.

National and state score reports, in principle, provide policy makers, educators, education writers, and the public with valuable information. But the reporting agencies need to ensure that the reporting scales are meaningful to the intended audiences and that the data displays are clear and understandable. This will almost certainly require the adoption and implementation of a set of guidelines for reporting that includes the field-testing of all reports to ensure that they are being interpreted fully and correctly. Special attention will need to be given, too, to the use of figures and tables, which can convey substantial amounts of data clearly when they are properly designed.

references

Beaton, A. E., & Allen, N. L. (1992). Interpreting scales through scale anchoring. *Journal of Educational Statistics, 17*(2), 191–204.

Beaton, A. E., & Johnson, E. G. (1992). Overview of the scaling methodology used in the National Assessment. *Journal of Educational Measurement, 29*(2), 163–176.

Bourque, M. L., Champagne, A. B., & Crissman, S. (1997). *1996 science performance standards: Achievement results for the nation and the states.* Washington, D.C.: National Assessment Governing Board.

Cleveland, W. S. (1985). *The elements of graphing data.* Monterey, Calif.: Wadsworth.

Forsyth, R. A. (1991). Do NAEP scales yield valid criterion-referenced interpretations? *Educational Measurement: Issues and Practice, 10*(3), 3–9, 16.

Hambleton, R. K. (1994). Scales, scores, and reporting forms to enhance the utility of educational testing. Invited presentation at the meeting of the National Council on Measurement in Education, New Orleans.

Hambleton, R. K., & Slater, S. (1995). Using performance standards to report national and state assessment data: Are the reports understandable and how can they be improved? In *Proceedings of the Joint Conference on Standard Setting for Large-Scale Assessments,* pp. 325–343. Washington, D.C.: NCES–NAGB.

Hambleton, R. K., Slater, S., & Allalouf, A. (in progress). Steps for preparing displays of educational data. *Educational Measurement: Issues and Practice.*

Hambleton, R. K., Swaminathan, H., & Rogers, H. J. (1991). *Fundamentals of item response theory.* Newbury Park, Calif.: Sage Publications.

Henry, G. T. (1995). *Graphing data: Techniques for display and analysis.* Thousand Oaks, Calif.: Sage Publications.

Jaeger, R. (1992). General issues in reporting of the NAEP trial state assessment results. In *Assessing student achievement in the states,* eds. R. Glaser & R. Linn, pp. 107–109. Stanford, Calif.: National Academy of Education.

———. (1999). *Reporting the results of the National Assessment of Educational Progress* (NVS NAEP Validity Studies). Washington, D.C.: American Institutes for Research.

Johnson, E. G. (1992). The design of the National Assessment of Educational Progress. *Journal of Educational Measurement, 29,* 95–110.

Kirsch, I. S., Jungeblut, A., Jenkins, L., & Kolstad, A. (1993). *Adult literacy in America: A first look at the results of the National Adult Literacy Survey.* Washington, D.C.: U.S. Government Printing Office.

Koretz, D., & Deibert, E. (1993). *Interpretations of National Assessment of Educational Progress (NAEP) anchor points and achievement levels by the print media in 1991.* Santa Monica, Calif.: Rand.

Linn, R. L. (1998). Validating inferences from National Assessment of Educational Progress achievement-level reporting. *Applied Measurement in Education, 11*(1), 23–47.

Linn, R. L., & Dunbar, S. B. (1992). Issues in the design and reporting of the National Assessment of Educational Progress. *Journal of Educational Measurement, 29*(2), 177–194.

Misley, R. J. (1998). Implications of market-basket reporting for achievement-level setting. *Applied Measurement in Education, 11*(1), 49–64.

Mislevy, R. J., Forsyth, R., Hambleton, R. K., Linn, R., & Yen, W. (1996). *Design/feasibility team report to the National Assessment Governing Board.* Washington, D.C.: National Assessment Governing Board.

Mislevy, R. J., Johnson, E. G., & Muraki, E. (1992). Scaling procedures in NAEP. *Journal of Educational Statistics, 17,* 131–154.

Mullis, I. V. S. (1991, April). The NAEP scale anchoring process for the 1990 Mathematics Assessment. Paper presented at the meeting of AERA, Chicago.

Mullis, I. V. S., Dossey, J. A., Owen, E. H., & Phillips, G. W. (1993). *Executive summary of the NAEP 1992 mathematics report card for the nation and the states.* Washington, D.C.: Department of Education.

Phillips, G. W., Mullis, I. V. S., Bourque, M. L., Williams, P. L., Hambleton, R. K., Owen, E. H., & Barton, P. E. (1993). *Interpreting NAEP scales.* Washington, D.C.: Department of Education.

Wainer, H. (1992). Understanding graphs and tables. *Educational Researcher, 21*(1), 14–23.

———. (1996). Using trilinear plots for NAEP data. *Journal of Educational Measurement, 33,* 41–55.

———. (1997a). Improving tabular displays: With NAEP tables as examples and inspirations. *Journal of Educational and Behavioral Sciences, 21,* 1–32.

———. (1997b). Some multivariate displays for NAEP results. *Psychological Methods, 2*(1), 34–63.

———. (1997c). *Visual revelations.* New York: Springer-Verlag.

Wainer, H., Hambleton, R. K., & Meara, K. (1999). Alternative displays for communicating NAEP results: A redesign and validity study. *Journal of Educational Measurement, 36*(4), 301–335.

Wainer, H., & Thissen, D. (1981). Graphical data analysis. *Annual Review of Psychology, 32,* 191–241.

Williams, P. L., Reese, C. M., Campbell, J. R., Mazzeo, J., & Phillips, G. W. (1995). *NAEP 1994 Reading: A first look.* Washington, D.C.: Department of Education.

11 How Will We Get Valid Among-State and International Comparisons and What Will They Tell Us?[1]

ALBERT E. BEATON[2]

Boston College

[1]This paper was delivered at the conference "Assessments in Educational Reform: Both Means and Ends" at the University of Maryland on June 5, 2000.
[2]This material is based upon work supported by the National Science Foundation under Grant #REC-9815180. Any opinions, findings, and conclusions or recommendations expressed in this material are those of the author and do not necessarily reflect the views of the National Science Foundation.

Over the past few years, assessments have been widely used to compare different educational systems. In the United States, the National Assessment of Educational Progress (NAEP) has been used to compare participating states and, internationally, the Third International Mathematics and Science Study (TIMSS) has been used to compare the countries that chose to be part of the study. The results of these assessments have been seized upon by the various media, including newspapers, television, radio, news magazines, and so forth. The public and the policy makers have shown great interest in the results and have used them to reconsider and sometimes change educational policies. The question to be addressed here is whether the information generated by these studies is sufficiently valid for the decisions that are made therefrom.

The title of this paper implies a model for future assessments that will produce more valid among-state and international comparisons. I believe that the present assessment models are the best that we know how to do at this time and will not make radical suggestions for the future. Perhaps a personal comment will help clarify my position. I have had a long career in large-scale assessments: as the Director of Data Analysis for the Equality of Educational Opportunity Survey (the Coleman Report, 1966), as the first Director of Data Analysis for the National Longitudinal Study of the Class of 1972, as the Director of Design, Research, and Data Analysis for the NAEP (1983–1989), and the International Study Director of TIMSS (1993–). In other words, I have been observing what has been happening and have been very much a part of the emerging design and implementation of these large scale assessment models. I have had—and taken advantage of—my many opportunities to improvise in the assessment designs. If I knew of better, feasible ways to make state and national comparisons, they would have been implemented in my past work. This is not to say that improvements should not be made, but radical changes will have to come from somewhere else—and meet the validity criteria set by past assessments.

The present assessment models are actually compromises among competing demands, such as the subject-matter experts' demand for broader coverage and the school administrators' demand for less interruption of teaching activities. Ultimately, the available funding must restrict any model's implementation. Trade-offs must be made to find an acceptable model for the many stakeholders in an assessment. Radical innovations must consider the many audiences before attempting to fund and implement changes.

It should be noted that the development of and innovation in these assessments have come largely as answers to increased demands on the data generated. The Coleman Report used off-the-shelf tests, multiple-choice items, and number-right scoring; its sampling would not pass today's minimum standards. In answer to the best available thinking about knowledge and learning, the tests now have a broad coverage of subject-matter content and some open-ended items, use item-response theory, and collect performance-assessment data. For example, the demand for increased subject-matter coverage first resulted in the matrix sampling used in the early NAEP and then the balanced incomplete block (BIB) spiraling introduced later, and these led to the use of item-response theory and the invention of plausible values. Again and again, the demand placed on the data has left statisticians and psychometricians with difficult problems to solve. The present models will require further modifications as the demands change; for example, there is a new demand for the introduction of individual score reports in NAEP.

Although I think that the present designs of NAEP and TIMSS are quite good responses to today's demands, their implementation needs to be improved. Despite extraordinary efforts to ensure the quality of the data—and, in my opinion, the collection of very high quality data—there is always some room for improvement. I will discuss some improvements here. Perhaps in a better-funded and more relaxed assessment situation in the future, these improvements can be implemented.

In the discussion of validity in this paper, I will focus mainly on the TIMSS project because it had to address many of the same issues as the NAEP state-by-state comparisons but had also to address additional issues, such as language and cultural differences. The starker differences among the countries make the issues concerning comparisons clearer.

The debate about educational policy and the changes made in practice have been worldwide. Although in many cases the changes have been made after careful analyses of the available data, most of the debate is generated from the national rankings or "league tables." Curiously, TIMSS did not actually publish rankings, although the rankings were easily identified in those tables that were ordered by national averages. Essays about the effect of TIMSS in different countries have been collected and published by Robitaille, Beaton, and Plomp (2000).

The issue of the validity of student scores is not relevant for TIMSS or NAEP. Because of their designs, both tests are inappropriate for individual decisions. In order to have their tests cover a wide range of student skills, both assessments used balanced incomplete block (BIB) spiraling (see Messick, Beaton, & Lord, 1983) to form their test booklets. Using this method, students received different, not necessarily parallel, tests, so a student's scores on the individual tests might differ sharply. Furthermore, subscale scores are built on short tests and thus have poor reliability. However, both TIMSS and NAEP are designed to produce estimates of the parameters of large populations, and individual scores are not important. Neither test actually produces individual scores—they produce "plausible values" instead. Each student is assigned five plausible values for a test, each one a random draw that is a plausible test score for that student. The plausible value includes what we know about the student's performance but also the uncertainty in that knowledge. These plausible values can be shown to produce consistent estimates of the population parameters. The plausible values are better considered as partial computations of the population estimates than as scores for the students. For more details, see Mislevy et al. (1992).

The validity of the tests for the purposes for which they are used is, of course, important. When comparing countries, it is important to realize the great differences among them. Educational systems differ in the age at which children enter and in their student retention policies. They differ in what they intend to accomplish, as indicated by their curricula. They differ in so many ways that one must wonder if any "fair" comparisons are possible.

First, it is important to realize that the detecting and recording of differences in the way the educational systems are organized and in their intended curricula is one of the main purposes of an international study. It is also important to take the differences into account when interpreting and using the data. For example, the children in Scandinavian countries start school a year later than those in most other countries. Comparing 9-year-old students from Sweden with those from other countries puts the Swedish students at a disadvantage because they have had one year fewer of formal schooling; comparing fourth graders gives Sweden a slight advantage because its fourth graders are a year older. We cannot remove these national differences from an international assessment and do not want to. The question is: Do the differences make any comparisons impossible?

As now conceived, validity must be looked at for each purpose for which an assessment is used. Validity is never perfect; it is only approached as more evidence is accumulated. Validity studies are a process by which the pros and cons of particular uses are identified. Using assessment data for decisions always involves some uncertainty. One can err by making simplified decisions using the data without concern for the data's complexity and application in a particular situation. On the other hand, one can err by not taking advantage of the data for fear of an imperfect decision. Both types of error can be reduced by the careful consideration of the assessment's properties.

The properties of the assessment can be studied by examining the design and implementation of the assessment. The design involves critical decisions about who and what will be assessed. A careful design defines the population of students to be tested, how they will be selected, and how we can be sure that the selection will be carefully done. The design includes developing the test specifications so that the test coverage is defined and implemented. The careful implementation and documentation of the design plans are critical to establishing the quality of the data and their appropriateness for educational decisions.

Not all aspects of the implementation of an assessment can be examined empirically, but some can. TIMSS went out of its way to check itself wherever appropriate. Some of these checks will be described next.

In the following section of this paper, I will describe the decisions and processes that went into the design and implementation of the TIMSS study. These should be helpful in judging whether TIMSS is appropriate for a particular purpose. Some of the many empirical checks that TIMSS did to check its data will also be described. The final section will discuss the implications of the findings.

The Design and Implementation of TIMSS

TIMSS was the result of the collaboration of the many participating countries, subject-matter experts from around the world, and assessment professionals. The collaboration of all of these persons was necessary to carry out the political process of making the assessment. Certainly, not all desiderata from the participants could be included in the design, but it was essential that the different points of view be aired, discussed, and agreed-upon decisions made. A test constructed to cover only topics covered everywhere would be a trivial subset of the subject-area content; a test constructed to include everything covered anywhere would be very thin in important areas. The aim was to have a test that was "equally unfair to all" and to have the participants see, however, that its development was in fact fair to all participants.

The organizational structure of TIMSS was complex. Each country appointed a national research coordinator to participate in assessment discussions and decisions and also to direct the implementation within that country. Some countries chose educational researchers as their coordinators and others chose personnel from government ministries. The study was coordinated from the TIMSS International Study Center at Boston College and the TIMSS International Coordinating Center at the University of British Columbia. Following the data flow is perhaps the best way of describing the important contributions of the several subcontractors. After testing, the national research coordinators shipped their results to the IEA Data Processing Center in Hamburg, Germany, where the data were carefully checked and any unusual occurrences investigated and adjudicated. The data were then moved to Statistics Canada in Ottawa to look for sampling irregularities and compute sampling weights. The data were then moved to the Australian Council for Educational Research, where the item-response theoretic scaling was done. The data finally went to the International Study Center for analysis and reporting. In other words, the data moved around the world from continent to continent and from hemisphere to hemisphere, making use of the best personnel that were available.

The main design decisions and implementation features were as follows:

Population Definition

The decision to assess in-school students only[3] was arrived at early in the design process; the cost of chasing out-of-school students was prohibitive for most countries. It was also decided to test students at an early point in their school years, other students in the middle of their school experiences, and others at the end of secondary schooling.

Next, a decision had to be made about whether to assess by age or grade. Age is tempting because it has the same meaning in all countries, making comparisons sharper. On the other hand, school policies are made by grade and in-depth analysis of school processes requires that intact classrooms be sampled so that the relationship between teacher characteristics and student performance could be studied. Furthermore, age sampling in most countries causes more school disruption, as students are removed from their regular classes and moved to separate testing rooms. To make the data most valuable, the assessment populations were defined as

Population 1: The two adjacent grades that contained the most 9-year-olds.

Population 2: The two adjacent grades that contained the most 13-year-olds.

Population 3: Students in their last year of secondary school.

Sampling two adjacent grades had several compelling features. First, in most countries—especially at the lower grades—an age cohort is largely located in a pair of grades, and in such cases the age distribution parameters could be estimated. Even in countries where the students were spread over more than two grades, age distribution can be approximated, and so TIMSS published its results both by age and by grade. Another

---

[3]In some countries, some students become apprentices in a trade and continue in school on a day or half-day a week basis. These apprentices were included in the population definition.

[4]For sampling efficiency, NAEP selects students randomly within a school; TIMSS chose to sample intact classrooms for administrative ease and for the use of hierarchical linear modeling in data analysis.

advantage is that average student progress between the two adjacent grades could be estimated.

Population 3, which included students at the end of their secondary school education, was especially problematic. Defining the population by two adjacent grades made no sense, given the intention to assess students at the end of their schooling. However, at this level the international differences were enormous. First, the percent of students remaining in secondary school until graduation varies sharply from country to country, with many young persons in an age cohort not tested. Although most countries provide 12 years of education, there is some international variation. Furthermore, not all students in all countries take mathematics or physics, the subjects that were tested in Population 3. It is unlikely that any simple comparison of national averages will be of use unless the national differences are considered. And yet, the report on Population 3 that detailed national differences was an interesting report that brought new understandings to national differences.

Sampling from the populations was done very carefully. Most countries prepared a list of their schools for each population, and the estimated number of students within those schools provided a basis for sampling proportional to size. Some countries, such as the United States, used a multistage sample in which geographical areas (e.g., counties or metropolitan statistical areas) were sampled first and then schools were sampled within those areas. Within schools, intact mathematics classes[4] were listed, and students not taking mathematics were placed in a pseudoclassroom. In most countries, one, but in some countries two, of these classrooms were randomly selected for assessment.

The sampling frame was compared to official national statistics for consistency. Under the watchful eye of TIMSS sampling consultants, a sampling plan was prepared for each country and schools were selected. The countries were required to meet rigid participation rates, and most of them did. Getting school participation is difficult in most countries where participation is not required. As will be noted later, the final sample was checked against the plans to determine any irregularities.

Test Development

At an early point, it was decided that the assessments would cover mathematics and science in Populations 1 and 2 but cover mathematics and science literacy in Population 3. In addition, students in Population 3 who specialized in mathematics or physics were selected for special tests in those subjects. Curriculum analyses (Schmidt et al., 1997a, 1997b) were done to find out what subject matter was covered at those levels in the participating countries. The final test specifications were published (Orpwood and Garden, 1998).

All countries were asked to submit test items that matched the test specifications. Items were translated into English from their original languages and then discussed and classified by the subject-matter experts and the national research coordinators, who were responsible for operations in their own countries. After several rounds of discussion, the national research coordinators or their staff viewed the test as a whole and had the right to object to particular items. After achieving general agreement on a test, the test was translated into the languages of the participating countries. This test development process was repeated for the pretest, field test, and for the final test forms.

Translation

The translation of the test items is a very important part of an international assessment. In fact, the TIMSS tests were translated into over 30 different languages. Moreover, minor adaptations had to be made for cultural differences; for example, the English tests had to be adjusted for different English-speaking countries such as Australia, Canada, England, Ireland, and the United States. To be comparable, the translated test item must not only have exactly the same meaning but require the same reading level as well. There is, however, no known way to ensure equivalence.

Past studies have used back translations, that is, having an independent translator convert the item back into English and then comparing the original against the doubly translated item. Unfortunately, this process does not necessarily catch differences; for example, the word *new* in English can be translated either to *neuf* or *nouveau* in French, which will have different meanings. However, both French words will translate back to *new* in English.

Instead of using this procedure, TIMSS found bilingual persons to review the translated version and judge whether the translation was equivalent to the English version. Differences were noted and brought to the attention of the country's national research coordinator. The items were edited as necessary.

Quality Assurance

The secret to successful data collection is extensive training. To ensure similar testing and grading procedures, the national research coordinators or their assistants went through training sessions on all phases of the study. The national research coordinators were required to run similar sessions in their own countries.

Quality assurance personnel were hired by the TIMSS International Study Center to interview the national research coordinators and to observe several testing sessions in participating countries, where feasible. The results are presented in Mullis and Martin (1996).

Data entry systems that checked for consistency of the input data were provided to the participating countries, and the data were carefully checked when they arrived at the IEA Data Processing Center in Hamburg. Unusual occurrences were brought to the attention of the national research coordinators and corrections were made as appropriate. The data were checked again by the TIMSS International Study Center and the Australian Council for Educational Research, which did the test analyses and scalings for TIMSS.

Data Analysis

TIMSS used item-response theory (IRT) to organize and summarize its data. As developed for TIMSS, IRT has the advantage of calibrating the different tests for a population into plausible values for estimating population parameters. The processes were carefully done and documented in Adams, Wu, and Macaskill (1997). The standard errors for published statistics were computed using the jackknife method (see Gonzalez & Foy, 1997).

Reporting

Before the actual results were available, dummy tables for all of the results to be published were developed and discussed with the national research coordinators. Revisions and additions were made as a result of the discussions. The national research coordinators had the opportunity to check their results before final publication.

Documentation

If TIMSS is to be judged by what its data represent, its design and implementation must be known. Both TIMSS and NAEP have been exceptionally well documented so that the decisions and the data can be reviewed by any interested evaluator. First, there is a report that gives an overview of the various educational systems that participated in TIMSS (Robitaille, 1996).

TIMSS has produced six major reports containing summaries of its data. For primary school students, there is a mathematics report (Mullis et al., 1997) and a science report (Martin et al., 1997). For the middle school years there is a mathematics report (Beaton et al., 1996a) and a science report (Beaton et al., 1996b). There is a report on both mathematics and science for students at the end of secondary school (Mullis et al., 1998). In addition, there is a report on the TIMSS performance assessment (Harmon et al., 1997).

TIMSS has also produced a series of technical reports to document its procedures. They are on TIMSS design and development (Martin & Kelly, 1996), on the implementation of TIMSS for primary and middle schools (Martin & Kelly, 1997), and on implementation at the final year of secondary school (Martin & Kelly, 1998). There is also a report on quality assurance (Mullis & Martin, 1996).

All of the data and reports for the study are available on the Internet at www.timss.org. There is also a user's guide (Gonzalez & Smith, 1997a) to help persons make use of the data.

Empirical Checks

The sampling procedures of TIMSS were supervised by Statistics Canada, and there was also a sampling referee, Keith Rust of Westat, to adjudicate sampling inconsistencies.

The sampling process provides several important checks on the adequacy of the sample. The process begins with a sampling frame for each country that covers all students in a population. The basic unit in a sampling frame is generally the school, but, in some larger countries, counties or other administrative sections may be used as primary sampling units. For each basic unit, there is an estimate of the number of eligible students. The sum of these estimates is an estimate of the number of eligible students in the country and can be checked against population estimates from other sources such as national census bureaus. If the estimate from the sampling frame is quite different from the national statistics, the frame must be revised or explained.

In most countries, some students cannot be tested because they do not speak the language of the test or they have physical or behavioral disabilities. There may also be areas of the country that are inaccessible or too expensive to locate and test. TIMSS allowed a small percentage of such untested students but carefully kept track of the number of students who were not tested and reported the percent in its reports.

After the tests were administered and the data collected, the sampling weights were computed and a number of checks on the samples were performed. In its simplest terms, a student sampling weight is in inverse of the probability of that student being selected for the sample. The sum of the sampling weights should be within sampling error of the population size from the sampling frame. However, a number of factors must be considered such as population characteristics and the participation rates, for example. Clearly, such variables as the percent of boys or girls in the sample can be checked against other statistics as can the percent of parents with secondary school or college educations. In many countries, schools may refuse to participate and sometimes do. The TIMSS rules required that at least 85% of the schools participate and whether this criterion was met could be established by comparing the actual data with the sampling frame. Adjustments for nonparticipation were made, but such adjustments bring into question the quality of the data, and so TIMSS presented its results in categories:

1. Countries that met all TIMSS sampling standards
2. Countries that required replacement schools to meet standards[5]
3. Countries not satisfying guidelines for participation rates
4. Countries not meeting age/grade specifications
5. Countries with unapproved sampling procedures at classroom level

Countries with extreme data problems were reported in appendices or not reported at all.

The validity question here is whether these samples are good enough for comparisons. There is no flat yes-or-no answer to such a question. All real-world samples are flawed to some degree and therefore so are the TIMSS samples. TIMSS set high standards for participation because the belief of sampling experts was that some countries would aim for the minimum and not try harder. But there is nothing special about the 85% of schools rule except that it was agreed to by the participants. Eighty-six percent would be better, but 84% does not suggest that the data are worthless. It is a judgment that someone using the data must make for a particular usage.

TIMSS Coverage Index (TCI)

One of the major issues concerning the quality of an assessment's data is the fact that some students drop out of school and are therefore not in the population. If a country's lower-scoring students tend to be the dropouts, then the country's average will be artificially

---

[5]TIMSS had specific rules so that the replacement schools would be similar to the nonparticipating schools.

high. This is not a matter of real concern for Populations 1 and 2 because of compulsory education laws in the TIMSS countries. However, it is a serious issue in terms of students at the end of secondary school because a substantial portion of these students may drop out. In past assessments, the poorer performance of the countries that kept a large proportion of students in school was used to explain that performance; it was alleged that the United States did poorly because its general population was being compared to the educational elite of other countries. And this may have been the case in the past.

TIMSS decided to investigate this issue for Population 3. For this purpose, Keith Rust suggested the TIMSS coverage index, which is the ratio of the number of students in the final year of secondary to the number of young persons in the total population. The numerator is derived from the TIMSS sample in a country; the denominator, the number of students aged 15 to 19 in that country divided by 5, is derived from census statistics. This ratio is an estimate of the percent of young persons in the population who were in secondary school for the TIMSS assessment.

The results of this analysis were unexpected (see Table B.5 in Mullis et al., 1998). The TCI for the United States was 63%, which places it 14th among the 24 countries in Population 3. This estimate has been carefully checked and is consistent with some other data sources, including NAEP. However, because a larger proportion of young persons are in school in other countries, the argument that the general population in the United States is being compared with the elite of other countries does not hold.

Test–Curriculum Matching Analysis (TCMA)

Another issue in comparing countries is whether the students in a country have had the opportunity to learn the test content and processes that are being measured. TIMSS curriculum analyses (Schmidt et al.,1997a, 1997b) have shown that there are substantial differences in curricula and therefore the opportunity to learn has been unequal. Is this inequality enough to invalidate the TIMSS results?

First, we must recognize that the differences in opportunity to learn are important, and it is these differences that TIMSS has looked for and documented. The question is: Is it "fair" to those countries whose students had less of an opportunity to learn the test content? In fact, we expect these differences to affect the national results substantially. But it seems to me that the countries, not TIMSS, are unfair to their students. If a country does not teach subject matter that other countries do teach, then that country must wonder why it does not so challenge its students.

As mentioned earlier, TIMSS was intended to be "equally unfair" to all countries. To estimate the unfairness, TIMSS asked the national research coordinators to have each test item reviewed for appropriateness for at least 50% of the students their countries. Appropriateness was defined as being in the intended curriculum of at least 50% of the students in each tested grade. It was recommended that the national research coordinators choose curriculum specialists who were very knowledgeable about what was taught in school to rate the items. If an item was administered at more than one grade, then it was to be rated separately by grade. The results were returned to the TIMSS International Study Center before the actual test results were distributed.

TABLE 11.1　Test-Curriculum Matching Analysis Results—Mathematics—Upper Grade (Eighth Grade*)

Average Percent Correct Based on Subsets of Items Specially Identified by Each Country as Addressing Its Curriculum

Instructions:　Read *across* the row to compare that country's performance based on the test items included by each of the countries across the top.
　Read *down* the column under a country name to compare the performance of the country down the left on the items included the country listed on the top.
　Read along the *diagonal* to compare performance for each different country based on its own decisions about the test items to include.

Country	Average Percent Correct on All Items	Singapore	Japan	Korea	Hong Kong	Belgium (F1)	Czech Republic	Slovak Republic	Switzerland	Austria	Hungary	France	Slovenia	Russian Federation	Netherlands	Bulgaria	Canada	Ireland	Belgium (F1)	Australia	Israel
(Number of Score Points Included)	162**	144	153	140	150	140	150	152	133	147	162	160	151	126	116	119	147	145	138	154	159
Singapore	79 (0.9)	79	79	80	79	79	79	79	80	80	79	79	79	81	79	80	79	79	79	79	79
Japan	73 (0.4)	73	73	74	73	73	73	73	75	74	73	73	73	74	73	73	74	73	73	74	73
Korea	72 (0.5)	71	72	73	72	71	72	71	72	72	72	71	71	72	70	72	72	71	71	72	72
Hong Kong	70 (1.4)	70	70	71	70	70	70	70	71	71	70	70	70	71	69	71	70	70	69	70	70
Belgium (F1)	66 (1.4)	65	65	67	65	65	65	65	68	66	66	66	65	67	64	65	66	65	65	66	66
Czech Republic	66 (1.1)	65	66	67	66	66	66	66	68	66	66	66	66	67	64	65	66	66	65	66	66
Slovak Republic	62 (0.8)	63	63	64	63	63	63	63	65	63	62	63	63	64	61	63	63	62	63	63	62
Switzerland	62 (0.6)	61	62	63	61	61	61	62	64	62	62	62	61	62	62	60	63	61	60	62	62
Austria	62 (0.8)	62	62	63	62	61	62	62	64	62	62	62	61	63	61	61	63	62	61	62	62
Hungary	62 (0.7)	61	61	63	61	61	61	61	63	62	62	61	61	62	60	61	62	61	61	62	62
France	61 (0.8)	61	61	62	61	60	61	61	63	61	61	61	61	62	60	60	62	61	60	62	61
Slovenia	61 (0.7)	61	61	62	61	61	61	61	63	61	61	61	61	63	59	61	62	61	61	62	61
Russian Federation	60 (1.3)	61	60	61	60	59	60	60	62	61	60	60	60	62	58	61	61	60	60	61	60
Netherlands	60 (1.6)	59	60	60	59	58	59	59	61	60	60	59	59	59	59	58	61	59	58	60	60
Bulgaria	60 (1.2)	60	59	61	59	59	59	59	61	60	60	59	59	61	57	60	60	59	59	60	60
Canada	59 (0.5)	58	58	59	58	58	58	58	60	59	59	58	58	59	58	57	60	58	57	59	59
Ireland	59 (1.2)	58	58	59	58	58	58	58	60	59	59	58	58	59	58	57	59	58	57	59	59
Belgium (F1)	59 (0.9)	58	58	60	58	58	58	58	61	59	59	59	59	59	57	58	59	58	58	59	59
Australia	58 (0.9)	57	58	59	57	57	58	58	60	58	58	57	57	58	57	56	59	57	56	58	58
Israel	57 (1.3)	57	57	59	57	57	57	57	59	58	57	57	57	59	55	57	58	57	57	58	58
Sweden	56 (0.7)	55	55	56	55	54	55	55	57	55	56	55	54	55	56	53	57	55	54	56	56
Germany	54 (1.1)	53	54	55	53	52	54	53	56	54	54	54	53	54	53	52	55	54	52	54	54
New Zealand	54 (1.0)	53	54	54	53	52	53	53	55	54	54	53	53	53	53	51	55	53	52	54	54
Norway	54 (0.5)	53	53	54	53	52	53	53	56	54	54	53	53	53	53	51	54	53	52	54	54
England	53 (0.7)	52	53	53	52	51	52	52	54	53	53	52	52	52	52	49	54	52	50	53	53
United States	53 (1.1)	52	53	54	52	52	53	52	54	53	53	52	52	53	52	51	54	52	51	53	53
Denmark	52 (0.7)	51	52	52	52	51	51	52	54	52	52	51	51	52	52	49	53	51	50	53	52
Scotland	52 (1.3)	51	51	52	51	50	51	51	53	51	52	50	51	51	51	48	52	51	49	52	52
Latvia (LSS)	51 (0.8)	51	51	52	51	51	51	51	53	52	51	51	51	53	50	51	52	51	51	52	51
Spain	51 (0.5)	50	51	52	51	50	51	51	52	51	51	50	51	51	48	50	51	50	50	51	51
Iceland	50 (1.1)	49	50	50	49	48	49	49	52	49	50	49	49	49	49	47	50	49	48	50	50
Greece	49 (0.7)	49	49	50	49	49	49	49	51	49	49	49	49	50	48	49	50	49	49	50	49
Romania	49 (1.0)	49	49	50	49	49	49	49	50	50	49	49	49	51	47	50	49	49	49	49	49
Lithuania	48 (0.9)	49	49	49	49	48	49	49	51	49	48	48	48	50	47	48	50	48	48	49	48
Cyprus	48 (0.5)	48	47	49	47	47	48	47	49	48	48	48	47	49	46	48	48	47	47	48	48
Portugal	42 (0.7)	42	43	43	43	42	43	43	45	43	43	42	42	43	41	41	44	42	41	43	43
Iran, Islamic Rep.	38 (0.6)	38	38	39	38	38	38	38	39	38	38	38	38	39	37	38	39	37	37	38	38
Kuwait	30 (0.7)	29	30	30	29	29	29	29	31	29	30	29	30	30	29	28	30	29	29	30	30
Colombia	29 (0.8)	29	29	30	29	29	29	29	31	29	29	29	29	29	28	28	30	29	28	30	29
South Africa	24 (1.1)	23	24	25	24	24	24	24	25	24	24	23	24	24	23	24	24	24	24	24	24
International Average	55 (0.9)	55	55	56	55	54	55	55	57	55	55	55	55	56	54	54	56	55	54	55	55

*Eighth grade in most countries.

**Of the 151 items in the mathematics test, some items had two parts and some extended-response items were scored on a two- or three-point scale, resulting in 162 total score points.

( ) Standard errors for the average percent of correct responses on all items appear in parentheses.

Because results are rounded to the nearest whole number, some totals may appear inconsistent.

Countries shown in italics did not satisfy one or more guidelines for sample participation rates, age/grade specifications, or classroom sampling procedures.

Because population coverage falls below 65% Latvia is annotated LSS for Latvian Speaking Schools only.

Source: IEA Third International Mathematics and Science Study (TIMSS), 1994–95.

Sweden	Germany	New Zealand	Norway	England	United States	Denmark	Scotland	Latvia (LSS)	Spain	Iceland	Greece	Romania	Lithuania	Cyprus	Portugal	Iran, Islamic Rep.	Kuwait	Colombia	South Africa
(Number of Score Points Included)																			
127	155	145	150	130	162	135	125	161	158	133	75	143	155	124	152	147	140	133	129
79	79	79	79	81	79	80	80	79	79	80	79	79	79	80	79	79	79	80	79
73	73	75	74	75	73	75	74	73	73	74	74	74	73	73	73	74	74	74	73
71	72	73	72	73	72	73	72	72	72	73	72	72	71	71	72	72	72	72	70
69	70	71	70	71	70	71	70	70	70	70	70	70	70	70	70	70	70	71	70
67	66	67	66	68	66	67	67	66	65	67	65	66	65	65	65	66	66	66	65
66	66	67	66	67	66	67	66	66	65	67	68	66	66	65	68	66	66	66	65
62	63	63	62	64	62	64	62	62	62	64	64	62	63	62	63	63	63	63	63
64	62	64	62	66	62	64	65	62	62	63	60	61	62	61	62	62	62	61	61
64	62	63	62	65	62	64	63	62	62	63	62	62	62	62	62	62	62	62	61
62	62	63	62	63	62	63	61	62	61	62	63	61	61	61	61	62	62	62	61
62	61	63	62	63	61	63	62	61	61	62	60	61	61	60	61	61	62	62	60
61	61	62	61	63	61	62	61	61	61	62	62	61	61	61	61	62	62	62	61
60	60	61	60	61	60	61	60	60	60	61	62	60	60	60	60	61	61	61	60
62	60	63	61	63	60	62	62	60	59	61	60	59	59	58	60	60	60	59	58
58	60	61	60	61	60	61	59	60	60	61	61	60	59	58	60	60	60	61	59
60	59	61	59	62	59	61	60	59	58	60	58	59	58	58	59	59	59	58	58
60	58	61	59	62	59	60	60	59	58	60	59	58	58	58	59	59	59	58	58
60	59	60	59	62	59	61	60	59	59	59	58	58	58	58	58	59	59	59	57
59	58	61	58	61	58	60	60	58	58	59	59	58	58	57	58	59	58	57	57
58	57	59	57	59	57	58	57	57	57	58	60	58	57	57	57	58	58	58	57
60	55	59	57	59	56	58	59	56	55	57	53	55	55	54	56	56	56	54	54
55	54	56	54	57	54	56	55	54	54	55	54	53	54	53	54	54	54	54	53
56	54	57	54	57	54	56	57	54	54	55	55	53	53	52	54	55	54	53	52
56	53	56	54	57	54	56	56	53	53	55	52	53	53	52	53	54	54	52	52
55	53	56	54	57	53	55	56	53	53	54	55	52	52	51	53	54	53	51	51
54	53	55	53	56	53	55	54	53	53	54	54	53	53	52	53	54	53	52	52
54	52	55	53	56	52	55	55	52	52	53	53	51	52	50	52	53	52	51	50
54	51	55	52	55	52	54	55	52	51	52	53	51	51	49	52	52	52	50	50
51	52	53	51	53	51	53	52	51	51	52	53	51	51	50	51	52	52	52	51
51	51	52	51	53	51	52	51	51	51	52	53	51	51	50	51	51	51	51	50
53	49	53	50	54	50	53	53	50	49	51	49	49	49	48	49	51	50	49	48
50	49	51	50	52	49	51	50	49	49	50	50	49	49	49	49	50	50	49	48
48	49	50	49	50	49	49	48	48	49	49	50	49	49	49	49	50	49	51	49
49	49	50	49	50	48	50	49	48	49	49	50	48	49	47	49	49	49	49	48
48	48	49	48	50	48	48	48	48	48	48	48	48	47	47	48	48	48	49	47
44	43	45	43	45	43	45	44	43	43	43	44	42	43	41	43	44	43	43	41
37	38	38	38	40	38	39	38	38	38	39	39	38	38	37	38	38	38	39	37
29	30	32	30	31	30	30	30	30	30	30	32	30	30	28	30	30	30	30	28
30	29	31	30	32	29	30	30	29	29	30	31	29	29	28	29	30	30	29	28
24	24	25	24	25	24	24	24	24	24	25	24	24	24	23	24	24	24	24	23
56	55	57	55	58	55	57	56	55	55	56	56	55	55	54	55	56	55	55	54

The results for mathematics in grade 8 are shown in Table 11.1. At first, the results are disappointing in that the number of items identified as appropriate varies substantially from country to country. The appropriate score points by country are shown in the top row of the table. Allowing for some items that were assigned more than one point, the test, if all items were given to a student, would have a maximum score of 162 points. Although most of the countries considered most of the items appropriate, some countries considered many items inappropriate. Greece considered only 79 of the score points appropriate. The United States deemed all items appropriate.

Table 11.1 also shows how each country performed on the items that it deemed appropriate and how all other countries performed on the same items. What is interesting is how little the judgment of appropriateness affected the relative positions of the countries. Reading down the first column, we see that Singapore averaged 79 points out of the 144 score points that it considered appropriate. On Singapore's items, Japan averaged 73 points, Korea 71 points, and so forth. For the most part, the item selection did not affect the order of the countries in the table.

These results are puzzling. On the one hand, they suggest that the variation in opportunity to learn does not substantially affect the relative positions of the participating countries. On the other hand, we must wonder why, because the curriculum is a substantial lever for educational reform. Perhaps the judges are not knowledgeable enough or the test is not precise enough to detect such differences. More work is in progress to see if these results hold up in the different content categories.

Discussion

The point here is that validity must be viewed with reference to the uses to which the data will be put. And there is no straightforward answer of "valid" or "invalid"; validity will be a matter of degree. The designers of a study have certain data uses in mind and create a study that tries to collect the best possible data for addressing those uses. Their success is a matter of judgment.

For judging the validity of a study for its original purposes, one must examine the quality of the process that generated the data, and it is incumbent upon those who perform the study to make detailed information available. Both NAEP and TIMSS have been exemplary in providing the technical information necessary for such judgments. By making such information available, both studies have improved the art and science of assessment.

Those who implement an assessment can never conceive of all of the purposes to which the data will be put. As noted, TIMSS chose to be a little less efficient in sampling by choosing to sample intact classrooms to encourage hierarchical modeling; in the future, studies might sample two or perhaps all classrooms in a school to improve such modeling. There are plenty of places where small adjustments in the design might improve the usefulness of the data. However, given a set of data, it is necessary for the secondary user to make a judgment about appropriateness of the data and for the readers of the secondary reports to accept or reject the judgment. As mentioned, there are two kinds of error possible: the error of using inappropriate data or the error of not using appropriate data. There is no way, simple or otherwise, to avoid the judgment and associated risks.

r e f e r e n c e s

Adams, R. J., Wu, M. L., & Macaskill, G. (1997). Scaling methodology and procedures for the mathematics and science scales. In *Third international mathematics and science study: Technical report, volume II: Implementation and Analysis*, M. O. Martin & D. L. Kelly, eds. Chestnut Hill, Mass.: Boston College.

Beaton, A. E., Mullis, I. V. S., Martin, M. O., Gonzalez, E. J., Kelly, D. L., & Smith, T. A. (1996a). *Mathematics achievement in the middle school years: IEA's Third International Mathematics and Science Study (TIMSS)*. Chestnut Hill, Mass.: Boston College.

Beaton, A. E., Martin, M. O., Mullis, I. V. S., Gonzalez, E. J., Smith, T. A., & Kelly, D. L. (1996b). *Science achievement in the middle school years: IEA's Third International Mathematics and Science Study (TIMSS)*. Chestnut Hill, Mass.: Boston College.

Coleman, J. S., Campbell, E. Q., Hobson, C. J., McPartland, J., Mood, A. M., Weinfeld, F. D., & York, R. L. (1966). *Equality of educational opportunity*. Washington, D.C.: U.S. Government Printing Office

Gonzalez, E. J., & Smith, T. A. (Eds.). (1997a). *User guide for the TIMSS international database: Primary and middle school years*. Chestnut Hill, Mass.: Boston College.

Gonzalez, E. J., & Foy, P. (1997b). Estimation of sampling variability, design effects, and effective sample sizes. In *Third International Mathematics and Science Study: Technical report, volume II: Implementation and analysis*, M. O. Martin & D. L. Kelly, eds. Chestnut Hill, Mass.: Boston College.

Harmon, M., Smith, T. A., Martin, M. O., Kelly, D. L., Beaton, A. E., Mullis, I. V. S., Gonzalez, E. J., & Orpwood, G. (1997). *Performance assessment in IEA's Third International Mathematics and Science Study (TIMSS)*. Chestnut Hill, Mass.: Boston College.

Martin, M. O., & Mullis, I. V. S. (1996). *Third International Mathematics and Science Study: Quality assurance in data collection*. Chestnut Hill, Mass.: Boston College.

Martin, M. O., Mullis, I. V. S., Beaton, A. E., Gonzalez, E. J., Smith, T. A., & Kelly, D. L. (1997). *Science achievement in the primary school years: IEA's Third International Mathematics and Science Study (TIMSS)*. Chestnut Hill, Mass.: Boston College.

Martin, M. O., & Kelly, D. L. (1996). *Third International Mathematics and Science Study: Technical report, volume I: Design and development*. Chestnut Hill, Mass.: Boston College.

———. (1997). *Third International Mathematics and Science Study: Technical report, volume II: Implementation and analysis*. Chestnut Hill, Mass.: Boston College.

———. (1998). *Third International Mathematics and Science Study: Technical report, volume III: Implementation and analysis of the final year of secondary school*. Chestnut Hill, Mass.: Boston College.

Messick, S. M., Beaton, A. E., and Lord, F. M. (1983). *National assessment of educational progress reconsidered: A new design for a new era*. Princeton, N.J.: Educational Testing Service.

Mislevy, R. J., Beaton, A. E., Kaplan, B., & Sheehan, K. (1992). Estimating population characteristics from sparse matrix samples of item responses. *Journal of Educational Measurement, 29*, 163–175.

Mullis, I. V. S., & Martin, M. O. (1996). *Quality assurance in data collection: The IEA Third International Mathematics and Science Study*. Chestnut Hill, Mass.: Boston College.

Mullis, I. V. S., Martin, M. O., Beaton, A. E., Gonzalez, E. J., Kelly, D. L., & Smith, T. A. (1997). *Mathematics achievement in the primary school years: IEA's Third International Mathematics and Science Study (TIMSS)*. Chestnut Hill, Mass.: Boston College.

———. (1998). *Mathematics and science achievement in the final year of secondary school: IEA's Third International Mathematics and Science Study (TIMSS)*. Chestnut Hill, Mass.: Boston College.

Orpwood, G., & Garden, R. A., Eds. (1998). *TIMSS monograph No. 4: Assessing mathematics and science literacy*. Vancouver, B.C.: Pacific Educational Press.

Robitaille, D., Ed. (1996). *National contexts for mathematics and science education: An encyclopedia of the education systems participating in TIMSS*. Vancouver, B.C.: Pacific Educational Press.

Robitaille, D. F., Beaton, A. E., & Plomp, T., Eds. (2000). *The Impact of TIMSS on the teaching and learning of mathematics and science*. Vancouver, B.C.: Pacific Educational Press.

Schmidt, W. H., McKnight, C. C., Valverde, G. A., Houang, R. T., & Wiley, D. E. (1997a). *Many visions, many aims volume 1: A cross-national investigation of curricular intentions in school mathematics*. Dordrecht, The Netherlands: Kluwer Academic Publishers.

Schmidt, W. H., Raizen, S. A., Britton, E. D., Bianchi, L. J., & Wolfe, R. G. (1997b). *Many visions, many aims volume 2: A cross-national investigation of curricular intentions in school science*. Dordrecht, The Netherlands: Kluwer Academic Publishers.

index